Viral Rhetoric

Robert Samuels

Viral Rhetoric

Psychoanalysis, Philosophy, and Politics after Covid-19

palgrave
macmillan

Robert Samuels
Writing Program
University of California
Santa Barbara
Goleta, CA, USA

ISBN 978-3-030-73894-5 ISBN 978-3-030-73895-2 (eBook)
https://doi.org/10.1007/978-3-030-73895-2

This Palgrave Macmillan imprint is published by the registered company Springer Nature Switzerland AG
The registered company address is: Gewerbestrasse 11, 6330 Cham, Switzerland

To the Living Memory of Jacqueline Samuels

Contents

CHAPTER 1

Introduction: Philosophy and Politics After COVID-19

Abstract This chapter outlines the main argument of the book and provides an outline for each chapter. In turning to a psychoanalytic understanding of rhetoric, the introduction reveals how language itself has many properties that make it appear to be a virus. As something that comes from the outside, but lives inside of us, language can be uncontrollable and alienating. Language also breaks down the border between the self and the other as it shapes how we see the world and ourselves. Since we learn language through imitation and identification, we often do not understand our own thoughts, and these thoughts can be both fictional and actual.

Keywords Viral · Rhetoric · Language · Psychoanalysis · Imitation · Identification

This book uses psychoanalytic concepts to examine the representation of viruses in rhetoric, politics, and popular culture. In utilizing Jean Baudrillard's concept of virality, I examine what it means to use viruses as a metaphor.[1] For instance, what is the effect of saying that a video has gone viral?[2] Does this use of biology to explain culture mean that our societies are determined by biological forces? Moreover, does the rhetoric

R. Samuels, *Viral Rhetoric*,
https://doi.org/10.1007/978-3-030-73895-2_1

of viral culture display a fundamental insensitivity towards people who are actually suffering from viruses?

The study of how rhetoric is used to represent viruses is so important because people and governments are basing their decisions on false connections among biology, culture, and psychology. Not only do we project intentionality onto nature, but we often see our social hierarchies as natural. In the case of the global response to the COVID-19 pandemic, the biological virus has been politicized as people read the infection as a message from nature or some higher power. Moreover, the protest against wearing masks or social distancing rules has been in part driven by the spread of conspiracy theories on the Web. While some see this fast circulation of misleading information as an example of viral culture, I argue that this use of the term "viral" blocks us from understanding how culture and language actually work.

As I document throughout this book, we are currently seeing a mixing of disciplines that produces confusion and misleading representations. At the same time that people talk about viral culture, they also relate biological viruses to computer viruses. This combination of culture, technology, and biology is in part driven by the way people see DNA as a language that we read. In fact, the representation of biology as a code is matched by the use of digital code in computer programming. Moreover, as people base their understanding of cultural memes on the biology of genes, the difference between nature and culture begins to dissolve.

One reason why I think it is essential to separate nature from language is that we need to affirm the limits of our scientific understanding. If we project language and culture onto nature, we take on the position of being able to know everything, and then when we fail to comprehend something, like how to stop a virus, people turn against science and scientists. One problem is that most people do not understand that science uses probabilities and approximations of reality, and it works through trial and error and consensus.

In turning to a psychoanalytic understanding of rhetoric, I hope to reveal how language itself has many properties that make it appear to be a virus. As something that comes from the outside, but lives inside of us, language can be uncontrollable and alienating. Language also breaks down the border between the self and the other as it shapes how we see the world and ourselves. Since we learn language through imitation and identification, we often do not understand our own thoughts, and these thoughts can be both fictional and actual. When we misunderstand how language actually works, we then project it onto nature and the outside world, and this process not only distorts our perceptions of our own minds, but it also prevents us from comprehending nature itself.

In order to understand why people buy into self-destructive conspiracy theories in relation to the novel coronavirus, it is necessary to separate culture, nature, and psychology. While Freud posited that mental contagions explain how ideas and behaviors spread in a group, he also provided a non-biological theory of the unconscious circulation of mental material.[3] Through his concepts of identification, idealization, and projection, we are better able to understand the ways ideology functions to shape our response to COVID-19.

For Baudrillard, the use of viruses as a metaphor is related to his theory that we have lost our cultural immune systems. As I show in Chapter 2, Baudrillard turns to AIDS as a symbol of our liberation from all traditional modes of cultural filtering.[4] He thus uses this medical condition as a metaphor for contemporary life, and one of the effects of this rhetoric is that the distinction between biology and culture breaks down. His implicit argument is that as we liberate ourselves from past social restraints, we also liberate ourselves from meaning itself. Therefore, once words no longer relate to fixed referents and meanings, they are able to circulate around the world without any resistance.

Chapter 3 examines James Gleick's *The Information* to show that a key move was made when people started seeing DNA as a form of language and information.[5] This rhetorical process enabled scientists the ability to eliminate the difference between nature and culture as nature itself was represented as a text that needed to be read. It thus becomes important to examine the effects of seeing nature in cultural terms and culture in natural terms. In fact, the very notion of memes as a cultural form of genes points to the dual process of objectifying humans and anthropomorphizing objects.[6]

Chapter 4 claims that one reason why it is necessary to maintain the distinction between mental and physical viruses is that without this difference, our view of ourselves and our societies becomes obscured. In reading Douglas Rushkoff's *Media Virus!*, I show how his early idealization of the Internet is coupled with a promotion of viral rhetoric.[7] He not only sees the media as a virus, but his own naïve investment in the future of social media is generated out of his confusion between mental and biological forces.

Chapter 5 discusses Freud's theory of the contagion in order to examine how ideas and emotions are able to spread from person to person. In looking at his text *Group Psychology and the Analysis of the Ego*, I outline a psychoanalytic understanding of viral culture. This theory helps us to comprehend how laughter can be contagious, and why empathy is often a destructive force.[8] Freud's interpretation also explains how ideology and media can free us from critical introspection and the testing of reality. The danger then of viral media is that it eliminates the separation of fact from fiction as it also frees people from the inhibition of aggressive drives. We will use this theory to reveal hidden aspects of contemporary left-wing and right-wing politics as we distinguish between actual biological viruses and the spread of ideas in the form of conspiracy theories.

In Chapter 6, I look at Ernesto Leclau's discussion of mental contagions in his *On Populist Reason*.[9] I turn to this work to reveal the way that political ideologies rely on unconscious rhetorical processes. Through the combination of identification, idealization, and projection, irrational political coalitions are able to be formed and maintained. In fact, I will show how this process of creating social solidarity relies on metaphor and metonymy as central rhetorical figures.

In Chapter 7, I examine Slavoj Zizek's initial response to the coronavirus.[10] In reading his *Pandemic*, I will focus on why it so tempting for people to politicize natural processes. While Zizek does at times seek to distinguish among biological, cultural, and technological viruses, he ends up contradicting himself by using the coronavirus as a way to promote his particular ideological investments.

As I argue in the conclusion of this work, the role played by rhetoric in shaping how we see ourselves and the world around us has profound effects, and this means that the teaching of rhetoric is more necessary than ever. In fact, I will argue that one way of defending the humanities against the current over-emphasis on the STEM disciplines is to show how much of scientific discourse is based on rhetorical manipulation. Therefore, if we want to understand science and how it shapes our world, we have to understand how rhetoric works.

Notes

1. Baudrillard, Jean. *The transparency of evil: Essays on extreme phenomena*. Verso, 1993.
2. Southgate, Duncan, Nikki Westoby, and Graham Page. "Creative determinants of viral video viewing." *International Journal of Advertising* 29.3 (2010): 349–368.
3. Freud, Sigmund. "Group psychology and the analysis of the ego." *The standard edition of the complete psychological works of Sigmund Freud, Volume XVIII (1920–1922): Beyond the pleasure principle, group psychology and other works* (1955): 65–144.
4. Fraiberg, Allison. "Of AIDS, cyborgs, and other indiscretions: Resurfacing the body in the postmodern." *Postmodern Culture* 1.3 (1991).
5. Gleick, James. *The information: A history, a theory, a flood*. Vintage, 2011.
6. Dawkins, Richard. *The selfish gene*. Oxford University Press, 2016.
7. Rushkoff, Douglas. *Media virus!: Hidden agendas in popular culture*. Random House Digital, Inc., 1996.
8. Massen, Jorg JM, and Andrew C. Gallup. "Why contagious yawning does not (yet) equate to empathy." *Neuroscience & Biobehavioral Reviews* 80 (2017): 573–585.
9. Laclau, Ernesto. *On populist reason*. Verso, 2005.
10. Zizek, Slavoj. *PANDEMIC!: Covid-19 Shakes the World*. Wiley, 2020.

CHAPTER 2

Baudrillard and Viral Rhetoric

Abstract Baudrillard's work offers an important insight into the way that a viral mode of rhetoric has been used to represent viruses and other aspects of biology, culture, and psychology. However, what if this entire way of seeing nature, culture, and psychology is simply the result of a mass delusion based on rhetorical manipulation? In other words, what if genetic codes and digital codes are two completely different things, and the reason why we are now thinking about these distinct domains through the same set of concepts and words is that our societies seek to bridge the gap between nature and culture by seeing culture as natural and nature as cultural.

Keywords Baudrillard · AIDS · Viruses · Rhetoric · Infection · Language

Jean Baudrillard's work offers an important insight into the ways that a viral mode of rhetoric has been used to represent viruses and other aspects of biology, culture, and psychology.[1] A key defining aspect of this mode of persuasion is the notion that due to the open nature of our social and cerebral networks, we are prone to being infected by uncontrollable external forces. This risk, then, of an "open society" is that it has lost its ability to stop and filter incoming germs and ideas, and once these

R. Samuels, *Viral Rhetoric*,
https://doi.org/10.1007/978-3-030-73895-2_2

elements enter into the system, they are able to replicate and circulate at will. However, what if this entire way of seeing nature, culture, and psychology is simply the result of a mass delusion based on rhetorical manipulation? In other words, what if genetic codes and digital codes are two completely different things, and the reason why we are now thinking about these distinct domains through the same set of concepts and words is that our societies seek to bridge the gap between nature and culture by seeing culture as natural and nature as cultural?[2]

This globalizing use of metaphor and analogy is centered on displacing the way language works onto non-linguistic entities. If we think of language as an external, automated influence that is internalized on an unconscious level, then we can begin to comprehend that the desire to see biology as a code and to project human understanding onto computers derives from the same drive to repress and project internal mental processes onto the external world.[3]

Baudrillard and AIDS

Baudrillard argues that our minds, cultures, and bodies are now shaped by a viral spread of images and signals:

> All these forms are viral - fascinating, indiscriminate - and their virulence is reinforced by their images, for the modern media have a viral force of their own, and their virulence is contagious. Ours is a culture in which bodies and minds are irradiated by signals and images; little wonder, then, that for all its marvels this culture also produces the most murderous viruses. The nuclearization of our bodies began with Hiroshima, but it continues endemically, incessantly, in the shape of our irradiation by media, signs, programs, networks. (36–37)

The main point in this passage appears to be that just as bodies can be infected by viruses, we also find that minds and cultures can be infiltrated by the spread of uncontrollable replications, and the central cause for this virality is the loss of our cultural immune system.[4] Since, according to Baudrillard, we have been liberating ourselves from all past constraints, we have no way of stopping new ideas and images from infecting our cultures and minds. As a cultural form of the acquired immune deficiency syndrome (AIDS), we have lost our ability to filter ideas, and the result is that these influences affect us in a viral way.

It is important to highlight that what we are witnessing in the world today is the global spread of viruses, like the novel coronavirus, which is made possible by our international systems of travel and social interaction.[5] Although the viruses themselves are purely biological entities that infect people and replicate within the host, their spread is facilitated by the connections made through non-biological transportation structures. Moreover, these open systems are matched by an integrated global media order that traces and represents the movement of the viruses. We also see that due to our lack of a global healthcare system, the biological spread cannot be contained through nation-based institutions.[6]

While it may appear that Baudrillard's discourse is just the rhetoric of an extreme, unhinged philosopher, we shall see throughout this book that the use of viruses as a metaphor for psychology, culture, and technology has spread throughout different areas of knowledge and life. In fact, there is a viral spread of viral metaphors, and this representation of viruses is derived from several fundamental factors. One of the main causes is that once we started seeing genetic material as a code, and we began to program computers through codes, the perceived differences between technology and biology began to break down.[7] The next stage in this process was to perceive the human mind itself as an information-processing machine determined by cellular machinery.[8] We then witnessed the simultaneous rise of AIDS and computer viruses through a shared language of infection and replication.[9] This combination of biology and computer technology was followed by the notion that memes are the cultural equivalent of genes, and so biology and culture could be said to be structured by the same set of processes: replication, mutation, combination, and selection.[10] Accompanying this biological model of culture was the notion of videos going viral as a way of representing the mass spread of material on the Web.[11]

All of these connections among nature, culture, and technology force us to ask if we are moving to a single trans-discipline, where everyone is starting to use the same set of shared concepts or has there been a massive confusion of discourses? To start to answer this important question, I want to first look at some quotes from high-level scientists, philosophers, and cultural theorists to show that this viral rhetoric is not just Baudrillard's fantasy. In examining the representations of these contemporary thinkers, I hope to reveal why it is important to take a critical perspective on this new mode of discourse.

Viral Rhetoric Across the Disciplines

In the following scientific description of the viral theory of cancer, we find a constant intermixing of diverse disciplines:

> Viral oncogenes disrupt the normal cellular gene expression and signal transduction pathways. The signal transduction pathway is responsible for altering cellular gene expression in response to a wide range of external and internal signals. It is a complex net of regulatory proteins which means that a given gene product can be (de)activated by many different stimuli and that a single stimuli can (de)activate many different genes. They do this by virtue of altered structures or overproduction. The end result is an altered transcriptional profile which favours cell division.[12]

The use of terms like "expression," "signal," and "transcription" to describe the functioning of genes shows how the language of computer science and linguistics has affected the discourse of biology. Moreover, the deployment of these borrowed metaphors creates the dual sense that biology functions like a machine, and at the same time, biology expresses itself like a human language.

While some may say that this example of intermixing disciplines is just an attempt of expert scientists to communicate to the general public, it is important to point out that this passage reflects how high-level scientists communicate with each other. In fact, we find the same type of interdisciplinary rhetoric in the discourse of expert computer scientists. This mixing of biology, technology, and linguistics can be detected in a description of a computer virus:

> Worms are programs that replicate themselves from system to system without the use of a host file. This is in contrast to viruses, which requires the spreading of an infected host file. Although worms generally exist inside of other files, often Word or Excel documents, there is a difference between how worms and viruses use the host file. Usually the worm will release a document that already has the "worm" macro inside the document.[13]

In the case of computer viruses, the very notion of a machine contracting a "virus" reveals a combination of biology and technology. Furthermore, by stressing the biological process of infection, computer scientists perform a double rhetorical function of naturalizing technology and instrumentalizing nature. One of the possible effects of this linguistic cross-over is that technological functions take on the sense of being inevitable (natural), while natural processes appear mechanical and changeable.

It is interesting to note that for Marx, this process of objectifying nature and naturalizing objects is the key to what he called commodity fetishism and the mystification of capitalism.[14] From this modern perspective, capitalists treat people like things and things like people. However, in contemporary culture, this fetishistic process is expanded so that humans are treated like machines, while machines are treated like people. Thus, a technological infection is not only called a "virus" that "infects" another entity, but a biological process which is described in highly mechanistic terms.

In another description of a computer virus, we see how his mixing of biology and technology creates a sense of automated psychology: "W32/Batrans-B is an email aware worm which uses MAPI to spread. The worm forwards itself to addresses found on the infected computer as an email message with no message text. The worm finds addresses to send itself to by searching the address book." The notion that the computer virus is "aware" and that it can "search," "find" and "forward" messages illustrates how new media technologies are being anthropomorphized. Therefore, just as human beings are becoming increasingly connected to their technologies, new media technologies themselves are represented as acting with human intentionality.[15]

In this humanization of automation, we see how the combination of autonomy and automation in automodernity is reversible.[16] Thus, just as humans seek individual control by using new media technologies, these same instruments are presented as having a mind of their own. In terms of our globalizing techno-culture, this dual reversal between humans and machines produces the ideology that we cannot stop technological progress or the viral spread of globalized capital.[17]

For Baudrillard, the use of biological metaphors points to the dominance of AIDS as a fundamental description of both our cultural and biological systems:

> AIDS is a reflection not so much of an excess of sex or sexual pleasure but as of sex's decomposition through its general spread into all areas of life, its venting through all of the trivial variants of sexual incantation. The real loss of immunity concerns sex as whole, with the disappearance of sexual difference and hence of sexuality per se. (8)

In this use of AIDS as a social metaphor, Baudrillard posits that just as this virus spreads because the individual's immune system is not working, a society that no longer has strict moral or traditional boundaries is subject to be infected from all other cultures. Likewise, a discipline or discourse that can no longer police its own boundaries becomes subject to being contaminated by other fields. Moreover, since sex is used to sell everything in our culture, sex itself loses meaning, and with this mode of trans-sexuality, the traditional function of sex as reproduction or gender opposition is overcome.[18]

In the case of new media, the notion of "viral videos" reveals how technology is being presented as a system of replication that avoids all attempts at cultural control. In fact, the World Wide Web is often depicted as being a media platform that spreads through all cultures and undermines all traditional beliefs, values, and authorities.[19] From this perspective, we really have lost our cultural immune systems, and we are now faced with the incontrollable infection of diverse discourses and influences.

A strong elaboration of this theory of "viral" cultural "infection" can be found in Richard Dawkins' "Viruses of the Mind."[20] In this text, Dawkins, an evolutionary biologist, posits that in our general condition of immune deficiency, we are no longer able to stop the influence of foreign and discredited ideas:

> A human child is shaped by evolution to soak up the culture of her people. Most obviously, she learns the essentials of their language in a matter of months. A large dictionary of words to speak, an encyclopedia of information to speak about, complicated syntactic and semantic rules to order the speaking, are all transferred from older brains into hers well before she reaches half her adult size. When you are pre-programmed to absorb useful information at a high rate, it is hard to shut out pernicious or damaging information at the same time. With so many mindbytes to be downloaded, so many mental codons to be replicated, it is no wonder that child brains are gullible, open to almost any suggestion, vulnerable to subversion, easy prey to Moonies, Scientologists and nuns. Like immune-deficient patients, children are wide open to mental infection s that adults might brush off without effort.

Within this rhetorical melding of biology and technology, humans are represented as being pre-programmed machines that circulate memes just like they replicate and circulate genes. Moreover, this notion of the meme is used to create a cultural equivalent to genetic code, and like Baudrillard,

Dawkins establishes a total equivalence between genetic processes and cultural structures. Therefore, in the same way that genes replicate, circulate, and mutate, ideas in automodern culture are seen as codes that are constantly being sampled, re-mixed, and transformed.[21] Likewise, the loss of the biological immune system is matched by the loss of our cultural filters, and so we are now victims of an uncontrollable biological-cultural infection. To further complicate things, we do not know if this mixing of biology and culture is a purely linguistic confusion or if this combination points to the creation of a new unified discourse where there is no longer any distinction made between biological and social processes. In other terms are we witnessing a confusion of tongues, or are we entering a new social period where biology, technology, and culture are one?

One of the reasons why it is so essential to try to determine what is really going on in this metaphorical equation between biology and culture is that we have to understand the threat posed by conspiracy theories circulating around the world through the Internet. For instance, during the time of the global COVID-19 pandemic, the ability to fight the biological virus was at times disrupted by our inability to contain false theories and pseudo-scientific explanations.[22] Due to the open nature of our communication networks, we have lost many of our protections against the spread of false information, and this lack of social filtering makes us prone to being manipulated by the repetition of misleading ideas.

The Rhetorical Universe

In looking at the Baudrillard's own rhetoric, we see how this mixing of disciplines relies on the metaphorical process of finding connections between different things:

> Nothing more closely resembles the chain reaction of terrorism in our irradiated societies than the chain reactions associated with AIDS, with Wall Street raiders or with software saboteurs. (And, by the way, what are these societies irradiated by? By the superfusion of happiness and security, information and communication? By the disintegration of symbolic nexuses, fundamental rules, or social contracts? It is anybody's guess.) The contagiousness of terrorism, its fascination, is every bit as enigmatic as the contagiousness of these other phenomena. When a programmer introduces a 'soft bomb' into his software and uses his resultant destructive

> power as a threat, is he not in effect taking the program and all its applications hostage? Likewise, are corporate raiders not taking and holding businesses hostage when they speculate on their demise or resurrection in the stock market? All these phenomena operate on the same model as terrorism (hostages have a quoted price just like shares or pictures), but one might just as easily explain terrorism in terms of a parallel with AIDS, with computer viruses, or with public stock offerings. (38)

In drawing an equivalence among terrorism, AIDS, and the stock market, Baudrillard seeks to associate these diverse domains by their shared traits of infection and replication. This metaphorical system, then, works by borrowing terminology from one discipline and applying it to another based on common characteristics.[23] In other words, the combination of discourses is rhetorical, and therefore, rhetoric becomes a key way to understand how we think about the world today.[24]

It is vital to realize that when one thinks with a metaphor, one is not only connecting two different things, but one also tends to borrow attributes from one object and apply them to another object to which they may not belong. Metaphors are also reversible feedback loops in the sense that the different objects being equated influence how we see each one of them. For instance, if I understand biology as information processing, I am not only applying computer science to nature, but I am also applying biology to computer technologies.[25] In fact, Baudrillard does show an awareness of this rhetorical structure when he questions his own metaphorical system:

> This is not to say that AIDS, financial crashes, computer viruses and terrorism are somehow interchangeable, merely that they do have a family resemblance. Thus AIDS is certainly a sort of crash in sexual values, while computers played a 'virulent' role in the Wall Street crash of 1987; meanwhile computers are themselves at risk of viral infection - of 'crashes' in the information market. Moreover, infection is no longer confined within a given system but can leap from one system to another. (37)

In this passage, he moves from simply equating these distinct domains to showing how they each affect the other. He thus shifts from a rhetoric of metaphor to one of metonymy because the basis of the connection is no longer similarity; instead, different things are being associated with their contingent connections.[26] For example, since the stock market uses computers, it is prone to computer viruses, and as a result of high-tech globalization, computer technology is infiltrating all aspects of our lives as it spreads to all parts of the world.

Added to the use of metaphor and metonymy in contemporary rhetoric, we also find a series of poetic devices that are not based on meaning or associative connections. For example, in the following passage, Baudrillard's own discourse is full of words that either sound the same or share the same letters:

> All integrated and hyperintegrated systems - the technological system, the social system, even thought itself in artificial intelligence and its derivatives - tend towards the extreme constituted by immunodeficiency. Seeking to eliminate all external aggression, they secrete their own internal virulence, their own malignant reversibility. When a certain saturation point is reached, such systems effect this reversal and undergo this alteration willy-nilly - and thus tend to self-destruct. Their very transparency becomes a threat to them, and the crystal has its revenge. (62)

At the very moment that he is claiming that all systems are being combined, he uses words like "virulence," "reversibility," and "revenge" because even in translation, these words share many of the same sounds and letters. Like a poet, Baudrillard highlights here what Lacan calls the insistence of the letter in the unconscious, which means that we can connect words not based on their meaning but on the repetition of their sounds or marks.[27] Here, we find an example of what Baudrillard indicates as the liberation of words from their referents and their meanings. For Lacan, the repetition of letters and sounds points to the way the primary processes in the unconscious utilize the materiality of language to fulfill our desire.[28]

A Conservative History of Liberation

At the start of *The Transparency of Evil*, the origin of our current cultural and rhetorical situation is traced to the modern and postmodern liberation movements:

> If I were asked to characterize the present state of affairs, I would describe it as 'after the orgy'. The orgy in question was the moment when modernity exploded upon us, the moment of liberation in every sphere. Political liberation, sexual liberation, liberation of the forces of production, liberation of the forces of destruction, women's liberation, children's liberation,

> liberation of unconscious drives, liberation of art. The assumption of all models of representation, as of all models of anti-representation. This was a total orgy - an orgy of the real, the rational, the sexual, of criticism as of anti-criticism, of development as of the crisis of development. We have pursued every avenue in the production and effective overproduction of objects, signs, messages, ideologies and satisfactions. Now everything has been liberated, the chips are down, and we find ourselves faced collectively with the big question: WHAT DO WE DO NOW THE ORGY IS OVER? (3)

This cultural history is actually quite conservative because it posits that we have not only liberated certain minority groups from their oppression, but we have also liberated ourselves from all personal and social constraints. As an argument against modernity, Baudrillard is implying that once we broke with premodern religion, monarchy, and feudalism, we lost our cultural immune system, and so now we are left in a situation where there are no boundaries or limits.

The liberation from past cultural restraints also entails for Baudrillard a liberation from representation, meaning, or value. Since we no longer believe in the ideas and structures that determined the foundations of our culture, all we can do is replicate and circulate in a viral manner all of the past social categories and representations:

> Now all we can do is simulate the orgy, simulate liberation. We may pretend to carry on in the same direction, accelerating, but in reality we are accelerating in a void, because all the goals of liberation are already behind us and because what haunts and obsesses us is being thus ahead of all the results - the very availability of all the signs, all the forms, all the desires that we had been pursuing. But what can we do? This is the state of simulation, a state in which we are obliged to replay all scenarios precisely because they have all taken place already, whether actually or potentially. The state of utopia realized, of all utopias realized, wherein paradoxically we must continue to live as though they had not been. But since they have, and since we can no longer, therefore, nourish the hope of realizing them, we can only 'hyper-realize' them through interminable simulation. We live amid the interminable reproduction of ideals, phantasies, images and dreams which are now behind us, yet which we must continue to reproduce in a sort of inescapable indifference. (3–4)

Baudrillard argues here that because we have liberated ourselves from all values and cultural filters, we simulate these ideas from a position of indifference. Of course, one could say in response to this cynical discourse that there are still many people who have not been liberated, and we still have many premodern ideologies and institutions, but Baudrillard wants to claim that once language itself became liberated from its relation to reality or meaning, all past and present value systems were hollowed out.[29]

The flip-side, then, of the viral combination of diverse discourses is the erasure of meaning from each domain. From this dark perspective, the effect of all of the revolutions and liberation movements has been to produce a culture of total viral contamination:

> The fact is that the revolution has well and truly happened, but not in the way we expected. Everywhere what has been liberated has been liberated so that it can enter a state of pure circulation, so that it can go into orbit. With the benefit of a little hindsight, we may say that the unavoidable goal of all liberation is to foster and provision circulatory networks. The fate of the things liberated is an incessant commutation, and these things are thus subject to increasing indeterminacy, to the principle of uncertainty. (4)

According to this logic, when ideas and symbols are liberated from their referents and meanings, they are able to circulate and replicate freely without any concern for resistances or filtering. The end result of this process is a total state of indifference and uncertainty because there is no longer any possible perspective or viewpoint to make a judgment on anything.[30]

The Irony of Theory

The major problem that I see with Baudrillard's analysis is that he is simply replicating in his own rhetoric the worst tendencies that he sees in contemporary culture, which makes sense since he wants to deny the possibility of any critical distance or social analysis. However, his discourse is dominated by the rhetorical tropes of hyperbole, metaphor, metonymy, and wordplay, and so instead of offering a different view of what he sees, he is instead repeating what he is critiquing.[31] Yet, we can still learn a lot from his words because he does in fact point to real events that do have real meanings and value, and in this way, his entire discourse is ironic because it is made possible by the very processes that he claims are no longer valid.[32] In other words, he still writes and wants to be understood at the same time he denies the possibility of communication, meaning, and understanding.

This use of irony is an important part of viral rhetoric because it reflects on the way that our world is increasingly structured by language, but this language often appears to have no set meaning. In fact, Baudrillard provides a historical explanation for how we have moved through different cultural periods shaped by distinct forms of value:

> Once, out of some obscure need to classify, I proposed a tripartite account of value: a natural stage (use-value), a commodity stage (exchange-value), and a structural stage (sign-value). Value thus had a natural aspect, a commodity aspect, and a structural aspect. ... For after the natural, commodity, and structural stages of value comes the fractal stage. The first of these stages had a natural referent, and value developed on the basis of a natural use of the world. The second was founded on a general equivalence, and value developed by reference to a logic of the commodity. The third is governed by a code, and value develops here by reference to a set of models. At the fourth, the fractal (or viral, or radiant) stage of value, there is no point of reference at all, and value radiates in all directions, occupying all interstices, without reference to anything whatsoever, by virtue of pure contiguity. At the fractal stage there is no longer any equivalence, whether natural or general. Properly speaking there is now no law of value, merely a sort of *epidemic of value,* a sort of general metastasis of value, a haphazard proliferation and dispersal of value. Indeed, we should really no longer speak of 'value' at all, for this kind of propagation or chain reaction makes all valuation impossible. (5)

This historical model begins with the premodern use value followed by the modern emphasis on exchange value.[33] The next postmodern stage is equated with the use of codes and models, while the final post-postmodern, automodern stage describes our current cultural infection of the viral epidemic of value. In this last cultural period, representations are said to be no longer equivalent to anything else, and so they are free to spread around the world without any resistance.

What many commentators miss is that Baudrillard's model is itself inherently conservative because it is based on the idea that in the initial use of language, words had a direct connection to reality, and their meanings were defined by tradition. As Marx argued, these premodern structures were undermined by modern capitalism as exchange value replaced all of the previous cultural values.[34] Baudrillard then seeks to go beyond Marx by showing how the postmodern investment in social structures was followed by the post-postmodern anti-social proliferation of meaningless signs.

What does appear to be missing in Baudrillard's discourse is any resistance to language itself. From Lacan's perspective, there is always a fundamental divide between the Symbolic order of language and the Real, which lacks nothing and has no inherent meaning.[35] As a product of natural replication, biological viruses can be considered to be Real, while our representations of these natural forces point to an attempt to use language to approximate and control the resistant Real.[36] From this perspective, what gives language its ability to make meaning is that it is limited by its inability to represent the Real. Similar to Kant's claim that since we cannot know the thing-in-itself, all we can know is how we use knowledge, Lacan offers a way of thinking about the limits of knowledge and thought.[37]

Lacan's fundamental divide between the Symbolic and the Real points to Freud's claim that science only emerges from primitive animism and premodern religion when people realize the limits of their own thoughts and knowledge.[38] Furthermore, Freud defines the reality principle as the acceptance of death and the necessities of life.[39] While in primitive animism, people are dominated by the "omnipotence of thought," the modern scientist has to overcome this mental omnipotence by separating symbolic memories from perceptions of reality. Part of this process requires moving beyond the pleasure principle by dis-investing from past attachments and fixations. The psychoanalytic process is thus a form of mourning where one must learn to accept loss, while one disinvests from delusional thoughts and one's unconscious dependency on others.[40]

A guiding paradox of psychoanalysis is that as a practice entirely centered on speech and language, it ends up emphasizing the limits of discourse and representation. If as Hegel wrote "the word is the death of the thing," then psychoanalysis has to deal with this process of mortification by showing how the Real of life itself resists symbolization. One way, then, of thinking about the coronavirus is to see it as a reminder of our inability to completely control the natural Real, and this encounter with the resistance of the Real forces us to think about the limits of language and society. However, this encounter with the Real is blocked by the way that we project nature onto culture and confuse the human mind with the biological brain. Likewise, Baudrillard's own discourse reflects a new form of animism where cultural structures are seen as natural and real, while the Real itself is taken to be Symbolic.

This projection of the omnipotence of thought into nature is evident in the following passage:

> Once again we are put in mind of microphysics: it is as impossible to make estimations between beautiful and ugly, true and false, or good and evil, as it is simultaneously to calculate a particle's speed and position. Good is no longer the opposite of evil, nothing can now be plotted on a graph or analysed in terms of abscissas and ordinates. Just as each particle follows its own trajectory, each value or fragment of value shines for a moment in the heavens of simulation, then disappears into the void along a crooked path that only rarely happens to intersect with other such paths. This is the pattern of the fractal - and hence the current pattern of our culture. (5–6)

In this combination of concepts derived from physics with ideas based on cultural values, the distinction between the Symbolic and the Real is lost. The key move in this projection is to equate the scientific principle of uncertainty with nature itself.[41] Thus, our own inability to think in terms of position and speed at the same time is seen as pointing to the uncertain nature of particles themselves. In turn, this uncertainty is then projected onto culture so that our lack of understanding is seen as undermining any stable cultural or social order.

However, since we think in terms of cultural oppositions, the collapse of these differences threatens to make communication itself impossible, and yet Baudrillard continues to write and communicate with others. Although his discourse appears to match the type of language use Freud finds in animism, psychotic delusions, and dreams, what makes his rhetoric non-psychotic is the fact that it is shaped by an ironic combination of opposing perspectives on language.[42] On the one hand, he wants to highlight how all meaning and reference to reality has been lost, but on another hand, he still wants to be read and understood. His discourse is therefore split between two very different perspectives that are able to be maintained at the same time.

We shall see that a central issue for our contemporary period is that we are witnessing both an over-abundance of meaning-making media and a nihilistic rejection of meaning itself. For Baudrillard, one possible explanation for this combination of meaning and non-meaning is that when signs are liberated from their significations, they are able to more freely circulate around the world:

> When things, signs or actions are freed from their respective ideas, concepts, essences, values, points of reference, origins and aims, they embark upon an endless process of self-reproduction. Yet things continue to function long after their ideas have disappeared, and they do so in total indifference to their own content. The paradoxical fact is that they function even better under these circumstances. (6)

From this perspective, what has made global capitalism and the World Wide Web possible is that ideas are able to freely circulate because they no longer conflict with cultural traditions and individual understandings, and the reason why these viral representations avoid resistance is that they have denied their own value and meaning.[43]

This global liberation of representation from meaning and reference can be understood through Freud's theory of the pleasure principle, which he defined by the drive to eliminate all mental and physical tension.[44] As a reactionary force, pleasure is here determined to be a means for escaping from conflict, anxiety, responsibility, and ultimately reality. Just as Aristotle defined catharsis as the release of the emotions of fear and pity, we can affirm that viral culture represents the liberation of people from social conflict and cultural mediation.[45] Thus, Baudrillard's rejection of the possibility of political liberation dovetails with the right-wing, libertarian attempt to deny the value of social movements and social welfare programs: since the problems of the world can be denied by escaping into the realm of virtual pleasure, then there is no need to try to change anything.[46]

This drive to meaningless enjoyment through endless media consumption is then coupled with a rhetoric that effaces the differences among nature, culture, and psychology: not only can we escape society through the private consumption of entertainment, but we can deny the importance of society itself by affirming that we are simply the products of our uncontrollable genes. Similar to Margaret Thatcher's claim there is no society, the libertarian Right wants to deny the importance of social mediation so that one can enjoy without guilt, shame, or responsibility.[47] The nihilism of this culture is apparent in the following passage by Baudrillard:

> The idea of wealth that production once connoted has disappeared, yet production itself continues more vigorously than ever. Indeed, it picks up speed precisely in proportion to its increasing indifference to its original aims. Of the political sphere one can say that the idea of politics has disappeared but that the game of politics continues in secret indifference to its own stakes. Of television, that it operates in total indifference to its own images (it would not be affected, in other words, even were mankind to disappear). Could it be that all systems, all individuals, harbour a secret urge to be rid of their ideas, of their own essences, so as to be able to proliferate everywhere, to transport themselves simultaneously to every point of the compass? In any event, the consequences of a dissociation of this kind can only be fatal. A thing which has lost its idea is like the man who has lost his shadow, and it must either fall under the sway of madness or perish. (8)

The notion that television would continue even after all humans have been eliminated represents the logical conclusion of the replacement of reality with media representations: we have been socialized to believe that all of the culture we are internalizing is just meaningless escape, and this trained indifference helps to turn every experience into a marketable commodity as political resistance is eliminated.[48] Our civilization has therefore finally attained its ultimate goal of self-destruction: in our effort to avoid all tension, we have turned life itself into a meaningless set of objects. As Freud insisted, the pleasure principle results in the death drive because the desire to keep anxiety at its lowest level requires a return to a state of inanimation.[49]

Since we are driven to use as little mental and physical energy as possible, we have effectively outsourced our physical labor and our mental processes to technology. The end point of this global project of automation is to eliminate humans from their own need to think or work.[50] If we can get computers to do things like perform our math and correct our grammar, we can escape from the need to think on our own, and in this system, education, parenting, and governing become unnecessary. Of course, I am presenting an extreme case of our current situation, but as we see in reading Baudrillard's own hyperbolic rhetoric, a view of the logical extension of our current actions can help us to understand the threats posed by contemporary trends.

The ultimate paradox is that the more that we turn to evolutionary science to explain technology and culture, the more we make science seem totalizing as it is represented as being able to explain anything. However, this idealized version of science makes people reject it when it produces errors or it fails to resolve pressing problems. Since people expect science to be all-knowing, it is easy to turn against it when a crisis like COVID-19 arises. Conspiracy theories are this in part caused by the conflation of biological processes and cultural formations. It is the hope of this book that by learning how to read the rhetorical foundations of our perceptions of nature, culture, subjectivity, and technology, we can take a more realistic approach to our social and political issues.

Notes

1. Baudrillard, Jean. *The transparency of evil: Essays on extreme phenomena*. Verso, 1993.
2. Rose, Steven, Richard Charles Lewontin, and L. Kamin. "Not in our genes: Biology, ideology and human nature." *The Wilson Quarterly* 152 (1984).
3. Samuels, Robert. *Psychoanalyzing the politics of the new brain sciences*. Springer, 2017.
4. Gerofsky, Susan. "The impossibility of 'real-life' word problems (according to Bakhtin, Lacan, Zizek and Baudrillard)." *Discourse: Studies in the Cultural Politics of Education* 31.1 (2010): 61–73.
5. Hollingsworth, T. Déirdre, Neil M. Ferguson, and Roy M. Anderson. "Will travel restrictions control the international spread of pandemic influenza?" *Nature Medicine* 12.5 (2006): 497–499.
6. Søreide, Kjetil, et al.. "Immediate and long-term impact of the COVID-19 pandemic on delivery of surgical services." *The British Journal of Surgery* (2020).
7. Hood, Leroy, and David Galas. "The digital code of DNA." *Nature* 421.6921 (2003): 444–448.
8. Waldrop, M. Mitchell. "The workings of working memory; the central thesis of cognitive science is that the mind is an information processor; the study of reading gives a unique insight into how that processor works." *Science* 237 (1987): 1564–1568.
9. Helmreich, Stefan. "Flexible infections: Computer viruses, human bodies, nation-states, evolutionary capitalism." *Science, Technology, & Human Values* 25.4 (2000): 472–491.
10. Dawkins, Richard. *The selfish gene*. Oxford University Press, 2016.
11. Burgess, Jean. "'All your chocolate rain are belong to us'? Viral video, YouTube and the dynamics of participatory culture." *Video Vortex Reader: Responses to YouTube* (2008): 101–109.
12. Sever, Richard, and Joan S. Brugge. "Signal transduction in cancer." *Cold Spring Harbor Perspectives in Medicine* 5.4 (2015): a006098.

13. https://www.iadvanceseniorcare.com/protecting-your-computers-from-invaders/.
14. De Angelis, Massimo. "Social relations, commodity-fetishism and Marx's Critique of Political Economy." *Review of Radical Political Economics* 28.4 (1996): 1–29.
15. Zheng, Jianqing Frank, and Sirkka Jarvenpaa. "Negative consequences of anthropomorphized technology: A bias-threat-illusion model." *Proceedings of the 52nd Hawaii International Conference on System Sciences*, 2019.
16. Samuels, Robert. "Auto-modernity after postmodernism: Autonomy and automation in culture, technology, and education." *Digital Youth, Innovation, and the Unexpected* (2008).
17. Dana, Leo-Paul, Len Korot, and George Tovstiga. "Toward a transnational techno-culture: An empirical investigation of knowledge management." *Globalization and Entrepreneurship: Policy and Strategy Perspectives* (2003): 183–204.
18. Jean, Baudrillard. "The end of the millennium or the countdown." *Economy and Society* 26.4 (1997): 447–455.
19. Berger, Jonah, and Katherine L. Milkman. "Social transmission and viral culture." *Philadelphia: The Wharton School of the University of Pennsylvania* (2010).
20. Dawkins, Richard. "Viruses of the mind." *Dennett and His Critics: Demystifying Mind* 13 (1993): e27.
21. Samuels, Robert. *New media, cultural studies, and critical theory after postmodernism: Automodernity from Zizek to Laclau*. Springer, 2009.
22. Mian, Areeb, and Shujhat Khan. "Coronavirus: The spread of misinformation." *BMC Medicine* 18.1 (2020): 1–2.
23. Lakoff, George, and Mark Johnson. *Metaphors we live by*. University of Chicago Press, 2008.
24. Samuels, Robert. *Zizek and the rhetorical unconscious: Global politics, philosophy, and subjectivity*. Springer Nature.
25. Glucksberg, Sam. "The psycholinguistics of metaphor." *Trends in Cognitive Sciences* 7.2 (2003): 92–96.
26. Radden, Günter, and Zoltán Kövecses. "Towards a theory of metonymy." *Metonymy in Language and Thought* 4 (1999): 17–60.
27. Lacan, Jacques. "The insistence of the letter in the unconscious." *Yale French Studies* 36/37 (1966): 112–147.
28. Lacan, Jacques. "The function and field of speech and language in psychoanalysis: Écrits." *Trans. B. Fink. New York NY: WW Norton & Company* (2006): 197–268.
29. Kellner, Douglas. *Jean Baudrillard: From Marxism to postmodernism and beyond*. Vol. 179. Stanford University Press, Stanford, CA, 1989.
30. King, Anthony. "Baudrillard's Nihilism and the end of theory" (1998).

31. Fisher, Mark. *Capitalist realism: Is there no alternative?* John Hunt Publishing, 2009.
32. Magill, R. Jay. *Chic ironic bitterness*. University of Michigan Press, 2009.
33. Kroker, Arthur. "Baudrillard's Marx." *Theory, Culture & Society* 2.3 (1985): 69–83.
34. Marx, Karl, and Friedrich Engels. *The communist manifesto*. Penguin, 2002.
35. Miller, Jacques-Alain, ed. *The seminar of Jacques Lacan: Book 1: Freud's papers on technique 1953–1954*. CUP Archive, 1988.
36. Samuels, Robert. *Between philosophy and psychoanalysis: Lacan's reconstruction of Freud*. Routledge, 2014.
37. Kant, Immanuel. *Immanuel Kant's critique of pure reason*. Vol. 1. Macmillan, 1881.
38. Freud, Sigmund, and Anna Freud. *Totem and Taboo and other works*. Vol. 13. Random House, 2001.
39. Freud, Sigmund. "Formulations on the two principles of mental functioning." *The standard edition of the complete psychological works of Sigmund Freud, Volume XII (1911–1913): The case of Schreber, papers on technique and other works*, 1958. 213–226.
40. Samuels, Robert. "Science and the reality principle." *Freud for the twenty-first century*. Palgrave Pivot, Cham, 2019. 5–16.
41. Robertson, Howard Percy. "The uncertainty principle." *Physical Review* 34.1 (1929): 163.
42. Samuels, Robert. "The unconscious and the primary processes." *Freud for the twenty-first century*. Palgrave Pivot, Cham, 2019. 27–42.
43. Varela, Julio Armando. "Vortex to virus, myth to meme: The literary evolution of nihilism and chaos in modernism and postmodernism" (2004).
44. Samuels, Robert. "The pleasure principle and the death drive." *Freud for the twenty-first century*. Palgrave Pivot, Cham, 2019. 17–25.
45. Halliwell, Stephen. *Aristotle's poetics*. University of Chicago Press, 1998.
46. Brennan, Jason. *Libertarianism: What everyone needs to know®*. Oxford University Press, 2012.
47. Thatcher, Margaret. "No such thing as society." *Intervista per Woman's Own* 23 (1987).
48. Postman, Neil. *Amusing ourselves to death: Public discourse in the age of show business*. Penguin, 2006.
49. Freud, Sigmund. *Beyond the pleasure principle*. Penguin UK, 2003.
50. Chessell, Darren. "The jobless economy in a post-work society: How automation will transform the labor market." *Psychosociological Issues in Human Resource Management* 6.2 (2018): 74–79.

CHAPTER 3

How the Rhetoric of Information Took over Our World

Abstract This chapter examines James Gleick's *The Information: A History, a Theory, a Flood* in order to examine the history behind our current replacement of reality with language. My central argument is that through a mixing of distinct discourses, the separation of nature and culture has been broken down, and this loss of difference has profound social and psychological implications. On the most basic level, Gleick's text presents the projection of linguistics onto biology and technology as a purely scientific advancement with little need for concern; however, what is missing from his analysis is not only any sense of critical distance but also an understanding of how human language actually works. By offering a rhetorical analysis of his book, I hope to show how we can fight the growing power of this new form of cultural animism.

Keywords Gleick · Information · DNA · Digital code · Language · Viruses

This chapter examines James Gleick's *The Information: A History, a Theory, a Flood* in order to examine the history behind our current replacement of reality with language.[1] My central argument is that through a mixing of distinct discourses, the separation of nature and culture has been broken down, and this loss of difference has profound

R. Samuels, *Viral Rhetoric*,
https://doi.org/10.1007/978-3-030-73895-2_3

social and psychological implications. On the most basic level, Gleick's text presents the projection of linguistics onto biology and technology as a purely scientific advancement with little need for concern; however, what is missing from his analysis is not only any sense of critical distance but also an understanding of how human language actually works. By offering a rhetorical analysis of his book, I hope to show how we can fight the growing power of this new form of cultural animism and totalitarian scientism.

The History of Information

At the heart of Gleick's text is an effort to explain how the concept of information has been able to spread to all aspects of our lives. Not only are we shown that nature is structured by the processing of information, but computer technologies are also shaped by the same type of processes we find in nature:

> Information theory began as a bridge from mathematics to electrical engineering and from there to computing. What English speakers call "computer science" Europeans have known as informatique, informatica, and Informatik. Now even biology has become an information science, a subject of messages, instructions, and code. Genes encapsulate information and enable procedures for reading it in and writing it out. Life spreads by networking. The body itself is an information processor. Memory resides not just in brains but in every cell. No wonder genetics bloomed along with information theory. (8)

In this description of biology and computer science, Gleick is not saying that nature and culture can be interpreted in a similar way; rather, he is arguing that there is no real difference between nature and technology since they are both centered on codes, messages, and instructions.[2] In other words, nature is a language that we need to read, and computers are also structured by language.[3] Furthermore, by affirming that memories reside in every cell, and genes are just coded information, we see that what breaks down the difference between nature and technology is language itself.

It is my hypothesis that due to a misunderstanding of how language actually works, linguistic structures are projected onto non-linguistic domains. Moreover, the difference between our constructed knowledge and the object of our representations is lost so that the Real becomes the Symbolic, and the Symbolic becomes the Real. This collapsing of fundamental difference is evident in the following passage:

> DNA is the quintessential information molecule, the most advanced message processor at the cellular level—an alphabet and a code, 6 billion bits to form a human being. "What lies at the heart of every living thing is not a fire, not warm breath, not a 'spark of life,'" declares the evolutionary theorist Richard Dawkins. "It is information, words, instructions.... If you want to understand life, don't think about vibrant, throbbing gels and oozes, think about information technology." The cells of an organism are nodes in a richly interwoven communications network, transmitting and receiving, coding and decoding. Evolution itself embodies an ongoing exchange of information between organism and environment. (8)

In this total loss of disciplinary boundaries, language is seen as existing in natural entities as the throbbing and oozing aspects of nature are replaced by the fixed stability of information processors. It is therefore not just the extreme rhetoric of Baudrillard that proclaims the combination of nature, culture, and technology, but sophisticated scientists and mainstream journalists also believe in what we can call "science fictions."

Inventing Science Fictions

Science fictions represent the breakdown in the separation of truth and fiction through the projection of one discourse onto another. In Gleick's case, the model of computer-based information processors is used to describe biological, technological, and cultural entities through the same set of shared concepts. By saying that genes and computer codes are structured like a language, what is being repressed is the structure of human language itself. For example, the reason why viruses are described as hijacking internal processes bent on replication, recombination, mutation, and selection is that human language is represented as a viral infection that replicates, mutates, recombines, and then survives in particular contexts.[4] My overall argument here is that often when biologists describe genetics, what they are actually doing is projecting our own mental processes onto external reality, which is exactly how Freud describes the primitive culture of animism.[5]

One might respond to my theory by asking how is it possible for biologists to accomplish many things if they are simply engaged in the psychotic process of projection? The answer to this important question is that scientific projections are combined with reality testing and communication, and so unlike psychotic formations, the scientific method forces us to take into account both the reactions of the Real and the need to communicate our findings to others through a shared process of linguistic dialogue. This relation between scientific projections and social reason will be further explained in the next chapter, but for now, it is vital to understand how the new animism accomplishes the goal of combining premodern religion with modern science.

Equating Modern Science and Premodern Religion

We see this blending of premodern and modern discourses in the following description of the role of information in biology: "The information circle becomes the unit of life," says Werner Loewenstein after thirty years spent studying intercellular communication. He reminds us that information means something deeper now: "It connotes a cosmic principle of organization and order, and it provides an exact measure of that" (9). By equating information with a cosmic principle of organization and order, we see a return to the premodern idea that the world is shaped by natural and divine predetermination.[6] However, this return to a totalizing organization is coupled with the modern use of science to determine the structural features of order. While in the case of premodern societies, there is no difference between culture and nature, with modernity, we use cultural theories to understand nature. Modernity, then, requires affirming the difference between our knowledge and the Real of the natural world, and one way that this difference is affirmed is by seeing language as an artificial system utilized to approximate reality.[7] Yet, in many contemporary discourses, instead of recognizing the limits of our knowledge, we act as if we can read nature as a book. We shall see that this rhetoric represents a radical misunderstanding of both nature and culture.

As a key move in combining of biology and culture is presented through the concept of the meme:

> The gene has its cultural analog, too: the meme. In cultural evolution, a meme is a replicator and propagator—an idea, a fashion, a chain letter, or a conspiracy theory. On a bad day, a meme is a virus. Economics is recognizing itself as an information science, now that money itself is completing

> a developmental arc from matter to bits, stored in computer memory and magnetic strips, world finance coursing through the global nervous system. Even when money seemed to be material treasure, heavy in pockets and ships' holds and bank vaults, it always was information. Coins and notes, shekels and cowries were all just short-lived technologies for tokenizing information about who owns what. (9)

It may appear that the analogy between the meme and the gene is based on using theories derived from genetics to understand how culture works and circulates, but my argument is the opposite: our understanding of genetics has been largely determined by our foreclosed awareness of how language is structured.[8] The reason, then, why we can now equate culture and biology is because we are seeing biology through the lens of linguistic principles.

Related to this analogy between genes and memes is the representation of memory in biological processes. Although it appears that genes must have memories because they are able to follow predetermined instructions based on the retention and retrieval of information, Freud helps us to distinguish between human memory and biological processes. For psychoanalysis, memory is a system of signs that are organized in a network.[9] As Lacan insists, each signifier is related to other signifiers, and each meaning is associated with other meanings.[10] This structure entails that a signifier never represents itself, and the meaning of each representation or memory is constantly being re-interpreted through the addition of new signifiers. On the most basic level, Freud treats neurons as memories and memories as signifiers, and so on the level of the human mind, memory symbols are constantly being updated and revised.[11] Language, then is not information or a simple code because it is an intertextual system with no inherent meaning or essence.

In equating language with the genetic code or the digital code, the richness and variety of human discourses are replaced by a set number of variables that do not lead to meaning or understanding. Just as computers do not understand anything, genetic codes only have signs but no signifieds.[12] From this perspective, Baudrillard is correct to say that our signs and representations have been freed from their referents and meanings so that they can circulate without any resistance: what then makes the theory of genetic and digital information possible is the elimination of meaning and understanding from language.

As Gleick indicates, this process of replacing language with information is shaped in part by the focus on reductive oppositions in binary code: "Increasingly, the physicists and the information theorists are one and the same. The bit is a fundamental particle of a different sort: not just tiny but abstract—a binary digit, a flip-flop, a yes-or-no. It is insubstantial, yet as scientists finally come to understand information, they wonder whether it may be primary: more fundamental than matter itself" (9). Here, we see that not only are scientists replacing matter with binary digits, but they are also using this reduction of language to make reality itself appear to be abstract.[13]

Instead of recognizing the difference between language and the thing-in-itself, the new animists see reality as pure information:

> They suggest that the bit is the irreducible kernel and that information forms the very core of existence. Bridging the physics of the twentieth and twenty-first centuries, John Archibald Wheeler, the last surviving collaborator of both Einstein and Bohr, put this manifesto in oracular monosyllables: "It from Bit." Information gives rise to "every it—every particle, every field of force, even the spacetime continuum itself." This is another way of fathoming the paradox of the observer: that the outcome of an experiment is affected, or even determined, when it is observed. Not only is the observer observing, she is asking questions and making statements that must ultimately be expressed in discrete bits. "What we call reality," Wheeler wrote coyly, "arises in the last analysis from the posing of yes-no questions." He added: "All things physical are information-theoretic in origin, and this is a participatory universe." The whole universe is thus seen as a computer—a cosmic information-processing machine. (10)

At first, it may appear that scientists are only using the computer as a metaphor for reality, but then we find that this metaphor is taken literally. In moving from the figurative to the literal, machines become humanized as culture is naturalized. One of the effects of these rhetorical moves is to turn science into scientism since the gap of knowledge is now closed by a totalizing perspective.[14]

It is important to point out that for premodern cultures, there is no doubt expressed about the natural order of culture and society; everything has been predetermined by a god or some natural force.[15] However, for contemporary animists, the combination of culture and nature must be seen as a reactionary move against the recognition of the separation between the Symbolic and the Real. In other terms, our post-modern scientists have to recognize on some level that our concepts and theories are not the product of nature, and so there must be a difference between our conceptions of reality and reality itself, and yet, they tend to act as if these differences do not exist: "When photons and electrons and other particles interact, what are they really doing? Exchanging bits, transmitting quantum states, processing information. The laws of physics are the algorithms. Every burning star, every silent nebula, every particle leaving its ghostly trace in a cloud chamber is an information processor" (10). The ultimate move in this understanding of information is to declare that physical particles are themselves nothing but computers processing bits of information.[16] From the perspective of the biologist and the physicist, we have not only outsourced our thinking to computers, but we now see reality as just a combination of computer technologies.[17]

When you read these descriptions of science, it does appear that as Lacan insisted science is based on the psychotic foreclosure of the Symbolic, but what makes this discourse more of a perverse structure is that the fantasy-based equation of culture, nature, and technology is coupled with an awareness of reality testing and the need to communicate ideas and findings to others.[18] As Freud emphasized, perverse subjects recognize castration, but act as if it does not exist.[19] In a similar way, these scientists must recognize the limits of their knowledge, but they speak as if no limits exist. Likewise, in the transformation of changing nature into static objects of binary logic, we encounter a desire to objectify other people and entities so that they can be manipulated on an instrumental level.[20] Therefore, the magical thinking of the new animist is combined with the pragmatic manipulations of the amoral opportunist. From the totalizing perspective of scientism, every aspect of reality is simply a code to be manipulated.

The Contagion

On the one hand, we see that the transformation of nature into information-processing machines enables the scientist to believe in the total power of humans to control and predict natural processes, but the flip side of this movement is the sense that nature, culture, and technology are prone to be infected by viral entities that spread beyond our control: "The alphabet spread by contagion. The new technology was both the virus and the vector of transmission. It could not be monopolized, and it could not be suppressed" (34). Here, we see how the virus represents a counter to scientism since as a return of the repressed or an answer from the Real, viral infections force us to admit our impotence in front of uncontrollable natural forces.[21] It is interesting to note that Gleick makes a strange reversal by affirming that it is language itself that is the real virus. Thus, instead of seeing natural viruses as the limits of our knowledge and social control, this uncontrollable nature is equated with the spread of the human-made alphabet.[22]

Just as the fight against the coronavirus revealed the limitations of our science and public healthcare systems, the spread of viral contagions highlights the limits of our ability to master nature. However, Gleick projects this natural threat onto language, and here, we see the ways the misunderstanding of language results in the misunderstanding of our relation to reality. On one level, it is true that language is like a virus because it enters our bodies and spreads to all aspects of our life through a process of replication, mutation, and recombination. In fact, Freud's descriptions of the unconscious represent the mind as being in part determined by uncontrollable memories and thoughts that cannot be effaced or stopped.[23] These unconscious representations are based on the linguistic process of substation and displacement, but it would be wrong to equate the spread of language with the spread of a virus because language is a human-made artificial structure and not a biological entity.[24]

One reason why Gleick and others may want to confuse language with a virus is that they do not want to think about the ways their own artificial language shapes how they view reality. If language is just a natural virus, then it is unnecessary to affirm the essential distinction between the Symbolic and the Real, and it is also not necessary for them to acknowledge the limits of their knowledge. What is also neglected in this discourse is that in an effort to communicate to others their scientific findings, scientists cannot help but rely on the necessary but impossible ideals of transparency, understanding, reason, and referentiality.[25] By using language to communicate, we must act as if our words are transparent, other people can understand what we are saying, our audience will process our signs in a rational way, and our words relate to a shared reality. I call this theory of communication, pragmatic idealism, because it is based on a set of necessary but impossible ideals. After all, it should be clear that people do not often understand each other, and words are not simply transparent mediums, but we still manage to do things with language through a process of approximation and trial and error. Moreover, it is precisely this type of communication that is foreclosed by psychotics, who use language without the ability to communicate with others.[26]

Pragmatic idealism also helps us to understand the difference between modern science and contemporary scientism. From the position of modern science, we use symbols and theories to make models of reality, but we also realize that these representations are only ideal concepts that never fully grasp reality itself.[27] However, with scientism, the gap between our knowledge and reality is effaced, and so one believes that one is reading nature like a book. The appearance of natural resistances to our knowledge, like viruses, and the need to communicate with others, reveals the limits of scientism, but these limitations are often simply split off into another realm.

Since science advances through experimentation and trial and error, the process of discovery must be seen as a form of pragmatic idealism and not scientism because the scientist with a totalizing view already knows what to look for.[28] This dialectic between scientism and science is presented in Gleick's description of the discovery of DNA:

> Watson and Crick thought this must be the secret, and they raced to figure out its structure at the Cavendish Laboratory in Cambridge. They could not see these molecules; they could only seek clues in the shadows cast by X-ray diffraction. But they knew a great deal about the subunits. Each nucleotide contained a "base," and there were just four different bases, designated as A, C, G, and T. They came in strictly predictable proportions. They must be the letters of the code. The rest was trial and error, fired by imagination. (291)

On the one hand, Watson and Crick had to rely on trial and error in order to discover something new and to test their theories against the reality of their perceptions, but once they began to see the biological elements as letters of a code, they re-absorbed nature back into a totalizing and self-regulating symbolic structure.[29] Just as digital code translates everything into the binary opposition of ones and zeros, genetic code reduces all of human life into four variables that can then be interpreted as a language with only four letters (G, A, T, C). Since the manipulation of these four elements will follow the mathematical laws of a combinatory system, the discourse is given a logical and non-contradictory foundation.[30] What is really happening is that language is being replaced by math, and the manipulation of the signifier is being separated from meaning and understanding.

Since machines cannot understand and other animals do not think, it is only humans that have meaning, and so it is essential to determine what makes human understanding possible. This question brings us to the issue of interpretation and consciousness since we are able to transcend our material reality through the use of mental representations.[31] Although computer scientists and biologists seek to see the world as a system of codes and information-processing machines, we have to realize that our perceptions of the world and ourselves rely on the process of signification. Gleick attempts to explore this issue by looking at how geneticists sought to turn the combinations of four different elements into a language:

> A problem was how nature punctuated the seemingly unbroken DNA and RNA strands. No one could see a biological equivalent for the pauses that separate letters in Morse code, or the spaces that separate words. Perhaps every fourth base was a comma. Or maybe (Crick suggested) commas would be unnecessary if some triplets made "sense" and others made "non-sense." Then again, maybe a sort of tape reader just needed to start at a certain point and count off the nucleotides three by three. (293)

The first solution to the problem of turning four variables into the words of a language was the issue of punctuation as a way of stopping the endless chain of signifiers. However, punctuation alone does not allow us to jump from syntax to semantics. We may be able to read genetic elements as hieroglyphics, but we still cannot move to the level of meaning.[32]

Back to Baudrillard

For Baudrillard, this separation of signifiers from signifieds reflects a general cultural movement to remove meaning and reference from discourse:

> This is where the order (or rather, disorder) of metastasis begins - the rule of propagation through mere contiguity, of cancerous proliferation (even the genetic code of value having lost any force). On all sides we witness a kind of fading away of sexuality, of sexual beings, in favour of a return to the earlier (?) stage of immortal and asexual beings reproducing, like protozoa, by simple division of the One into two and the transmission of a code. Today's techno-logical beings - machines, clones, replacement

> body parts - all tend towards this kind of reproduction, and little by little they are imparting the same process to those beings that are supposedly human, and sexed. The aim everywhere - not least at the leading edge of biological research - is to effect a genetic substitution of this kind, to achieve the linear and sequential reproduction, cloning or parthenogenesis of little celibate machines. (7)

Baudrillard's point here appears to be that we are driven to translate all of life into the linear code of sequential reproduction, and this process is enabled by replacing metaphorical relationships with contingent associations. By turning everything into a binary code, we are able to transform human life itself into a mechanical process.

Baudrillard therefore turns to rhetoric to explain how we have moved from a culture based on metaphors to a society centered on meaningless associations:

> When sexual liberation was the order of the day, the watchword was 'Maximize sexuality, minimize reproduction'. The dream of our present clone-loving society is just the opposite: as much... reproduction and as little sex as possible. At one time the body was a metaphor for the soul, then it became a metaphor for sex. Today it is no longer a metaphor for anything at all, merely the locus of metastasis, of the machine-like connections between all its processes, of an endless programming devoid of any symbolic organization or overarching purpose: the body is thus given over to the pure promiscuity of its relationship to itself - the same promiscuity that characterizes networks and integrated circuits. (7)

Since it is metaphor that makes meaning possible, the move away from metaphor implies a loss of human understanding.[33] This lack of meaning also allows representations to circulate through integrated systems without any resistance or limitations.

Due to fact that we no longer insist on the separation of distinct disciplines or areas of life, we are subjected to what Baudrillard calls a trans-disciplinary discourse where every field infects other fields:

> The possibility of metaphor is disappearing in every sphere. This is an aspect of a general tendency towards transsexuality which extends well beyond sex, affecting all disciplines as they lose their specificity and partake of a process of confusion and contagion - a viral loss of determinacy which is the prime event among all the new events that assail us. Economics

> becomes transeconomics, aesthetics becomes transaesthetics, sex becomes transsexuality - all converge in a transversal and universal process wherein no discourse may have a metaphorical relationship to another, because for there to be metaphor, differential fields and distinct objects must exist. But they cannot exist where contamination is possible between any discipline and any other. Total metonymy, then - viral by definition (or lack of definition). (7–8)

As we saw in Gleick's book, the mixing of different discourses is coupled with a lack of meaning and metaphor since metaphor can only exist when two different distinct objects are being compared. Baudrillard thus turns to viral rhetoric to explain how the replacement of metaphor with metonymy opens the door for linguistic infection and contamination.

While we might think that Baudrillard himself is using the virus as a metaphor to describe the loss of metaphor, he wants to insist that his reference to viral contamination is not metaphorical:

> The viral analogy is not an importation from biology, for everything is affected simultaneously and under the same terms by the virulence in question, by the chain reaction we have been discussing, by haphazard and senseless proliferation and metastasis. Perhaps our melancholy stems from this, for metaphor still had its beauty; it was aesthetic, playing as it did upon difference, and upon the illusion of difference. Today, metonymy - replacing the whole as well as the components, and occasioning a general commutability of terms - has built its house upon the dis-illusion of metaphor. (8)

The argument here is that since we do not clearly differentiate between different disciplines, we are unable to see the metaphorical relationship between distinct objects. Metaphor thus is predicated on the recognition of difference that is then overcome through the mental connection based on common traits.[34]

Baudrillard therefore helps us to see that the study of rhetoric is essential for understanding culture and ourselves because we have to distinguish metaphor from metonymy as we recognize the need to clearly separate distinct discourses:

> Thus every individual category is subject to contamination, substitution is possible between any sphere and any other: there is a total confusion of types. Sex is no longer located in sex itself, but elsewhere - everywhere else,

> in fact. Politics is no longer restricted to the political sphere, but infects every sphere - economics, science, art, sport. ... Sport itself, meanwhile, is no longer located in sport as such, but instead in business, in sex, in politics, in the general style of performance. (8)

One of the things that Baudrillard is emphasizing here is that not only are biologists confusing computer programming with genetics and linguistics, but we no longer separate politics from entertainment and business. For instance, for national politicians to become elected, they have to raise large sums of money in order to purchase television commercials. In this context, it is hard to say if politicians are public servants, business people, or entertainers; the fact is that contemporary politicians have to be all three at once, and so what is lost is the modern separations between democracy and capitalism and art and capitalism.[35] The problem then is not only that the market spread to all aspects of our life, but entertainment and politics have also broken free from any limitations, and so each discourse combines with the other.

A central issue, thus, with the contemporary combination of biology, technology, and culture is that it undermines our ability to understand ourselves and our world. As I will discuss in the next chapter, just as scientists and philosophers started to see biology as a language and humans as computers, our understanding of culture was itself reshaped by seeing it as a virus.

Notes

1. Gleick, James. *The information: A history, a theory, a flood.* Vintage, 2011.
2. Dennett, Daniel C. *From bacteria to Bach and back: The evolution of minds.* WW Norton & Company, 2017.
3. Head, Thomas, Gheorghe Păun, and Dennis Pixton. "Language theory and molecular genetics: Generative mechanisms suggested by DNA recombination." *Handbook of formal languages.* Springer, Berlin, Heidelberg, 1997. 295–360.
4. Dawkins, Richard. *The selfish gene.* Oxford University Press, 2016.
5. Ornston, Darius. "On projection: A study of Freud's usage." *The Psychoanalytic Study of the Child* 33.1 (1978): 117–166.
6. Harvey, Graham. *Animism: Respecting the living world.* Wakefield Press, 2005.
7. Dupré, Louis K. *Passage to modernity: An essay in the hermeneutics of nature and culture.* Yale University Press, 1993.

8. Leigh, Hoyle. *Genes, memes, culture, and mental illness: Toward an integrative model*. Springer Science & Business Media, 2010.
9. Freud, Sigmund. "Project for a scientific psychology (1950 [1895])." *The standard edition of the complete psychological works of Sigmund Freud, Volume I (1886–1899): Pre-psycho-analytic publications and unpublished drafts*, 1966. 281–391.
10. Miller, Jacques-Alain, Paul Verhaeghe, and Ellie Ragland. *Jacques Lacan and the other side of psychoanalysis: Reflections on seminar XVII, sic vi*. Vol. 6. Duke University Press, 2006.
11. Samuels, Robert. *Freud for the twenty-first century: The science of everyday life*. Springer, 2019.
12. Weizenbaum, Joseph. "Contextual understanding by computers." *Communications of the ACM* 10.8 (1967): 474–480.
13. Heath, F. G. "Origins of the binary code." *Scientific American* 227.2 (1972): 76–83.
14. Haack, Susan. *Defending science-within reason: Between scientism and cynicism*. Prometheus Books, 2011.
15. Smith, David Livingstone. "Animism, realism and anti-realism." *Freud's philosophy of the unconscious*. Springer, Dordrecht, 1999. 102–111.
16. Steane, Andrew, et al.. "Speed of ion-trap quantum-information processors." *Physical Review A* 62.4 (2000): 042305.
17. Vora, Kalindi. *Life support: Bicoapital and the new history of outsourced labor*. University of Minnesota Press, 2015.
18. Lacan, Jacques. "Science and truth." *Newsletter of the Freudian Field* 3.1/2 (1989): 4–29.
19. Freud, Sigmund. "Fetishism." *The standard edition of the complete psychological works of Sigmund Freud, Volume XXI (1927–1931): The future of an illusion, civilization and its discontents, and other works*, 1961. 147–158.
20. Jameson, Fredric. "Reification and utopia in mass culture." *Social Text* 1 (1979): 130–148.
21. Zupančič, Alenka. *Ethics of the real: Kant, Lacan*. Verso, 2000.
22. Piattelli-Palmarini, Massimo, and Juan Uriagereka. "The immune syntax: the evolution of the language virus." *Variation and universals in biolinguistics*. Elsevier, Oxford, 2004.
23. Freud, Sigmund. *The unconscious*. Vol. 8. Penguin UK, 2005.
24. Cowley, Stephen J. "Taking a language stance." *Ecological Psychology* 23.3 (2011): 185–209.
25. Niemi, Jari I. "Jürgen Habermas's theory of communicative rationality: The foundational distinction between communicative and strategic action." *Social Theory and Practice* 31.4 (2005): 513–532.
26. Lacan, Jacques, Jacques-Alain Ed Miller, and Russell Trans Grigg. "The seminar of Jacques Lacan, Book 3: The psychoses 1955–1956." *Translation of the seminar that Lacan delivered to the Société Française de*

Psychoanalyse over the course of the academic year 1955–1956. WW Norton & Company, 1993.
27. Barrow, John D. *Impossibility: The limits of science and the science of limits*. Oxford University Press on Demand, 1999.
28. Witze, Alexandra. "Does innovation always come from science?" *Nature* 527.7576 (2015): 11–11.
29. Pray, Leslie. "Discovery of DNA structure and function: Watson and Crick." *Nature Education* 1.1 (2008).
30. Arpaia, Salvatore Roberto. "The logical levels of change: Notes on the epistemology of psychological sciences." *Methods, models, simulations and approaches towards a general theory of change*, 2012. 203–218.
31. Samuels, Robert. *Freud for the twenty-first century: The science of everyday life*. Springer, 2019.
32. Girard, Jean-Yves. "On the meaning of logical rules I: syntax versus semantics." *Computational logic*. Springer, Berlin, Heidelberg, 1999.
33. Spivey, Nancy Nelson. *The constructivist metaphor: Reading, writing and the making of meaning*. Brill, 1996.
34. Chaitin, Gilbert D. *Rhetoric and culture in Lacan*. Cambridge University Press, 1996.
35. Postman, Neil. *Amusing ourselves to death: Public discourse in the age of show business*. Penguin, 2006.

CHAPTER 4

Viral Culture

Abstract Written in 1994 before the rise of Web 2.0 and the current mode of social media, Douglas Rushkoff's *Media Virus!: Hidden Agendas in Popular Culture* demonstrates the risks posed by the metaphorical use of viruses as a way of seeing how culture works in the world today. I will reveal how his overly optimistic perspective concerning the democratic possibilities of new media is in part based on his desire to see cultural media as a living, organic thing. By not clearly distinguishing between biology and culture, he ends up taking his own viral rhetoric literally.

Keywords Viral media · Hackers · Genetics · Digital code · Popular culture

Written in 1994 before the rise of Web 2.0 and the current mode of social media, Douglas Rushkoff's *Media Virus!: Hidden Agendas in Popular Culture* demonstrates the risks posed by the metaphorical use of viruses as a way of seeing how culture works in the world today.[1] I will reveal how his overly optimistic perspective concerning the democratic possibilities of new media is in part based on his desire to see cultural media as a living, organic thing. Ultimately, by not clearly distinguishing between biology and culture, he ends up taking his own viral rhetoric literally.

R. Samuels, *Viral Rhetoric*,
https://doi.org/10.1007/978-3-030-73895-2_4

Is the Media the Message?

At the start of his work, he probes the question of what is the ontological status of media itself: "Why do we think of the media as a "thing" at all—much less one with a life and agenda all its own?" (ix). As his work will illustrate, we often see media as a living creature that has its own agenda.[2] Here, human psychological traits are projected onto culture as non-biological entities are experienced as being alive. This confusion of fundamental social and scientific categories derives in part from the fact that culture is generated from human beings, but it also transcends the control of individuals. From this perspective, media, culture, and language have the same relationship to us: we use language to express ourselves, but language goes beyond our own intentions and control. As Hegel insisted, I use the word "I" to refer to myself as a particular individual, but anyone can say "I," and so language is both individualistic and universal at the same time.[3]

Making the Fake Real

Not only does language threaten the boundary between the self and others, but it also is both inside and outside of us. Like culture and "the media," language can be seen as an entity that infects us and takes on a life of its own since it originates in the external world and is internalized through processes of identification and imitation.[4] Moreover, what we are currently seeing is a desire to think of media and culture as being Real and not Symbolic:

> What I've tried to show in this book is that the media's unbridled and chaotic character is precisely what allows it to restore a sense of nature and reality to our otherwise stymied and hollow cultural conversation. The media does have a life of its own, and it behaves like a living thing, in spite of our efforts to restrain it. It touches us all, forcing an intimacy between people and cultures who may have preferred to remain artificially distinct. Further, it forces issues out into the open that many people, particularly those who perceive themselves to be in power, would prefer to have kept locked away. (x)

For the most part, whenever Rushkoff writes the word "media," we can replace it with the word "language" because language stands between ourselves and external reality, and yet Rushkoff argues that media itself belongs to the Real since it has a life of its own and should be considered to be a living thing.[5] What he is arguing here is that language as the center of the Symbolic order cannot be contained or controlled by us so it must be considered to be a viral life form. Furthermore, he presents this language virus as a progressive political force because it threatens to undermine all traditional power structures.

In representing language, culture, and the media as living organisms, Rushkoff points to the contemporary desire for reality media, which I interpret as the ironic attempt to make scripted and filtered representations appear to be real, natural, authentic, and alive: "We are to voluntarily disregard our sensationalist impulses. What business do we have watching the raw footage of a real event?" (x). According to this perspective, the dominant culture wants us to focus on easily controlled scripted media, but we are drawn to live events with real people because these types of media objects match the aliveness of our impulses and sensations.[6] Here, sensationalism is valorized because it indicates the authenticity of a media experience.

It will be my argument that in a world full of media representations, people desire to escape from representational fakeness by making the Symbolic appear to be Real.[7] Likewise, societies know that the best way to get their subjects to comply to social regulations and limitations is to produce the fantasy of realness, authenticity, naturalness, and sexual freedom. In other terms, societies can control people by convincing them that the social order is able to deliver an access to what is anti-social. Ideology, then, works here in an ironic way because it seeks to produce its own outside, and in this way, it contains its own subversion.[8] In the effort to shape people through popular culture, the media can be considered to be an undead virus due to the fact that it is represented as being both alive and dead. As Slavoj Zizek has argued, this notion of the undead relates to language in the form of a death drive: like a zombie, media cannot be stopped, but it is also not a purely living thing.[9] Thus, one reason why we desire to have reality-based media is that we want to make language and culture come alive. Moreover, the proliferation of media about media represents the need to control language by showing our awareness of its constructed nature.[10]

In looking at how someone like Donald Trump was able to become president after being a reality-media star, we see that elite politicians have to convince people that they are just like them, and they do this in part by pretending to be real, natural, unscripted, and authentic.[11] Not only will politicians dress down for campaign events, but they will also try to show themselves as doing the same things as the lower classes, like going to county fairs and eating unhealthy food. In this effort to make the Symbolic appear to be Real, these politicians are creating a false sense of authenticity, which can also be seen when Trump goes off script or tweets directly to the people.

Rushkoff's work helps us to understand this drive to make the fake seem real because he documents the early stages of this process. However, his own discourse is undermined by his desire to see the media as a virus dedicated to undermining all traditional social boundaries: "But sometimes, in spite of our puritanical closed-mindedness (or even as a direct result of it), a media virus spreads and infects us anyway. Why? The same reason a biological one spreads to new hosts: because we are vulnerable to its attack" (x). In this use of viral rhetoric, the value of the media is tied to its viral nature since the only way that popular culture can disrupt the dominant culture is if it is seen as a biological infection countering all attempts at immunization. What Rushkoff, then, sees as a progressive force, I see as ideology working in its most pure form: by representing the media as an infecting virus, culture itself is equated with its own transgressive other. For instance, many advertisements today tell people that if they buy the same object as everyone else, they will be an individual who is alive, unique, authentic, and real.[12] The goal of the social order is to convince people that they are the most free when they are conforming to what other people are doing.[13] However, we have to ask, what do we mean by the social order?

New Media Animism

As Lacan shows in his use of the term "the Other," the concept of society includes other people, language, a generalized audience, and a higher being.[14] From this perspective, the media embodies the Other since it points to the role of language in structuring the social order, but this order is also embodied by other people and is mystified as a higher power. On the most basic level, society as the Other means that we address ourselves to an abstract, generalized audience, which we experience as a transcendent force.[15] As the embodiment of the necessary but impossible social contract, the Other represents our need to sacrifice our own self for the sake of society. When we then seek to prove our individuality and authenticity in the media, we are trying to turn the source of our submission into a sign of our freedom. Therefore, in seeing the media as a living virus, we make ourselves feel more real and authentic by making the Other also come alive.

A fundamental conflict for human beings is that we turn to language in order to represent ourselves, but language goes beyond our control, and so in an effort to regain our authentic existence, we turn mediated representations into real events. This process has the paradoxical effect of projecting life and intentionality onto the Other as we gain access to our own freedom by living vicariously through the freedom and enjoyment of media representations.[16] This whole system is unconscious and fantasy-based since it is founded on substitution, displacement, projection, and identification, and because it is unconscious, it is experienced as natural and real. Interestingly, Rushkoff does at times point to this psychoanalytic interpretation of our relation to culture, media, and language:

> The imagery has emerged from the psychic shadows—it is not controlling us any more than our dreams do, but neither can we attempt to control it without suffering the consequences. Dream deprivation leads to psychosis in an individual; I'd hate to find out what it would do to a culture whose collective dreamlife were repressed. But if we embrace the seeming darkness of this dream (as Carl Jung used to say) and attempt to reckon with its messengers, we stand a chance of learning a lot more about ourselves in the process. (xi)

What I think Rushkoff is arguing here is that if we learn how the media virus functions, then we can try to control it and understand more about our own unconscious process. However, by following Jung and not Freud, he turns to an animistic view of the unconscious since what he wants to posit is that due to their viral nature, our cultural representations are coming alive and have a spiritual essence.[17]

It is vital to stress that for Freud, animism is defined by the projection of internal human mental processes onto the external world.[18] In what he calls the "omnipotence of thoughts," animistic cultures confuse memories with perceptions as they see dead things as being alive, and they endow non-human beings with human attributes.[19] Yet, Freud also insists that these projected ideas come from culture, and people do not have control over their own thoughts. What then equates primitive cultures with psychotics, infants, and dreamers is that they are all dominated by projective hallucinations where internalized representations are experienced in the form of the perception of external reality.[20] From this perspective, language and consciousness are inherently psychotic because they are made possible by the confusion between inner thoughts and outer perceptions on the one hand, and external culture and internal thoughts on the other hand. In fact, right before Descartes says his famous "I think, therefore, I am," he relates that he does not know if he is awake or dreaming, but he does know that in both states he is thinking.[21] The radical conclusion we should draw from this analysis is that on the level of pure thought and language, there is no way of testing reality since we always could be just dreaming.

What Rushkoff and others do not see is that the desire to make the media come alive represents a return to animism and the suspension of the distinction between fact and fiction. However, as we saw in the last chapter, what prevents this perspective from being truly psychotic and primitive is that it is coupled with the desire to communicate. In fact, Freud posits that dreamers and psychotics are not trying to dialogue with others because they do not believe in the Other.[22] Thus, while Rushkoff does project human attributes onto the media, he also directs his discourse to a generalized audience by using the norms of rational discourse. Like most neurotics, the psychotic primary processes are repressed into the unconscious by establishing a relationship between the intentional ego and the abstract Other, and yet he also seeks to escape the limits of this doubled alienation by making the Other come alive:

> So the O. J. media frenzy, more than just forcing us to confront the fact that the media is alive (consider a time-elapsed photo of the growing camera clutter around the Los Angeles Courthouse in the weeks during the trial—what else grows at that rate except maybe a fungus?), demonstrated how we, the viewing public, are as much a part of this life-form as any newscaster or TV movie subject. The media is a culture-wide dance. (xiii)

This passage should push us to ask if Rushkoff really cannot see the difference between an actual living being and a media representation? I believe that he desires to see them as the same because he knows that they are different. In other words, like a fetishist, he acts as if there is no difference, but he is also aware that they cannot be the same.[23]

Similar to so many other contemporary thinkers, Rushkoff's Neo-Animism is presented through this projection of natural evolution onto culture: "Like the hidden code of DNA, unfolding only so much at a time, directing our evolution forward, media viruses emerge to articulate and inform our cultural experience as it occurs" (xiv). As an example of viral rhetoric, the spread of mass media is seen as analogous to the unfolding of DNA code within the natural process of biological evolution. Through this mixing of different disciplines, a new mode of media is valorized, and this idealization points to his failure to register the dark side of reality-based media and the spread of destructive conspiracy theories.

Enjoying the Suffering of Others

Not only does Rushkoff want to see the media as a natural virus, but his use of viruses as metaphors points to a lack of sensitivity toward those who really suffer from natural infections. In seeing illness as just a metaphor, the sickness of culture is denied as the suffering of people is trivialized.[24] As someone who wanted to sell books and who did become a kind of media star, Rushkoff's combination of science, entertainment, and business reflects the need for successful media personalities to turn human suffering into an object of vicarious pleasure. We see this insensitivity in his unempathetic discussion of crimes, tragedies, and disasters; from the perspective of the entertainment subject, the only value of an event is defined by its ability to catch and sustain our attention as it delivers us from the reality of our own lives.

One way that he seeks to valorize the destructive and attention-grabbing aspects of the media is by arguing that if we understand how the media really works, it does not matter what content it presents: "Hopefully, if we learn to embrace our media's evolutionary function rather than despair its sensationalist execution, it will provide us with some of the tools necessary to navigate through an increasingly interdependent and leaderless world" (xv). The central idea here is that if we acknowledge that the media is a part of natural evolution, then we will be able to ignore its sensationalism as we learn how to manage in a world without leaders. What is so interesting about this argument is that he ties the focus on form over content to the radical political vision of a society where the people take back power from the leaders of the past. In other words, he simply ignores the effects of destructive media representation as he promotes a false political revolution in the form of media production and consumption.[25]

One reason why he can equate the production of memes with political transformation is that he sees cultural representations as replacing the old order's investment in material goods: "We live in an age when the value of data, images, and ideologies has surpassed that of material acquisitions and physical territory" (3). As a common fantasy of New Age cyber-culture, Rushkoff claims that material possessions and physical places no longer matter as much as our media representations of these real things.[26] The flip side, then, of seeing the media as a living virus is to see real things as having less value than the things that represent them. As Baudrillard insists, the map has replaced the territory as the simulation has become more important than reality itself.[27]

Since Rushkoff appears to believe that viral media frees us from power structures and reality itself, he is able to claim that the ideological control over the people has now been undermined: "But even if the original intentions of the media were to manipulate the American psyche by deadening our senses and winning over our hearts and minds to prepackaged ideologies, this strategy has finally backfired" (5). Of course, he wrote this book right before social media took off, but it is interesting to ask if he thinks that Facebook is a revolutionary force helping the people escape from ideology and social influence? Many people would argue that this "democratic" platform is centered on people seeking to be liked by others by conforming to the expectations of particular audiences.[28] As a form of narcissistic filtering, many social media sites cater to people seeking to have their own ideologies and preferences verified and mirrored, and so it is hard to see how the new media virus has served as a liberation from ideological constraints.[29]

In many ways, Rushkoff's celebration of viral media comes off as an advertisement for new media libertarian capitalism: "No, the media web has neither captured nor paralyzed the American individual. It has provided her with the ability to chart and control the course of her culture. She's been empowered" (5). By using the feminine pronoun, he may be attempting to make his discourse appear to be progressive, but isn't this celebration of the empowered individual the basis of the libertarian, Right-wing promotion of the market over any other social or personal value.[30] The trick, then, of this ideology is that it tries to convince people that they are free individuals because they can now generate their own media productions:

> The advent of do-it-yourself (DIY) technology makes direct feedback even more far-reaching. Today, homemade camcorder cassettes are as likely to find their way onto CNN as professionally produced segments. Tapes ranging from "America's Funniest Home Videos" to the world-famous Rodney King beating are more widely distributed through the datasphere than syndicated reruns of "I Love Lucy." Alternative media channels like the computer networks or even telephone and fax "trees" (distribution lists) permit the dissemination of information unacceptable to or censored by mainstream channels and have been heralded as the new tools of revolution .... (6)

My point is not that new media technologies have not led to some revolutionary acts or progressive movements; rather, this one-sided presentation of viral media as being liberatory represses the many negative effects of this type of culture.

One destructive aspect of the media Rushkoff celebrates is evident in the real human suffering caused by computer viruses or by having your identity information stolen. However, Rushkoff appears to be insensitive to the people who have been the victims of the viral strategies he idealizes: "Pirate media, like illegal radio broadcasts and cable or satellite jamming, are even more blatant assertions of the power of individuals to hack the data network" (6). He thus focuses on the power of the individual and not on the social and personal consequences of illegal hacking and other related criminal activities.

This insensitivity can also be found in his desire to see media viruses as no different from actual biological infections:

> This term is not being used as a metaphor. These media events are not like viruses. They are viruses. Most of us are familiar with biological viruses like the ones that cause the flu, the common cold, and perhaps even AIDS. As they are currently understood by the medical community, viruses are unlike bacteria or germs because they are not living things; they are simply protein shells containing genetic material. The attacking virus uses its protective and sticky protein casing to latch onto a healthy cell and then inject its own genetic code, essentially genes, inside. The virus code mixes and competes for control with the cell's own genes, and, if victorious, it permanently alters the way the cell functions and reproduces. A particularly virulent strain will transform the host cell into a factory that replicates the virus.

In this use of viral rhetoric, he first claims that he is not using the term virus as a metaphor, and so he really does not believe that there is difference between someone suffering from AIDS and someone who is a victim of a computer virus. Since in both cases, a host has been taken over by an outside force for the purpose of replication, the distinctions among biology, culture, and technology are denied.

As Baudrillard insists, we have become indifferent to the world around us because the differences between distinct discourses and domains have broken down.[31] The problem is not that very different things are being equated; rather, the mixing of disciplines removes the possibility of critical distance, reality testing, and sensitivity to others. If AIDS is represented as being the same thing as a media virus, then why should people care about the suffering of other people who have the actual biological infection?

Naturalizing Media

As we have seen throughout this book, a key defining aspect of viral rhetoric is the projection of human traits onto natural forces. This type of Neo-Animism is evident in Rushkoff's description of how biological viruses actually function:

> It's really a battle for command of the cell, fought between the cell's own genetic programming (DNA) and the virus's invading code. Wherever the cell's existing codes are weak or confused, the virus will have a better chance of taking over. Further, if the host organism has a weak immune system, its susceptibility to invasion is dramatically increased. It can't recognize that it is being attacked and can't mobilize its defenses. The protein shell of a virus is the Trojan horse. The genetic codes are the soldiers hidden inside, battling our own genes in an attempt to change the way our cells operate. The only "intention" of the virus, if it can be said to have one, is to spread its own code as far and wide as possible—from cell to cell and from organism to organism.

In using words like "battle," "command," and "soldiers," he anthropomorphizes biological viruses, and one effect of this mixing of discourses is that nature is seen through the lens of cultural representations.[32] Moreover, since all metaphors are reversible, the more you treat nature as cultural, the more culture itself can be naturalized.

An important move in this confusion between culture, technology, and nature is the analogy drawn between biological circulation and media distribution:

> Media viruses spread through the datasphere the same way biological ones spread through the body or a community. But instead of traveling along an organic circulatory system, a media virus travels through the networks of the mediaspace. The "protein shell" of a media virus might be an event, invention, technology, system of thought, musical riff, visual image, scientific theory, sex scandal, clothing style or even a pop hero—as long as it can catch our attention. Any one of these media virus shells will search out the receptive nooks and crannies in popular culture and stick on anywhere it is noticed. Once attached, the virus injects its more hidden agendas into the datastream in the form of ideological code—not genes, but a conceptual equivalent we now call "memes." (10)

The idea of memes is itself an idea that has successfully entered into our discourse and our perceptions of the social world.[33] As the vehicles of ideological codes, these representations are able to circulate freely in our open, integrated media systems. Of course, one of the biggest ideological codes circulated here is the very idea that memes are equivalent to genes.[34] In repeating this metaphor, Rushkoff reinforces the idea that there is no real difference between biology and culture, and this lack of difference helps to idealize technology as the mediating force enabling open circulation.

Just as words shape how we see the world, memes are presented as being symbols with the power to affect minds and perceptions:

> Like real genetic material, these memes infiltrate the way we do business, educate ourselves, interact with one another—even the way we perceive reality. Media viruses spread rapidly if they provoke our interest, and their success is dependent on the particular strengths and weaknesses of the host organism, popular culture. The more provocative an image or icon—like the videotaped police beating or a new rap lyric, for that matter—the further and faster it will travel through the datasphere. We do not recognize the image, so we cannot respond automatically to it. (11)

Rushkoff indicates here that if we cannot anticipate an image, it is able to evade our psychological immune systems, and so the power of media viruses relies in part on their shock value.[35] What Rushkoff is trying to do here is to relate the way natural section works on a biological level to the way popular culture functions on a psychological basis. Since genetic material is selected if it is able to reproduce by surviving in a particular environment, the question is what allows memes to become successful.[36] Thus, in order for them to circulate widely, they need an open system (host), and they must attract an audience by being provocative or shocking.

It should be clear that genes do not become selected because they provoke their host, but Rushkoff needs to maintain the equivalence between genes and memes so that he can constantly reinforce the notion that culture and technology are biological. Like Baudrillard, his insensitivity to the people suffering from real viruses is displayed by his indifference to the distinction between biological and cultural filtering systems:

> Our interest and fascination is a sign that we are not culturally "immune" to the new virus. The success of the memes within the virus, on the other hand, depends on our legal, moral, and social resiliency. If our own attitudes about racism, the power of police, drug abuse, and free speech are ambiguous—meaning our societal "code" is faulty—then the invading memes within the media virus will have little trouble infiltrating our own confused command structure. There appear to be three main kinds of media viruses. The most obvious variety, like publicity stunts or activist pranks, are constructed and launched intentionally, as a way of spreading a product or ideology. There are also what we can call co-opted or "bandwagon" viruses—the Woody Allen/Mia Farrow debacle or the AIDS epidemic—that no one necessarily launches intentionally, but … Some highlights have been hidden or truncated due to export limits. (10)

From this trans-disciplinary perspective, there is little difference between AIDS and a computer virus or a conspiracy theory since all of these phenomena draw their power from their ability to transgress our resistances. As Rushkoff argues, we are prone to these cultural infiltrations because we are so confused about cultural values and boundaries, and yet, his own discourse is centered on adding to the confusion by mixing different realms together.

Idealizing Hackers

Rushkoff not only equates cultural memes to natural forces, but he also desires to represent a new culture of computer hackers as being progressive, revolutionary resistance fighters:

> Today's media activists understand the properties of media viruses. The designers of intentional viruses take into account both the aspects of the status quo they wish to criticize, as well as the kinds of packaging that will permit the distribution of their critique. Most, but certainly not all, intentional media viruses are cultivated from scratch. The "smart drugs" virus is an excellent example of such designer memes. By the late 1980s a small group of AIDS activists, pharmaceutical industry critics, and psychedelics advocates felt the need to call our current drug paradigm into question. The AIDS activists were upset by laws limiting the domestic use of unapproved or experimental drugs from overseas. The pharmaceutical industry critics were frustrated by the way that the profit motives of drug companies could limit rather than expand the number of helpful medications .... (11)

While it is possible that some media activists have been able to accomplish progressive political goals, it should be clear that many acts of viral media and hacking have been anything but progressive.[37] In many cases, hackers have simply disrupted systems, and even media activists with a clear agenda have often supported both productive and destructive causes.

As Rushkoff's rhetoric reveals, the problem is not only that we are equating genetic code with digital code, but we are also seeing society as a code that can be either replicated or infected: "The immune response of our culture to the virus was weak because of our ambivalent attitudes toward drug use. The memes themselves were able to infiltrate because of our ambiguous laws and policies—our faulty societal code" (14). From this perspective, our social codes help to provide immune responses, but when these codes become confused, they become prone to infection by outside forces.

The representation of immunity as a cultural, psychological, and biological process points to another mixing of discourses and also highlights the way viral rhetoric often does not distinguish among natural section, biological viruses, and the natural reaction to viruses. Immune responses react to viral infections by generating toxic anti-bodies that kill off infections but can also destroy surrounding vital processes.[38] These viruses represent a mutation of genetic material that is recombined with other genetic material. In turn, the immune response is triggered by the mutated structure. In terms of human cultural and psychological systems, censorship plays the role of blocking new ideas from groups and individuals, and the reaction to new ideas can do damage to the host system by releasing destructive defensive forces. However, we should not confuse censorship with biological immunity or viral infections because they function on different levels of human existence. In fact, as Rushkoff highlights that it is confusion itself that makes us prone to false ideas like his own claim that there are no real differences among biological, cultural, and technological processes. Conspiracy theories, like the idea that COVID-19 virus is a hoax, spread because people do not understand how nature and culture work, and the rhetorical confusion between different disciplines only serves to heighten this confusion.

A great example of this mixing of domains that should be kept separate for conceptual clarity can be found in his description of self-generated media viruses:

> Finally there exist what countercultural activists would consider "self-generated" viruses. These are concepts or events that arise in the media quite spontaneously, but spread widely because they strike a very resonant chord or elicit a dramatic response from those who are exposed to them. If all of civilization is to be seen as a single organism, then these self-generated viruses can be understood as self-corrective measures. They are ways for the organism to correct or modify its own code. This is what is known in evolutionary circles as "mutation." (14)

The first issue to be clarified here is the nature of genetic mutations: biological mutations are coding errors, and they do not have any purpose or intention.[39] Thus, it is incorrect to see them as corrective forces since they serve no function; they are only meaningless mistakes, which introduce difference into self-replicating genetic codes. It is also misleading to see all of civilization as a single organism because what in part defines societies is their break from natural, evolutionary determinism. Yet, in order to use biology to explain culture, Rushkoff has to efface the very things that make us human and differentiate us from other animals and natural beings. Since our use of language and thought separates us from nature and reality itself, this break cannot be healed by simply using language to make metaphors and analogies.

As a way of rationalizing and idealizing the countercultural media hackers and activists, Rushkoff also turns to new scientific and mathematical theories to support his case:

> The famous phrase "a butterfly flapping its wings in China can create a hurricane in New York" means that a tiny event in one remote area can lead to huge repercussions in another. It is no wonder that those attempting to demonstrate the fall of hierarchical systems and to debunk the notion of top-down control cherish the memes of the chaos math virus, which contradict these orderly notions of natural behavior. Activists love evidence that supports their minute-man tactics. (15)

There is a world of difference between the chaos theory claim that different systems affect each other and the notion that the tactics of media hackers undermine all hierarchical systems.[40] This injection of politics into math is yet another example of the mixing of discourses as an effort to justify activities that are often highly destructive and anti-social.

In analyzing Rushkoff's discourse, I have shown how the rhetorical manipulation of language determines how he sees nature, culture, and technology. However, since this rhetoric is rarely addressed, figurative language is taken to be literal as distinct discourses become confused. To help clarify how this viral rhetoric relates to politics and psychology, I will in the next chapter turn to Freud's work on group psychology. Of special importance to this analysis of viral rhetoric is the notion that destructive conspiracy theories are able to spread because people fail to clearly separate culture from nature.

Notes

1. Rushkoff, Douglas. *Media virus!: Hidden agendas in popular culture*. Random House Digital, Inc., 1996.
2. Strate, Lance. "Media ecology." *Communication Research Trends* 23.2 (2004): 1–48.
3. Hegel, Georg Wilhelm Friedrich. *The phenomenology of mind*. Courier Corporation, 2012.
4. Gewirtz, Jacob L., and Karen G. Stingle. "Learning of generalized imitation as the basis for identification." *Psychological Review* 75.5 (1968): 374.
5. Samuels, Robert. "Logos, global justice, and the reality principle." *Zizek and the rhetorical unconscious*. Palgrave Macmillan, Cham, 2020. 65–86.

6. Weimann, Gabriel. *Communicating unreality: Modern media and the reconstruction of reality*. Sage Publications, 1999.
7. Samuels, Robert. "Trump and Sanders on the Couch: Neoliberal populism on the left and the right." *Psychoanalyzing the left and right after Donald Trump*. Palgrave Macmillan, Cham, 2016. 61–76.
8. Grady, Hugh. "Containment, subversion—And postmodernism." *Textual Practice* 7.1 (1993): 31–49.
9. Zizek, Slavoj, and Slavoj Žižek. *The fragile absolute: Or, why is the Christian legacy worth fighting for?*. Verso, 2001.
10. Welsh, Timothy J. *Immersive fictions: Modern narrative, new media, mixed reality*. University of Washington, 2011.
11. Hearn, Alison. "Trump's "reality" hustle." *Television & New Media* 17.7 (2016): 656–659.
12. Frank, Thomas, and Matt Weiland, eds. *Commodify your dissent: Salvos from the baffler*. WW Norton & Company, 1997.
13. Samuels, Robert. "Grand theft automodernity: Globalizing individualism and cultural nihilism from Eminem to the matrix." *New media, cultural studies, and critical theory after postmodernism*. Palgrave Macmillan, New York, 2009. 123–144.
14. Lacan, Jacques. *The ego in Freud's theory and in the technique of psychoanalysis, 1954–1955*. Vol. 2. WW Norton & Company, 1991.
15. Pfaller, Robert. *Interpassivity: The aesthetics of delegated enjoyment*. Edinburgh University Press, 2017.
16. Van Oenen, Gijs. "Interpassivity revisited: A critical and historical reappraisal of interpassive phenomena." *International Journal of Žižek Studies* 2.2 (2016).
17. Jung, Carl Gustav, et al. *Man and his symbols*. Vol. 5183. Dell, 1964.
18. Fox, Robin. "Totem and Taboo reconsidered." *The Structural Study of Myth and Totemism* (1967): 161–178.
19. Freud, Sigmund, and Anna Freud. *Totem and Taboo and other works*. Vol. 13. Random House, 2001.
20. Samuels, Robert. "The unconscious and the primary processes." *Freud for the twenty-first century*. Palgrave Pivot, Cham, 2019. 27–42.
21. Descartes, René. *Discourse on method and the meditations*. Penguin UK, 1968.
22. Freud, Sigmund, and A. J. Cronin. *The interpretation of dreams*. Read Books Ltd., 2013.
23. Freud, Sigmund. "Fetishism." *The Standard edition of the complete psychological works of Sigmund Freud, Volume XXI (1927–1931): The future of an illusion, civilization and its discontents, and other works*, 1961. 147–158.
24. Sontag, Susan, and Heywood Hale Broun. *Illness as metaphor*. Farrar, Straus, 1977.

25. Rajagopal, Arvind, and Anupama Rao, eds. *Media and Utopia: History, imagination and technology*. Routledge, 2017.
26. Capitalism, Consumer, and Michael Billig. "Commodity fetishism and repression." *Theory Psychology* 9 (1999): 313.
27. Baudrillard, Jean. *Simulacra and simulation*. University of Michigan Press, 1994.
28. Carpenter, Christopher J. "Narcissism on Facebook: Self-promotional and anti-social behavior." *Personality and Individual Differences* 52.4 (2012): 482–486.
29. Pariser, Eli. *The filter bubble: What the Internet is hiding from you*. Penguin UK, 2011.
30. Iyer, Ravi, et al. "Understanding libertarian morality: The psychological roots of an individualist ideology." *Available at SSRN 1665934* (2010).
31. Kellner, Douglas. "Jean Baudrillard." *The Blackwell Companion to Major Contemporary Social Theorists* (2007): 310.
32. Nie, Jing-Bao, et al.. "Healing without waging war: Beyond military metaphors in medicine and HIV cure research." *The American Journal of Bioethics* 16.10 (2016): 3–11.
33. Shifman, Limor. *Memes in digital culture*. MIT press, 2014.
34. Dawkins, Richard. *The selfish gene*. Oxford University Press, 2016.
35. Rose, Nick. "Controversies in meme theory." *Journal of Memetics-Evolutionary Models of Information Transmission* 2.1 (1998): 43.
36. Coscia, Michele. "Competition and success in the meme pool: A case study on quickmeme. com." *arXiv preprint arXiv:1304.1712* (2013).
37. Sciglimpaglia Jr, Robert J. "Computer hacking: A global offense." *Pace International Law Review* 3.1 (1991): 199.
38. Yang, Yiping, Qin Su, and James M. Wilson. "Role of viral antigens in destructive cellular immune responses to adenovirus vector-transduced cells in mouse lungs." *Journal of Virology* 70.10 (1996): 7209–7212.
39. Goldsmith, Moshe, and Dan S. Tawfik. "Potential role of phenotypic mutations in the evolution of protein expression and stability." *Proceedings of the National Academy of Sciences* 106.15 (2009): 6197–6202.
40. Oestreicher, Christian. "A history of chaos theory." *Dialogues in clinical neuroscience* 9.3 (2007): 279.

CHAPTER 5

Freud's Contagion

Abstract This chapter examines Freud's *Group Psychology and the Analysis of the Ego* to see how his use of the term "contagion" both reinforces and undermines viral rhetoric. At times he uses biological metaphors to explain mental processes, but at other times, he seeks to distinguish his discourse from biological determinism. As a counter-discourse to the previous texts I have discussed, Freud offers a way of escaping from the confusing mixing of discourses and the promotion of Neo-Animism. One of the aims of Freud's text is to explain why psychoanalysis has something to offer to our understanding of society, culture, and politics. To bridge the gap between individual psychology and social formations, he utilizes the concept of identification, which on its most basic level describes how isolated individuals internalize social representations transcending the subject.

Keywords Freud · Identification · Hypnosis · Contagion · Neo-Animism · Projection

This chapter examines Freud's *Group Psychology and the Analysis of the Ego* to see how his use of the term "contagion" both reinforces and undermines viral rhetoric.[1] At times he uses biological metaphors to explain mental processes, but at other times, he seeks to distinguish his discourse

R. Samuels, *Viral Rhetoric*,
https://doi.org/10.1007/978-3-030-73895-2_5

from biological determinism.[2] As a counter-discourse to the previous texts I have discussed, Freud offers a way of escaping from the confusing mixing of discourses and the promotion of Neo-Animism.

Contagious Group Psychology

One of the aims of Freud's text is to explain why psychoanalysis has something to offer to our understanding of society, culture, and politics. To bridge the gap between individual psychology and social formations, he utilizes the concept of identification, which on its most basic level describes how individuals internalize social representations that transcend their own individualism.[3] One of the main forms of identification that he will isolate is derived from the past work of other psychologists and social scientists, and this concerns the concept of the contagion. We shall see that this term is problematic because it creates the illusion that just as biological infections can infect others, ideas and values can also spread like germs.[4] The problematic nature of the contagion is presented in Freud's reference to Le Bon's *Psychology of Crowds*[5]:

> The second cause, which is contagion, also intervenes to determine the manifestation in groups of their special characteristics, and at the same time the trend they are to take. Contagion is a phenomenon of which it is easy to establish the presence, but that it is not easy to explain. It must be classed among those phenomena of a hypnotic order, which we shall shortly study. In a group every sentiment and act is contagious, and contagious to such a degree that an individual readily sacrifices his personal interest to the collective .... (10)

The concept of the contagion is thus a key theory for understanding how individuals are shaped by other people, but we have to remind ourselves that ideas do not spread like viruses because they do not have a physical presence: ideas are signifiers relating to other signifiers and take on their meaning by being placed in a network of associations. The issue, then, is how can something be contagious, like laughter or a yawn, if it does not spread through material contact? Moreover, Freud ends up centering the very possibility of culture and society on the contagion, and so it is essential to determine how this process actually functions.

As a bridge between the mental and the physical, Le Bon posits that suggestion is the most important aspect of contagious social behavior:

> A third cause, and by far the most important, determines in the individuals of a group special characteristics which are quite contrary at times to those presented by the isolated individual. I allude to that suggestibility of which, moreover, the contagion mentioned above is only an effect. 'To understand this phenomenon it is necessary to bear in mind certain recent physiological discoveries. We know to-day that by various processes an individual may be brought into such a condition that, having entirely lost his conscious personality, he obeys all the suggestions of the operator who has deprived him of it, and commits acts in utter contradiction with his character and habits. The most careful investigations seem to prove that an individual immersed for some length of time in a group in action soon finds himself — either in consequence of the magnetic influence given out by the group, or from some other cause of which we are ignorant –in a special state, which must resemble the state of 'fascination' in which the hypnotized individual finds himself in the hands of the hypnotizer. (10–11)

What Freud draws from this theory is the connection between the individual in the group and the person being hypnotized. Since Freud started out his therapeutic technique by hypnotizing his patients, he has a great deal of knowledge about this topic, but it also should be mentioned that Freud developed psychoanalysis by breaking away from hypnosis, and so in many ways, the psychoanalytic process is in opposition to suggestion.[6]

It is also vital to realize that Le Bon had a tendency to base psychological concepts in biological theories, and so he participates in an early form of Neo-Animism.[7] Freud breaks from this naturalization of culture by positing that the artificial social group functions by effacing the will of the individual subject:

> In order to make a correct judgement upon the morals of groups, one must take into consideration the fact that when individuals come together in a group all their individual inhibitions fall away and all the cruel, brutal and destructive instincts, which lie dormant in individuals as relics of a primitive epoch, are stirred up to find free gratification. But under the influence of suggestion groups are also capable of high achievements in the shape of abnegation, unselfishness, and devotion to an ideal. While with isolated individuals personal interest is almost the only motive force, with groups it is very rarely prominent. It is possible to speak of an individual having his moral standards raised by a group. (15)

In this approach to suggestion and contagious behavior, Freud sees these processes as having both positive and negative effects; thus suggestion can allow us to escape our own narcissism to accomplish important social goals, but it also can function to free us to express our inhibited destructive impulses. However, by pointing to the role of uninhibited instincts, Freud is not returning to a purely biological model of human impulses because he is clear to distinguish between animal instincts and human drives, yet the translators often lose this distinction by confusing these two opposed terms.[8]

The Primitive Crowd

Since anything can be a source of pleasure for humans, they make a break with evolution and natural biological impulses. According to his early work on sexuality, what makes us human is in part this separation from nature through the movement beyond reproduction.[9] The drives are shaped by what he calls polymorphous perversity because the means of sexual excitement can replace the end of sexual reproduction, and in this structure, biological determinism is subverted. Therefore, if the crowd enables people to release their usually inhibited impulses, this does not mean that they return to a purely animalistic mode of being.

It is also vital to emphasize that Freud's notion of the primitive is also divorced from the purely natural or biological because he stresses how primitive cultures are determined by the "omnipotence of thought," and therefore when he talks about a return to primitive states of being, he is referring to the way our original mode of consciousness is structured by the internalization of representations derived from culture.[10] Since humans not only break from nature through their drives, but they also break from reality by replacing matter with their minds, there is no way of returning to a natural state of being determined by evolutionary processes. In contrast to the social Darwinism of the Neo-Animists, Freud separates natural viruses from mental viruses since he removes biological determinism from human subjectivity.

However, a problem with reading Freud is that he often uses common words in an uncommon way, and so people are quick to re-absorb his theories into more traditional ways of seeing the world. This issue is clear in the following passage: "Whereas the intellectual capacity of a group is always far below that of an individual, its ethical conduct may rise as high above his as it may sink deep below it. Some other features in Le Bon's description show in a clear light how well justified is the identification of the group mind with the mind of primitive people" (15). In order to comprehend this passage, one must understand that for Freud, the category of the primitive represents a state of mind and social organization determined by the primary processes of substitution, displacement, and projection. Moreover, for Freud, primitive cultures are not immersed in nature since they experience everything through the lens of cultural representations. Just as consciousness is shaped by language, primitive thought is mediated by internalized representations, which then are taken to be real and natural. The regression in the crowd to the primitive mind, then, must be understood as a return to psychological and social processes structured by cultural concepts.

As Freud insists, primitive cultures are dominated by the omnipotence of thoughts, but these thoughts come from the Other. Furthermore, as Descartes states, since we never know if we are awake or dreaming, but we are thinking in both states, our thoughts do not have the ability on their own to distinguish between what is real and what is fictional.[11] This lack of reality testing is presented by Freud in his claim that what makes the social group so powerful is that it is able to suspend critical distance and the rational separation of fact from fiction: "And, finally, groups have never thirsted after truth. They demand illusions, and cannot do without them. They constantly give what is unreal precedence over what is real; they are almost as strongly influenced by what is untrue as by what is true" (16). Like the dreamer, the psychotic, the infant, or the animistic culture, the dominance of thinking entails that reality testing is suspended, and this leaves people prone to believing in illusions and other falsehoods. From this vantage point, what makes us susceptible to viral memes and conspiracy theories is that on the level of conscious thought, we are unable to separate facts from fictions.

Contagious thoughts and suggestibility are therefore not aberrant states: instead, they represent the foundations of our consciousness and social formations. The problem is thus is not why are we prone to be seduced by misleading ideas: the problem for Freud is how do we ever escape this primary way of thinking and being.[12] For Freud, the answer will be the slow acceptance of the reality principle and the limits of our own thinking, but this mode of reason is not there at the start and has to be slowly internalized through a process of trial and error where one learns that one cannot escape one's own memories or the reality of the external world.[13]

Since we are vulnerable to suggestion, we are also prone to submitting to powerful cultural figures who are placed in a position of social influence: "Moreover, he ascribes both to the ideas and to the leaders a mysterious and irresistible power, which he calls 'prestige'. Prestige is a sort of domination exercised over us by an individual, a work or an idea. It entirely paralyses our critical faculty, and fills us with astonishment and respect. It would seem to arouse a feeling like that of fascination in hypnosis" (18). Since our consciousness is determined by social categories, even if we think our ideas come from our own isolated minds, it is easy for us to submit to authority figures as we suspend our critical faculties. In the same way that we will do whatever the hypnotist tells us to do, we will also follow the commands of leaders without question once we have placed them in the position of power.

This submission to a higher power is coupled by Freud with the emotional feedback effect between members of the group: "The individual loses his power of criticism, and lets himself slip into the same emotion. But in so doing he increases the excitement of the other people, who had produced this effect upon him, and thus the emotional charge of the individuals becomes intensified by mutual interaction" (22–23). When the individual regresses to the primitive state of consciousness in front of the powerful leader, this suspension of reality testing through immersion is shared by other people who submit to the same power. There are thus two processes occurring here: individuals are subjected to the will of the leader, and the followers imitate each other's regressive thinking, Freud reveals here the key to political movements on the Left and the Right since they both often rely on the suspension of reality testing and the release of uninhibited drives through the submission to the same leader or idea.

Unlike any other discourse, psychoanalysis is able to explain seemingly irrational social and subjective processes because this theory is the only one to be founded on a break with nature and material reality.[14] While consciousness is an unresolved problem for philosophers and neuroscientists, psychoanalysis helps us to see how consciousness is itself centered on the internalization of social representations, which are then projected back onto the external world.

The Hypnotic Leader

In terms of politics and social organization, mental contagions are thus the result of our primary mode of consciousness, and what is added to this structure is the role played by the leader or idea as the source of submission and regression. Powerful figures then gain control by getting their followers to regress to the level of the primitive mind. A side-effect of this process is that the submissive followers will gain a sense of empowerment:

> This mechanism for the intensification of emotion is favoured by some other influences which emanate from groups. A group impresses the individual with a sense of unlimited power and of insurmountable peril. For the moment it replaces the whole of human society, which is the wielder of authority, whose punishments the individual fears, and for whose sake he has submitted to so many inhibitions. It is clearly perilous for him to put himself in opposition to it, and it will be safer to follow the example of those around him and perhaps even 'hunt with the pack'. In obedience to the new authority he may put his former 'conscience' out of action, and so surrender to the attraction of the increased pleasure that is certainly obtained from the removal of inhibitions. (23)

Freud explains here why people may join a cult or political movement since he connects subjective submission to the removal of inhibitions and the illusion of unlimited power in the face of extreme dangers.[15] Taking advantage of the viral and irrational nature of consciousness itself, leaders are able to influence our minds by turning our subjection into a source of perceived power and freedom.

As a type of shock doctrine, Freud posits that what often draws people to powerful leaders and ideologies is the panic and anxiety caused by the loss of social bonds: "A hint to the same effect, that the essence of a group lies in the libidinal ties existing in it, is also to be found in the phenomenon of panic, which is best studied in military groups. A panic arises if a group of that kind becomes disintegrated. Its characteristics are that none of the orders given by superiors are any longer listened to, and that each individual is only solicitous on his own account …" (35). When the social order dissolves, anxiety ensues and people regress to primary processes as they seek out a powerful leader or idea.[16] Freud uses this theory to argue that the example of panic reveals that the group has always been constituted by a need to escape from a lack of social order. He adds that the organizing principle can also be hatred of another group: "The leader or the leading idea might also, so to speak, be negative; hatred against a particular person or institution might operate in just the same unifying way, and might call up the same kind of emotional ties as positive attachment" (41). It is interesting that for Freud, a leader or an idea can play the role of organizer, and so on the level of social psychology, there is no real difference between people and ideas. As Lacan insists, our social reality is structured by signifiers, and so the social bond is based on the linking of symbolic representations.[17] From this perspective, we are never really dealing with other people since we only know them only as a collection of social signs. Moreover, since each signifier is defined in opposition to other signifiers, self-identity relies on being opposed to other people, and here we see why hatred can be such a powerful organizing principle: due to the fact that the group has to define itself in opposition to other groups, internal group identity often relies on the hatred of the out-group.

From the Symbolic to the Imaginary Contagion

Freud's primary theory of how ideas spread has been shown to be tied to his notion that our consciousness is itself shaped by social signifiers, but for most people, this primitive form of perception is repressed by defense mechanisms generated from the ego. In fact, what enables the formation of the unconscious is the repression of primary consciousness by the self, but this ego is itself a product of identification. As Lacan illustrates in his theory of the mirror stage, we first gain a sense of ourselves as being separate and unified by identifying with an image in the other or with another person around the same size and age.[18] Furthermore, Freud insists, the ego is not there from the start, and so it has to be developed through imitation and identification.[19] Although the psychotic subject is spoken by the Other and projects the Symbolic onto the Real, the neurotic subject represses psychotic consciousness and replaces it with symptoms and defenses.[20] We see the early stage of this structure in Freud's discussion of the formation of a hysterical symptom:

> Let us disentangle identification as it occurs in the structure of a neurotic symptom from its rather complicated connections. Supposing that a little girl (and we will keep to her for the present) develops the same painful symptom as her mother — for instance, the same tormenting cough. Now this may come about in various ways. The identification may come from the Oedipus complex; in that case it signifies a hostile desire on the girl's part to take her mother's place, and the symptom expresses her object love towards her father, and brings about a realisation, under the influence of a sense of guilt, of her desire to take her mother's place. (48)

The key point I want to stress here is that hysterical symptom is itself the result of an identification with the suffering of another person.[21] What makes emotions in hysteria circulate is the process of identification where the subject takes on the traits of someone the subject desires to replace. This identification with the suffering of others plays a crucial role in the "viral" spread of emotions since it represents the mental path of the contagion. Therefore, the reason laughter and other emotional reactions can appear to be contagious is that they rely on a process of identification, which itself is driven by desire and guilt.

The next stage in this process moves from the isolated hysteric to the hysterical group:

> There is a third particularly frequent and important case of symptom formation, in which the identification leaves any object relation to the person who is being copied entirely out of account. Supposing, for instance, that one of the girls in a boarding school has had a letter from someone with whom she is secretly in love which arouses her jealousy, and that she reacts to it with a fit of hysterics; then some of her friends who know about it will contract the fit, as we say, by means of mental infection. The mechanism is that of identification based upon the possibility or desire of putting oneself in the same situation. The other girls would like to have a secret love affair too, and under the influence of a sense of guilt they also accept the pain involved in it. It would be wrong to suppose that they take on the symptom out of sympathy. On the contrary, the sympathy only arises out of the identification .... (49)

Even though Freud returns in this passage to the language of biological infections, it should be clear that his theory of hysterical sympathy is centered on imaginary identification: the subjects in the group all express the same emotional reaction because they all identify with the same suffering person. A side-effect of this theory is that the psychoanalytic conception of sympathy and empathy relies on a symptomatic mode of identification.[22]

A reason why the hysteric does not know the cause of her symptom or what it means is that this form of expressed suffering is the result of an unconscious process of identification. For Freud, it is this imaginary identification that paves the way for a non-psychotic relation to the Other; however, this new emotional tie is itself unconscious and misrecognized:

> We already begin to divine that the mutual tie between members of a group is in the nature of an identification of this kind, based upon an important emotional common quality; and we may suspect that this common quality lies in the nature of the tie with the leader. Another suspicion may tell us that we are far from having exhausted the problem of identification, and that we are faced by the process which psychology calls 'empathy [Einfühlung]' and which plays the largest part in our understanding of what is inherently foreign to our ego in other people. (50)

Freud's radical gesture is to base our empathic understanding of others on an unconscious identification, and from this perspective, our initial comprehension of others relies on imitating their emotional responses.

After he develops the hysterical foundation of subjectivity and empathy, Freud turns to the formation of the super-ego as represented by the internal division between the ego and internalized social ideals:

> They [melancholics] show us the ego divided, fallen into two pieces, one of which rages against the second. This second piece is the one which has been altered by introjection and which contains the lost object. But the piece which behaves so cruelly is not unknown to us either. It comprises the conscience, a critical faculty [Instanz] within the ego, which even in normal times takes up a critical attitude towards the ego, even though never so relentlessly and so unjustifiably. (52)

Freud first gains insight to the formation of the super-ego by studying the extreme self-criticism of people suffering from acute melancholia, but he quickly realizes that the division of the self between the ego and its ideals plays a role in all subjects. His basic idea is that when we are attacking ourselves, we are really attacking another person with whom we identify.[23] As Lacan points out, since the neurotic ego is formed by identifying with an other, and this ego is then judged by the internalization of an ideal through identification, the subject is doubly alienated: the neurotic subject is an other for the Other.[24]

It is precisely this theory of identification that is often missing from most representations of viral rhetoric. Since people do not understand how ideas and ideals are internalized, they turn to the displaced realm of biological infection. An important step, therefore, in separating biology from psychology is to recognize how emotional ties are circulated through the processes of identification. Coupled with this clarification is Freud's effort to describe why the formation of neurotic symptoms and defenses is transcended by the development of sexual drives. In fact, it is this third theory that will help us to understand how the empathic circulation of ideas and emotions gets hooked up to the submission to an idealized Other.

Perverting the Other

One of Freud's basic concepts is his notion that there is often an opposition between neurotic narcissism and the state of falling in love.[25] Since he wants to equate the submission to a leader in a group with the submission of the lover to the beloved, he has to account for the ways love allows us to go beyond our own narcissism. Freud's paradoxical theory is that the state of love mirrors a hypnosis since the lover has to suspend reality testing and self-respect in order to submit to the will of the beloved:

> The tendencies whose trend is towards directly sexual satisfaction may now be pushed back entirely, as regularly happens, for instance, with the young man's sentimental passion; the ego becomes more and more unassuming and modest, and the object more and more sublime and precious, until at last it gets possession of the entire self-love of the ego, whose self-sacrifice thus follows as a natural consequence. The object has, so to speak, consumed the ego. Traits of humility, of the limitation of narcissism, and of self-injury occur in every case of being in love; in the extreme case they are only intensified, and as a result of the withdrawal of the sensual claims they remain in solitary supremacy. (56)

The sublime object of love is thus derived in part from the destruction of the lover's narcissism, which is demanded by the idealization of the beloved: the self-sacrificing lover becomes full of humility because the narcissistic ego has been transcended.

What is so interesting is that Freud once again equates the love of the other to an idea as he describes how the devotion to a love object matches the commitment to a social ideal:

> Contemporaneously with this 'devotion' of the ego to the object, which is no longer to be distinguished from a sublimated devotion to an abstract idea, the functions allotted to the ego ideal entirely cease to operate. The criticism exercised by that faculty is silent; everything that the object does and asks for is right and blameless. Conscience has no application to anything that is done for the sake of the object; in the blindness of love

> remorselessness is carried to the pitch of crime. The whole situation can be completely summarised in a formula: The object has taken the place of the ego ideal. (57)

The sublime object of ideology is here generated from the substitution of the object for the conscience, and so the lover is not only deaf and dumb but also criminal.[26] As a theory of how ideas become internalized and replicated, this theory of sublime love reveals that the more we devote ourselves to the ideas of others, the more we eliminate our ability to make moral and epistemological judgments. This suspension of conscience entails that the "viral" spread of ideas prevents us from taking a critical perspective on the cultural representations we internalize and idealize.

We have seen that on a primitive level, we are prone to being influenced by the ideas of others because our consciousness is shaped by the discourse of the Other, and on a secondary level, the way we escape from the primary state is by the development of symptoms and the ego through the process of identifying with other people. We now find that on a third level, we are still dominated by the ideas and ideals of others since our dedication to leaders, lovers, and ideals robs us of our critical faculties. As Freud insists, the model of the organized social group is the hypnotic relationship because the group requires our complete submission:

> From being in love to hypnosis is evidently only a short step. The respects in which the two agree are obvious. There is the same humble subjection, the same compliance, the same absence of criticism, towards the hypnotist just as towards the loved object. There is the same absorption of one's own initiative; no one can doubt that the hypnotist has stepped into the place of the ego ideal. (58)

This replacement of the ego ideal with the object in hypnosis and the social group means that a problem with social movements and social media is that they have the power to make us suspend all criticism as we become immersed in the object of our attention.[27] In fact, Freud emphasizes the idea that hypnosis is made possible by a form of deep focus: "The hypnotist is the sole object, and no attention is paid to any but him. The fact that the ego experiences in a dream-like way whatever he may request or assert reminds us that we omitted to mention among the functions of the ego ideal the business of testing the reality of things" (58). It is thus the focus on the object that effaces the subject and removes reality testing and moral judgment. In opposition to theories of viral rhetoric that base the uncontrollable spread of ideas and memes on biological process of replication and infection, Freud provides a way out of New-Animism, contemporary conspiracy theories and the submission to the authoritarian leader.

For Freud, when multiple people replace their ego ideals with the same object, a fanatical group is formed, and like any type of cult, this group loses its ability to employ the reality principle or the moral conscience:

> Some of its features — the weakness of intellectual ability, the lack of emotional restraint, the incapacity for moderation and delay, the inclination to exceed every limit in the expression of emotion and to work it off completely in the form of action — these and similar features, which we find so impressively described in Le Bon, show an unmistakable picture of a regression of mental activity to an earlier stage such as we are not surprised to find among savages or children. (60)

Freud's theory of group regression helps us to comprehend why people submit to destructive leaders and follow irrational conspiracy theories. Instead of basing the circulation of ideas on a biological model of the contagion, Freud turns to his experience with hypnosis to introduce a radical theory of the foundation of social formations.

Freud's pessimistic conclusion is that the due to way we become absorbed in the ideas and ideals of social others, we are prone to fanatism, racism, and other destructive attitudes:

> We thus have an impression of a state in which an individual's separate emotion and personal intellectual act are too weak to come to anything by themselves and are absolutely obliged to wait till they are reinforced through being repeated in a similar way in the other members of the group. We are reminded of how many of these phenomena of dependence are part of the normal constitution of human society, of how little originality and personal courage are to be found in it, of how much every individual is ruled by those attitudes of the group mind which exhibit themselves in such forms as racial characteristics, class prejudices, public opinion, etc. (63)

By ending with public opinion, Freud points to how in our world of social media, the "viral" spread of ideas and emotions often entails a loss of conscience and reality testing, and yet Freud also seeks to develop a theory of the social that counters the negative aspects of the hypnotic group.

Freud and the Origins of Social Justice

So far, Freud's theory has helped us to separate biological viruses from culture and psychology, but it has left us with a form of subjectivity and social structure that is void of justice, equality, or fairness. While viral rhetoric pushes us to believe that we cannot control the spread of both positive and negative ideas in culture because this uncontrollable circulation is the direct result of evolution and our natural tendencies, Freud turns to consciousness, identification, and idealization as the main causes for our lack of mental and social control. However, he does offer a way out, and this exit is centered on his theory of universal justice:

> Something like it grows up first of all, in a nursery containing many children, out of the children's relation to their parents, and it does so as a reaction to the initial envy with which the elder child receives the younger one. The elder child would certainly like to put its successor jealously aside, to keep it away from the parents, and to rob it of all its privileges; but in face of the fact that this child (like all that come later) is loved by the parents in just the same way, and in consequence of the impossibility of maintaining his hostile attitude without damaging himself, he is forced into identifying himself with the other children. (66)

From Freud's perspective, the desire for equality and social justice is derived from envy and hostility as the child decides to identify with others instead of trying to replace them:

> So there grows up in the troop of children a communal or group feeling, which is then further developed at school. The first demand made by this reaction-formation is for justice, for equal treatment for all. We all know how loudly and implacably this claim is put forward at school. If one cannot be the favourite oneself, at all events nobody else shall be the favourite. This transformation — the replacing of jealousy by a group feeling in the nursery and classroom — might be considered improbable, if the same process could not later on be observed again in other circumstances. (66)

Freud's model of the social contract therefore is derived from hostile feelings of jealousy and envy, which are then transformed into a plea for equal treatment: since no child can get as much as he or she wants, no one should be able to get more than others.[28]

Paradoxically, Freud's argument for how to move beyond destructive social opinion and defensive individual psychology is to turn selfishness into its opposite:

> What appears later on in society in the shape of Gemeingeist, esprit de corps, 'group spirit', etc., does not belie its derivation from what was originally envy. No one must want to put himself forward, everyone must be the same and have the same. Social justice means that we deny ourselves many things so that others may have to do without them as well, or, what is the same thing, may not be able to ask for them. This demand for equality is the root of social conscience and the sense of duty. (67)

One reason why I am focusing on this strange theory of social justice is that this argument allows Freud the ability to reject the biological model of the herd instinct. Instead of relying on some mythical evolutionary process of group selection, Freud bases the formation of the just society on the unconscious choice to replace envy with equal treatment.[29]

In the next chapter, I will examine how Ernesto Laclau extends Freud's project by developing a theory of political populism that bases the spread of ideas on rhetoric and not biological viruses. While Laclau does draw from Freud and Lacan to discuss the role played by contagions in political ideologies, he offers a mostly formalistic approach, which often does not take into account the different unconscious mechanisms that we have seen shape Freud's approach to the hypnotic spread of ideas and ideologies.

Notes

1. Freud, Sigmund. *Group psychology and the analysis of the ego*. WW Norton & Company, 1975.
2. Samuels, Robert. *Psychoanalyzing the politics of the new brain sciences*. Springer, 2017.
3. Compton, Allan. "The concept of identification in the work of Freud Ferenczi, and Abraham: A review and commentary." *The Psychoanalytic Quarterly* 54.2 (1985): 200–233.
4. Meerloo, Joost AM. "Mental contagion." *American Journal of Psychotherapy* 13.1 (1959): 66–82.

5. Le Bon, Gustave. *Psychology of Crowds (annotated).* Sparkling Books, 2009.
6. Freud, Sigmund. "The dynamics of transference." *The standard edition of the complete psychological works of Sigmund Freud, Volume XII (1911–1913): The case of Schreber, papers on technique and other works*, 1958. 97–108.
7. Chertok, Léon, and Isabelle Stengers. *A critique of psychoanalytic reason: Hypnosis as a scientific problem from Lavoisier to Lacan.* Stanford University Press, 1992.
8. Lacan, Jacques. *The four fundamental concepts of psycho-analysis.* Vol. 11. WW Norton & Company, 1998.
9. Freud, Sigmund. *Three essays on the theory of sexuality: The 1905 edition.* Verso Books, 2017.
10. Freud, Sigmund. "Totem and Taboo: some points of agreement between the mental lives of savages and neurotics (1913 [1912–13])." *The standard edition of the complete psychological works of Sigmund Freud, Volume XIII (1913–1914): Totem and Taboo and other works*, 1955. VII–162.
11. Descartes, René. *Discourse on method and the meditations.* Penguin UK, 1968.
12. Freud, Sigmund. "Formulations on the two principles of mental functioning." *The standard edition of the complete psychological works of Sigmund Freud, Volume XII (1911–1913): The case of Schreber, papers on technique and other works*, 1958. 213–226.
13. Freud, Sigmund. "Negation." *Organization and pathology of thought: Selected sources.* Columbia University Press, 1951. 338–348.
14. Rensmann, Lars. *The politics of unreason: The Frankfurt School and the origins o modern antisemitism.* Suny Press, 2017.
15. Spitz, Renée A., and Hella Freud Bernays. "The genesis of magical and transcendent cults." *American Imago* 29.1 (1972): 2–10.
16. Klein, Naomi. *The shock doctrine: The rise of disaster capitalism.* Macmillan, 2007.
17. Miller, Jacques-Alain, Paul Verhaeghe, and Ellie Ragland. *Jacques Lacan and the other side of psychoanalysis: Reflections on seminar XVII, sic vi.* Vol. 6. Duke University Press, 2006.
18. Muller, John. "Lacan's mirror stage." *Psychoanalytic Inquiry* 5.2 (1985): 233–252.
19. Freud, Sigmund. *On narcissism: An introduction.* Read Books Ltd., 2014.
20. Lacan, Jacques, Jacques-Alain Ed Miller, and Russell Trans Grigg. "The seminar of Jacques Lacan, Book 3: The psychoses 1955–1956." *Translation of the seminar that Lacan delivered to the Société Française de Psychoanalyse over the course of the academic year 1955–1956.* WW Norton & Company, 1993.

21. Samuels, Robert. "Catharsis: The politics of enjoyment." *Zizek and the rhetorical unconscious*. Palgrave Macmillan, Cham, 2020. 7–31.
22. Bloom, Paul. *Against empathy: The case for rational compassion*. Random House, 2017.
23. Freud, Sigmund. "The ego and the id id." *The standard edition of the complete psychological works of Sigmund Freud, Volume XIX (1923–1925): The ego and the id and other works*, 1961. 1–66.
24. Lacan, Jacques. "Aggressivity in psychoanalysis: Ecrits" (1948): 21.
25. Crockatt, Philip. "Freud's 'On narcissism: An introduction'." *Journal of Child Psychotherapy* 32.1 (2006): 4–20.
26. Žižek, Slavoj. *The sublime object of ideology*. Verso, 1989.
27. Samuels, Robert. "Victim politics: Psychoanalyzing the neoliberal conservative counter-revolution." *Psychoanalyzing the left and right after Donald Trump*. Palgrave Macmillan, Cham, 2016. 7–29.
28. Samuels, Robert. "Logos, global justice, and the reality principle." *Zizek and the rhetorical unconscious*. Palgrave Macmillan, Cham, 2020. 65–86.
29. Greisman, Harvey C. "Herd instinct and the foundations of biosociology." *Journal of the History of the Behavioral Sciences* 15.4 (1979): 357–369.

CHAPTER 6

Populism as a Cultural Virus

Abstract The concept of viral rhetoric points to two opposing ideas: one notion is that the metaphor of the virus is being used to blur the distinctions among culture, biology, psychology, and technology, and the other notion is that we can critique this collapsing of difference through an understanding of a psychoanalytic model of rhetoric. This chapter discusses Ernesto Laclau's *On Populist Reason* as he extends Freud's work through a focus on the rhetorical nature of political ideologies. In fact, Laclau presents an extensive analysis of the rhetorical theory of the contagion, and part of the strength of his perspective derives from his elimination of biological determinism from this concept.

Keywords Laclau · Rhetoric · Populism · Contagion · Psychoanalysis

Throughout this book, I have employed the concept of viral rhetoric to point to two opposing ideas: one notion is that the metaphor of the virus is being used to blur the distinctions among culture, biology, psychology, and technology, and the other notion is that we can critique this collapsing of difference through an understanding of a psychoanalytic model of rhetoric. By looking at Freud's work on group psychology, I stressed that he helps us to accomplish the latter task by explaining how

R. Samuels, *Viral Rhetoric*,
https://doi.org/10.1007/978-3-030-73895-2_6

ideas spread in an uncontrollable way through the processes of identification and idealization. In this chapter, I will discuss Ernesto Laclau's *On Populist Reason* as he extends Freud's work through a focus on the rhetorical nature of political ideologies.[1] In fact, Laclau presents an extensive analysis of the rhetorical theory of the contagion, and part of the strength of his perspective derives from his elimination of biological determinism from this concept.

Political Rhetoric

In his combination of psychoanalysis and rhetoric, Laclau seeks to provide a new theory of populism on the Right and the Left: "What happens, however, if the field of logic fails to constitute itself as a closed order, and rhetorical devices are necessary to bring about that closure? In that case, the rhetorical devices themselves – metaphor, metonymy, synecdoche, catachresis – become instruments of an expanded social rationality, and we are no longer able to dismiss an ideological interpellation as merely rhetorical" (12). In this turn to rhetorical figures, we see how Laclau wants to supplement Freud's work through an emphasis on how the manipulation of language serves to structure our political investments.[2]

One of Laclau's key moves is his notion of the empty signifier: "So the imprecision and emptiness of populist political symbols cannot be dismissed so easily: everything depends on the performative act that such an emptiness brings about" (18). In other words, even if politicians use empty phrases, these signifiers produce real effects through a process of performative enactment.[3] Just as Trump creates his own reality by simply saying and repeating things that are not true, the political use of vague and overly-general terms helps to unite together people with diverse interests and values: "But obviously, if through rhetorical operations they managed to constitute broad popular identities which cut across many sectors of the population, they actually constituted populist subjects, and there is no point in dismissing this as mere rhetoric. Far from being a parasite of ideology, rhetoric would actually be the anatomy of the ideological world" (12). While for Baudrillard, the separation of words from their referents and meanings points to a viral spread of contingent associations, for Laclau the employment of empty signifiers can function as an empty mirror that is able to receive the projections of different groups and individuals.[4] He adds that instead of seeing rhetoric as a parasitic force, we should realize its essential role in constructing social belief systems.

Returning to Le Bon's work on the irrationality of crowds, Laclau highlights how signifiers gain their power through affirmation, repetition, and contagion:

> The dissociation between the 'true signification' of words and the images they evoke requires some rhetorical devices to make it possible. According to Le Bon, there are three such devices: affirmation, repetition and contagion. 'Affirmation pure and simple, kept free of all reasoning and all proof, is one of the surest means of making an idea enter the mind of the crowds. The conciser an affirmation, the more destitute of every appearance of proof and demonstration, the more weight it carries.' As for repetition, its 'power is due to the fact that the repeated statement is embedded in the long run in those profound regions of our unconscious selves in which the motives of our actions are forged. At the end of a certain time, we have forgotten who is the author of the repeated assertion, and we finish by believing it.' Finally, contagion: 'Ideas, sentiments, emotions and beliefs possess in crowds a contagious power as intense as that of microbes. This phenomenon is very natural, since it is observed even in animals when they are together in number … In the case of men collected in a crowd all emotions are very rapidly contagious, which explains the suddenness of panics. Brain disorders, like madness, are themselves contagious'. (24)

Like Freud, even though he returns to Le Bon's biological metaphors, Laclau seeks to remove the contagion from the biological, and he does this by combining psychoanalysis and rhetoric together. Instead of basing the spread of ideas on a viral circulation, he emphasizes the rhetorical tools of affirmation, repetition, and suggestion.

In terms of Le Bon's use of viral metaphors, Laclau is quick to show how earlier theories of social behavior tended to rely on natural metaphors to describe cultural structures:

> For Le Bon, contagion can only be a form of pathological transmission. Its explanation is to be found in the general phenomenon of 'suggestibility' which was, at the time, the Deus ex machina omnipresent in the discourse on mass psychology. What, however, explains suggestibility is something to which no attention whatsoever was paid. As Freud put it: 'My resistance took the direction of protesting against the view that suggestion, which explained everything, was itself exempt of explanation.' (28)

As we saw in the last chapter, Freud explains the contagion through the concept of suggestion, which he then attaches to his notions of identification and idealization. Thus, while Freud still uses the term "contagion," he seeks to separate it from biology and attach it to psychology.

In his efforts to distinguish the spreading of ideas from the spreading of germs, Laclau stresses the symbolic foundation of shared representations: "What, for instance, if contagion were not a disease but the expression of a common feature shared by a group of people, one which is difficult to verbalize in a direct way, and can be expressed only by some form of symbolic representation?" (28). From the perspective of rhetoric and psychoanalysis, we need to divorce the "viral" madness of the crowd from the medical model of diseases. In fact, by turning to the manipulation of symbols as the foundation of political formations, Laclau highlights the rhetorical nature of these investments.[5]

As Laclau points out, it was common to believe that the lower classes were more susceptible to the spread of ideas than the more sophisticated upper classes: "Within contemporary society, the danger of crowd infection is greater in some groups than in others: the aristocracy is less prone to mental contagion than are the popular classes, and women and children are more prone than men. The link between women and crowd behaviour is, in fact, not only Taine's idiosyncratic view; it was a general view at the time" (34). This class dimension to biological determinism is in part derived from the idea that the general populace was easily "infected" by natural forces; however, as we saw in Freud, the opposite perspective is presented since he argues that the "primitive" groups are shaped by the spread of social thoughts and not biological impulses. While Freud's use of the term "primitive" is highly divisive, his main point was that animistic cultures and unconscious minds are both shaped by the primary symbolic processes of substitution, displacement, and figural representation.[6] In other words, our minds are initially determined by rhetorical figures and not natural forces.[7] This theory also entails that consciousness itself is more about representations than perceptions.[8]

The Role of Antagonism

Laclau posits that the big step he makes beyond Freud's conceptual model is that he uses the concept of social antagonism as a central framing device for the construction of populist politics:

Preface

I have written on energy justice for many years now, and I was inspired to finally write this book in order to capture my own thoughts on this global issue. I also feel there is a lack of literature exploring energy justice as a concept in research, and also its potential value in practice. I see two roles for energy justice: first there is the role within research itself in setting a theoretical framework; and second, there is its implementation and use in practice. When we discuss this latter point, it is because justice has to be implemented either in law, or indeed it can be carried out within the court system, which is the final place where we can go within society in order to ensure that justice is done. This is the perspective I wanted to bring to the literature, and to ensure that all disciplines engage with these legal arguments.

I want to thank many people along my energy justice journey. At the start I was able to discuss these issues in 2012 with Darren McCauley and Hannes Stephen at the University of Stirling, UK. It was from those discussions that we built some initial ideas on energy justice, mixing poetry alongside Roman history, and we produced two small papers: one being the triumvirate of tenets; and the other relating justice with energy systems, or indeed, what's referred to as the energy value chain/supply chain. These two short papers marked the beginning of focused energy justice research for me.

In thinking of energy justice research, it is important to realise the significant growth in scholarship around the area of this discipline. It is incredibly exciting to see! There is widespread adoption across all disciplines of the energy justice concept. Of huge importance to me is that finally there is a common goal within the energy sector, a realisation that the energy sector has to produce just outcomes.

In the past people focused on different issues to try and explore justice without ever thinking about what justice they were looking for. For example, people spent time exploring issues of safety, energy security and delivering affordable energy to the population while some also were concerned with infrastructure. However, today it is great to see that many people have at the backs of their minds the goal of justice as the overarching aim of their research—i.e., making the world a better and more sustainable place to live in.

I have written this book to put forward my views on the concept, and coming from a legal perspective I think it's important for scholars to realise that when all is said and done, justice takes place in two ways: (1) a new law is introduced to ensure justice happens; and (2) we go to the national legal courts to advance justice on a certain issue. Researchers from all disciplines need to realise what they are seeking for and how new advancements might happen, i.e., which of the two ways mentioned above will be needed, or maybe they both will. This discussion around how justice is delivered is my contribution to energy justice research, and it has received little if any attention in the literature to date; and therein lies the contribution of this book.

Dundee, UK

Raphael J Heffron

Acknowledgements

I would like to thank all who contributed in some form to the development of this short book.

I would like to thank those who introduced me fully to the energy sector at the University of Cambridge (UK) and in particular, Professor William Nuttall and Professor Angus Johnston. Thanks also to those at the various institutions where I built up my knowledge of planning, environmental, climate and energy law and policy—these include the Energy Policy Research Group (University of Cambridge, UK), Massachusetts Institute of Technology (US), the University of Texas at Austin (US), the British Institute of International and Comparative Law (UK), the Honourable Society of King's Inns (Ireland), Trinity College Dublin (Ireland), University of St Andrews (UK), University of Stirling (UK), the University of Leeds (UK) and Queen Mary University of London (UK).

I also convey thanks to people I have worked with over the years from across the world, and from whom I have learned more on how the energy sector works and the justice issues that arise in the Europe, Asia-Pacific, Africa, Middle East, North America and Latin America.

Sincere thanks also go to my family for their assistance and understanding while I wrote this short text in Achill and Dundee. And finally, this book is:

Le haghaidh mo h-oileán

Contents

About the Author

Raphael J Heffron is *Professor for Global Energy Law & Sustainability* at the Centre for Energy, Petroleum and Mineral Law and Policy at the University of Dundee. As of July 2019 he is also *Jean Monnet Professor in the Just Transition to a Low-Carbon Economy* awarded by the European Commission. In 2020, he was also appointed as *Senior Counsel at Janson* law firm in Brussels (Belgium). Professor Heffron is a qualified Barrister-at-Law, and a graduate of both Oxford (MSc) and Cambridge (MPhil & PhD). His work has as its principal focus the achievement of a just transition to a low-carbon economy, and combines a mix of energy law, policy and economics. He has published over 140 publications of different types and is the most cited scholar in his field worldwide (1370+*Scopus*). Professor Heffron has given just over 125 keynote or guest lectures in forty-nine countries worldwide.

Raphael's energy research has involved funding from UK national research councils (the Economic and Social Research Council (ESRC) and the Engineering and Physical Sciences Research Council (EPSRC), the EU and currently through the European Commission Jean Monnet Professorship 2019–2022, the British Academy, UK Department for Business, Energy and Industrial Strategy and ERA-ACTOM. He has given professional expert advice on energy law and policy issues (low-carbon energy and electricity systems) to the EU, UN, Commonwealth Secretariat, World Bank and various international think tanks—he currently serves on the United Nations Economic Commission for Europe (UNECE) Group of Experts on Cleaner Electricity Systems. More recently, he has performed due diligence on low-carbon energy projects for the ten Member States of the Association of Southeast Asian Nations (ASEAN) Center for Energy; produced a law and policy report on the energy transition for the fifty-four Member States of the Commonwealth, advised Nigerian Ministries on oil and gas law and Colombian professionals on climate and green finance.

Raphael was elected to the Royal Society of Edinburgh Young Academy of Scotland in 2018. His research and teaching has been recognised by the award of a Jean Monnet Professorship by the European Commission twice, in 2016 (–2019) and 2019 (–2022). His teaching has also been recognised in the UK by his becoming a Senior Fellow of the UK Higher Education Academy in 2018. In addition, Raphael is a Fellow of The Royal Society of Arts.

He is a reviewer for the next Intergovernmental Panel on Climate Change (IPCC) Report. Raphael is on the Editorial Board of the *International Energy Law Review*, the *Renewable Energy Law and Policy Review* and is Consulting Editor of the current *Halsbury's Laws of England* volumes on Energy Law (the leading practitioner energy law series). Raphael is also co-editor of the forthcoming *Oxford University Press Handbook for International Energy Law* and Editor-in-Chief of the Edinburgh University Press journal *Global Energy Law & Sustainability.*

Raphael is currently holding or has previously held the following positions: Co-Chair of the UK Energy Law and Policy Association; Visiting Professor in Energy Law at the International Hellenic University (Greece); Associate Researcher at the Energy Policy Research Group at the University of Cambridge (*current*); Visiting Professor at Paris-Dauphine University (Paris, France—*current*), Queen Mary University of London (UK—*current*), the University of West Indies (Trinidad-based), Javeriana University (Colombia) and University Eduardo Mondlane (Mozambique—*current*), University of Brawijaja (Indonesia); Visiting Lecturer at the ESCP Business School (London and Paris); and a Visiting Scholar at MIT (US), University of Sydney (Australia), University of Texas at Austin (US) and the British Institute for International and Comparative Law (UK).

Raphael read for his PhD at Trinity Hall, University of Cambridge. He is also a trained Barrister-at-Law and was called to the Bar in July 2007 in the Republic of Ireland. He holds degrees from the University of Cambridge (MPhil-Darwin, PhD-Trinity Hall), the University of Oxford (Christ Church) (MSc), the University of St Andrews (MLitt), and Trinity College Dublin (BA, MA).

List of Figures

List of Tables

CHAPTER 1

Introduction: The Inevitable Emergence of Energy Justice

Abstract In Chap. 1 the need for the implementation of energy justice into practice is called for. This chapter advances the idea that there is a perfect storm within many countries that is creating a need for energy justice. These international conditions are giving rise to society focusing on the issue of justice in our economies. Climate change continues at pace, and unless action is taken across society the effects will be felt and our human rights will be infringed. With the energy sector being responsible for the majority of carbon dioxide emissions and many environmental impacts, justice need to begin to permeate the energy sector. In essence, human rights need to be applied at each stage of the energy life cycle.

Keywords Energy justice • Human rights • Energy justice risks • Energy life cycle • Sustainable world • Implementing energy justice

1.1 The Inevitable Emergence of Energy Justice

Energy justice was always going to emerge at some point in time, and it is a mystery why energy justice has not emerged within research long before now. It is a reflection of the energy sector itself that 'justice' was not one of its core concepts in terms of research, nor indeed was the justice concept much in existence until 2013. Of course, there were scholars touching a range of different issues that had an element of justice within them,

R. J. Heffron, *The Challenge for Energy Justice*,
https://doi.org/10.1007/978-3-030-80097-0_1

but there was no common approach that could be understood, if for example, you were interested in the extractive industry as opposed to the electricity sector. There are many people who view the energy sector as having a reputation for being corrupt and they are not wrong. There remain so many problems, such as revenue management (taxation) issues, seeking environmental and planning approval and impacts, and climate change contributions. It is beyond doubt that energy justice will remain very important in the future, and become a topic that keeps on growing.

My own experience with energy justice has had two common experiences rise to the fore. The first has been the levels of engagement I have witnessed; energy justice is a concept that people can engage with very quickly. For many persons even outside the arenas of research and academia, it is easy to see why this concept has become the heartbeat and the *raison d'être* of energy research. Probably, like me, they will be incredulous that it has taken so long. The second experience is that many people think it is such a clear concept that they tell me they had the idea (or similar) but they never put it down on paper either quickly or succinctly enough. Again, that is very positive to hear but it does raise the question, 'why?'

The answer to that question is that for many people the energy sector is seen as vital to the functioning of the national (and global) economy. Researchers (and practitioners) have formerly focused on the development of energy resources. Little attention was given to fairness, equity, equality and inclusiveness which all together can be stated to be energy justice. The energy sector was seen as large and fragmented into different areas: you would be classified as a mining researcher, an oil and gas specialist, a nuclear energy scholar or an electricity expert. Indeed, it seems to have suited the energy community to have the sector arranged that way, as it meant that different activities could continue unabated, without fear of stepping on each other's toes, and with people in dominant positions remaining so.

A classic highlight for me of what was wrong centres on competition in the electricity sector. In many cases energy sources that generate electricity were classed as cheap, when, if you looked up and down the energy life cycle, they received subsidies, i.e., subsidies in extraction, and what can be classed as a subsidy when there is no charge on carbon dioxide pollution. Immediately, low-carbon energy sources are at a disadvantage, and in general the public initially complained that subsidies were given to the low-carbon sector, and meanwhile the fossil fuel sector continued its heavily subsidised existence. Where was the fair competition? This was a notional competition in a market that was designed for fossil fuels and is a contributory cause to the rise in carbon dioxide emissions.

With energy justice however, the energy research community is beginning to change. Many now describe themselves as energy researchers and particularly those who classed themselves as oil and gas specialist. The research community sees the energy system and how different activities and issues are interrelated. Research no longer has to be so fragmented. In practice it has been more visible with more than several energy companies rebranding themselves to reflect change, where there is a realisation that the energy transition is happening and that there is a need to move beyond fossil fuels and into low-carbon energy sources. It has been to the advantage of the energy justice concept that the energy transition began and received huge momentum with the signing of the Paris Agreement in 2015; that 197 countries signed the Paris Agreement has finally persuaded the majority of people that action needs to happen and carbon emissions have to be reduced.

1.2 What Is Energy Justice: My View

I have been asked across the world, whether in-person or online, for my views about what energy justice is and what it means, by diverse audiences. Hence, I will clarify my perspective. Energy justice is centred on:

- the normative aim of contributing to make the world a better place, i.e., a more just and sustainable world;
- it is based on five core justice philosophies which are procedural, distributive, restorative, recognition and cosmopolitan justice; and
- its definition is that it is about applying human rights across the energy life cycle (see Fig. 1.1).

That final definition is vital. Applying human rights across the energy life cycle is what we are working towards within energy justice where we aim to protect our rights as these various energy activities continue. There will be evolutions and revolutions in energy activities, and they will continue considering the vital role energy plays in our economies today. It is down to the scholarship and practitioner communities to ensure that energy activity improves its outcomes, i.e., that the energy sector delivers just outcomes. These type of just outcomes will deliver energy justice and they will ensure that our rights are protected as the energy sector

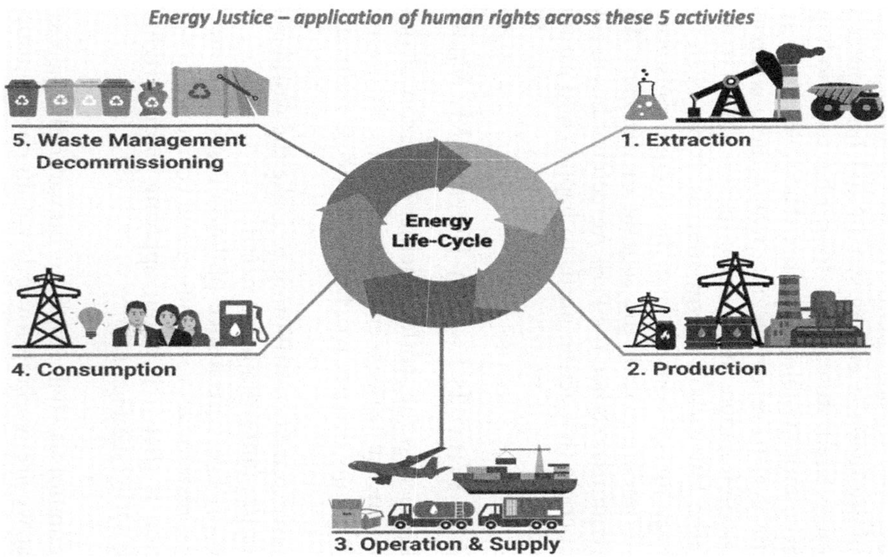

Fig. 1.1 Energy Justice and the Energy Life Cycle. *Source*: Created by the author (2021)

continues to develop. We are working towards a broad list of rights and these include mainly the following (though not limited to) rights of/for: life, health, minimum subsistence, freedom, human dignity, water, healthy environment, air, culture, property, adequate housing, security and a fair trial.

The essence of this book is to provide a first clear direction in research of how we have arrived at this point in terms of energy justice, and to provide the first research that orients the essence of energy justice to be about ensuring these rights are delivered, as a result of energy decision-making, activities and investment, so that it all ensures that our human rights are protected.

1.3 The Acceleration of Energy Justice: The Perfect Storm[1]

As stated earlier, in the past society has unfortunately not realised the need for justice all across the energy sectors and for thinking about it in a unified way. However, we are beginning to consider this issue now, for several reasons, as in essence public policy is shifting. It could be called a 'perfect storm of energy justice' whereby the opportunity for justice to permeate through the energy sector has arisen. What prompted this perfect storm was really the financial crisis of 2007–2009 as I will explain later. Indeed, Plato stated "*Accidents and calamities…are the universal legislators of the world.*" (Plato, *The Laws*).

As a result of the economic crisis of 2007–2009, largely remembered as the banking crisis, society began to reform and particularly so in the financial sector which is so vital to the energy sector. The availability of finance is absolutely crucial to a sector which needs to deliver more energy than ever before, to ensure more energy access and to replace old energy infrastructure (not to mention the need for more low-carbon energy to address climate change). After a crisis society's behaviour becomes risk averse, and in addition to the other changes that have occurred this has resulted in more justice within the transition.

There are presently ten key reasons why a perfect storm has been created, and which is accelerating justice into the energy transition—and when one reflects on these, the five forms of justice mentioned earlier are at the root of the rise of justice into the energy sector.

1. *Economics*

After the financial crisis a revision of economics has occurred. The education of economists across many countries has changed and universities are or have adjusted their curricula to accommodate more economic perspectives than the previous over-reliance on neoclassical economics. We have seen a rise in the popularity of economists working on addressing societal inequality (Thomas Piketty in *Capital* for example) and we also have seen Jean Tirole, a Nobel Prize Winning Economist state in essence that justice (via law) has a key role to play in ensuring that society can address the issues of the energy and climate crisis (in his book in *Our Common Ground*). Law change has increasingly begun to address issues of inequality across all parts of our societies and that includes the energy sector.

2. *Taxation*

Taxation is another area in the commercial world that has seen change. Post the 2007–2009 financial crisis society has begun to re-assess the role of taxation in our societies. The use of tax havens is now well documented and there have been major leaks that have promoted change (the Panama Papers and the Paradise Papers). Now more scrutiny is being paid to international transactions, particularly because energy companies were exposed as heavy users of tax havens. The Organisation for Economic Co-operation and Development (OECD) is aiming through several initiatives to examine the issues (particularly inequality) that the unfair world of international taxation is causing in the energy sector (and especially in the mining sector).

3. *Disclosure and Transparency*

There are several other issues that already have an impact on the energy sector, and all of which deserve mention and impact on disclosure and transparency. *Accounting* has changed, and international accounting standards require more disclosure specifically for energy projects. The international *Extractive Industries Transparency Initiative* (EITI) requires both a State and the Investor to disclose issues around the taxation relationship between both parties. A *Social-Licence-to-Operate* (SLO) requires more transparency between the energy project developer and the local community—and some projects have been stopped recently due to a failure to keep the SLO internationally. And finally an *Energy Finance Reserve Obligation* (EFRO) is causing an impact on the value of an energy asset, as it requires an operator to place an estimated amount of money that will pay for the decommissioning of the energy infrastructure and site into a neutral bank account, so as to avoid the scenario where the State has to pay should the operator go bankrupt or sell on the asset to a company without the financial capacity to pay for a clean-up.

4. *Insurance*

Again, after a crisis, insurance is more difficult to obtain. And in light of changes in the commercial world alongside climate change issues, insurance for energy projects has now become very difficult to obtain. Already this is the case for coal projects, and in 2019 such projects are now finding it very difficult to get insurance (Sheehan 2019). This will have a knock-on effect where there will be a rise in cases where the insurer of last resort—the State—will need to become much more active, and as a result the public will increasingly question all the benefits of fossil fuel development, and the support of its continuation.

5. *Environmental Impact Assessments (EIAs)*

EIAs have been around since the 1980s, but they have only now started to assist in developing a low-carbon economy. EIAs are a permitting procedure that is required before an energy project can be built, and it assesses in detail from an interdisciplinary perspective all the environmental and social impacts of the project. The legislation internationally has changed over the last decade in part in response to the economic crisis. It has become stricter at a national level, and also international banking rules (known as the *Equator Principles*) now require a developer also to have gone through an EIA process in order to get the project financed. It is via EIAs that projects on coal have been stopped in Australia (Nogrady 2019) and Kenya in 2019 (Bloomberg 2019). The data required by a project developer in which they can demonstrate their project will have limited environmental and/or social impact is increasing year-on-year. Project developers in both Australia and Kenya struggled to present this data, and the data did not make their coal projects attractive; even the positive economic contribution was considered an over-estimation.

6. *Legal Action on Climate Change*

Legal action is now beginning to influence company behaviour. One of the key court cases on climate change is *State of the Netherlands v Urgenda* in the Supreme Court in the Netherlands in a recent decision in 20 December 2019, where it was held that the Netherlands had an obligation to take action to prevent climate change and reduce greenhouse gas (GHG) emissions by at least 25 per cent at the end of 2020 compared to 1990 levels (Minnesma 2019). Further, it noted that this was on the basis of the European Convention on Human Rights (ECHR). This case will result in the recognition of human rights in energy development and the State obligation to act on climate change, and consequently it will have a major impact on energy projects over the coming years. Further, this court ruling will spread and create value in judicial decision-making in other countries and ensure more justice is applied in decision-making around energy policy development.

7. *Legal Action on Rules of Foreign Investment*

The role of energy arbitration is relatively unknown to interdisciplinary scholars, however, this will change. It is clear that recent cases—in Bolivia, Peru and Kenya[2]—have highlighted key legal issues such as the importance of EIAs, SLOs, the EFRO and energy justice issues. However, a more recent case which is still ongoing is *Process & Industrial Developments Limited v The Federal Republic of Nigeria*, [2019] EWHC 2241, a circa $9 billion case, and this case will be transformative for several reasons. The first is whether such investments should be protected and the question then arises: can an energy dispute (arbitration) case be included in public policy decision-making? The answer should be a resounding 'yes' especially as an energy case involves energy, environmental and climate change issues and generally also includes closely related issues such as international development, finance and taxation. The UK Court in August 2019 stated there was no public policy issue. However, if the energy transition is to happen, rules around investor protection will have to change. Poor or unjust investment choices should not be supported or protected by rules of foreign investment. This will be an area of transformation over the next decade and will put pressure on energy projects, particularly on fossil fuel which within the context of climate change could be classified as an unjust or poor investment choice.

8. *The 2015 Paris Agreement*

In 2015 the Paris Agreement was signed at COP21 with 188 countries signing and ratifying it within circa three years, which is very fast for any international agreement. The agreement is already prompting change. It requires countries to produce a plan of how they will reduce their carbon dioxide emissions. A key impact of this treaty is that it also gets people to think of the energy transition as a 'just' transition to a low-carbon economy. What this essentially means is that we do not want a Business-as-Usual (BaU) approach to the energy transition. We need one that has justice at its core as there is a desire to have a more fair and equitable economy in the future.

9. *Personal Technology and the Role of Imagery*

Personal technology is also having a major impact in terms of utilising imagery to change public policy. It should be remembered that pictures (images) already have and continue to play a role in our legal systems in cases of criminal law and for civil liability. That this should spread into mainstream society in terms of the effects of climate change should be no surprise, but it is having a major effect. Key issues around personal decisions as where to live, lifestyles and tourism will change and are already influencing societal development.

10. *UN Sustainable Development Goals (SDGs)*

There are seventeen UN SDGs and they are having a major impact. Countries have signed up to these and they are beginning to think about how these SDGs are considered in a range of different policies across society. The energy sector is obviously crucial here and one metric proposed that demonstrates this is how the UN SDG 7 on energy is the most influential of all UN SDGs, and if the latter is resolved it will have a major impact on whether we meet the rest of the SDGs (Nerini et al. 2018).

1.3.1 Final Thoughts

This 'perfect storm' of energy justice issues has created the opportunity for justice to be at the heart of the energy transition. All of these issues increase the commercial risk of investment decisions by energy countries and also affect public policy-making. The result is that a project developer not only has to meet the demands of public policy on the energy sector but also meet their internal requirements on investment risk where there will also be obligations from external investors (such as those providing project finance, insurance, etc.). These demanding requirements will mean that projects which can play a role in the energy transition become much more attractive.

The energy industry can no longer afford to only focus on profits but has to consider how the project will result in 'just' outcomes, where considerations of social and environmental impacts are of vital importance alongside meeting new standards of commercial practice and its limitations. It can be stated therefore that justice in the energy transition is set to become the key influencer in State and firm strategy and behaviour. We are at the precipice of a just transition to a low-carbon economy.

1.4 Structure of the Book

The major contribution of this text centres on the focus on human rights and energy justice, and is the first literature in this direction and of vital importance in terms of implementing energy justice into practice. The book builds up to a crescendo on this important human rights issue. Hence, in Chap. 2, it covers the emergence of energy justice and sets out its interdisciplinary nature. Chapter 3 centres on exploring the issue of economics and energy justice. This is an underexplored area and to a certain point, energy economists are only slowly taking to energy justice as a concept. Many energy economists do approach the issues from an 'equity' perspective, but more work is needed in this area, and energy justice scholars also need to connect with and to complete more economics-driven research. After all, and as noted in this chapter, economists still influence policy-makers in a major way, so it is important to connect with those persons who deliberate on the financing of the energy transition.

Continuing with the finance theme, Chap. 4 focuses on a case study of distributive justice. For me, distributive justice is very important, particularly in addressing the major issue of societal inequality, an issue that is distributed across our societies. Here the focus is on taxation and resource revenue management; and it highlights the possible use of a sovereign wealth fund to manage resources in a more sustainable way. A functioning taxation system is vital to an economy, and the area of energy taxation and justice is under-researched, hence this will be an area of future growth.

The penultimate Chap. 5 builds on all the previous chapters and advances the issue of human rights and energy justice. The aim is to explore how energy justice can be implemented. There is limited research on this and yet there is some momentum going forward, with US President Joe Biden appointing an academic to his administration specifically on energy justice. The chapter explores energy justice from the perspective of the opportunity of last resort, i.e., what is the final opportunity that we have of enforcing energy justice in society? This 'opportunity of last resort' is the national courts and is the place where societies can seek to have justice enforced through the protection of a variety of human rights. One hundred legal cases from around the world covering the activities of the energy life cycle are analysed to highlight the key human rights and forms of justice that are being implemented today. This represents a starting point, and the aim is that society needs to go far beyond this in order to ensure our future climate goals and ambitions for a sustainable world.

Chapter 6 concludes the book and offers some of my own perspectives on energy justice risks alongside my future outlook for energy justice research and practice, and lessons for the next generation of energy justice scholars.

Notes

1. This sub-section is in part based on previous work I completed for the following mini-review, and I thank the publisher for permission for the adapted re-use of the information: Heffron, R. J. 2020. Justice in the Energy Transition. Special Issue 'Decarbonisation Pathways for Oil and Gas'. The Oxford Institute for Energy Studies, March 2020, Issue 121. Available at: https://www.oxfordenergy.org/wpcms/wp-content/uploads/2020/03/OEF121.pdf (last accessed 1 May 2021).
2. The case references are: Kenya—Cortec Mining Kenya Limited, Cortec (Pty) Limited and Stirling Capital Limited v. Republic of Kenya, ICSID Case No. ARB/15/29; Peru—Bear Creek v. Peru Bear Creek Mining Corporation v. Republic of Peru, ICSID Case No. ARB/14/2; and South American Silver Limited (Bermuda) v. the Plurinational State of Bolivia, PCA Case No. 2013-15.

References

Bloomberg. 2019. New Energy Outlook Annual Report Executive Summary 2019. Accessed 1 May 2021. https://bnef.turtl.co/story/neo2019/page/2/2?teaser=true.

Minnesma, M. 2019. Not Slashing Emissions? See you in Court. *Nature*, 576, 379–381.

Nerini, F., Tomei, J., To L.S., Bisaga, I., Parikh, P., Black, M. et al. 2018. Mapping Synergies and Trade-offs between Energy and the Sustainable Development Goals. *Nature Energy* 3 (1): 10–15. https://doi.org/10.1038/s41560-017-0036-5.

Nogrady, B. 2019. Landmark Australian Ruling Rejects Coal Mine Over Global Warming, Nature, (11 February 2019). Accessed April 2021. https://www.nature.com/articles/d41586-019-00545-8.

Sheehan, M. 2019. Coal Exclusions Double in 2019 as Action Spreads Beyond Europe. 2 December 2019, Reinsurance News. Accessed April 2021. https://www.reinsurancene.ws/coal-exclusions-double-in-2019-as-action-spreads-beyond-europe/.

CHAPTER 2

The Concept of Energy Justice Across the Disciplines

Abstract Energy justice has taken on an increasing role and value within the energy sector and particularly in the research community where it is now a recognised interdisciplinary concept. This chapter presents a critical account of the emergence of the concept alongside a diagrammatical image of how in a normative way energy justice works from theory to practice. The chapter also explores energy education as well as some of the pitfalls of the energy concept to date.

Keywords Energy justice • Interdisciplinary energy research • Restorative justice • Energy infrastructure development • Sustainable world • Energy justice framework

2.1 Introduction

As stated earlier, 'energy justice' is a concept that is being used across many academic disciplines within energy research at the present time. This development has occurred over the last decade and is currently accelerating. There is one main research question that drives this chapter: what is the role of the 'energy justice concept' across the disciplines? In answering this question, there are a sub-set of questions and these include exploration of the ways in which the energy justice concept has emerged: how will it continue to emerge, how has it emerged, and will it become engaged in practice and therefore become relevant to policy? This chapter details the

R. J. Heffron, *The Challenge for Energy Justice*,
https://doi.org/10.1007/978-3-030-80097-0_2

exploration of this core concept which is emerging across all disciplines that conduct energy research, and is a concept that could become an 'ethos' and provide society's ethical framework for decision-making in the energy sector.[1]

This chapter contributes to the research literature in a number ways. It offers a first historical overview of how energy justice emerged. It also analyses energy research within universities which demonstrate why 'energy justice' as a concept is likely to increase in its value to a range of disciplines across the sciences and social sciences at universities. Further, it demonstrates a number of ways in which 'energy justice' is emerging in practice and how it can be adopted and utilised in policy (through restorative justice) and become an economic policy relevant to the energy sector.

The chapter begins in Sect. 2.2 by providing a critical account of the emergence of the energy justice concept. This involved the identification of three specific stages in its development and how these have influenced the development of the energy justice concept. It discusses the reasons for why there is a need and an opportunity to work on further building of the energy justice concept and for having a common concept across the disciplines. It presents a diagrammatical representation of energy justice for researchers and policy-makers to interact with, which has been adopted in the literature and most significantly utilised by Professor Shalanda Baker and her team in *The Energy Justice Workbook*.[2] Professor Baker has been appointed to US President Biden's team as a Deputy Director in Energy Justice.

Restorative justice is also examined as a way of ensuring energy justice is applied within policy and how three recent examples demonstrate this: (1) Environmental Impact Assessments and the post-acceptance monitoring phase; (2) a Social-License-to-Operate that will ensure the development of cooperation with the local community over the life-span of the energy infrastructure; and (3) the Energy Financial Reserve Obligation where the company needs to demonstrate they have the financial capacity to clean and restore the mine.

Section 2.3 details the importance and role of energy research at universities and how this provides support for more integrative research on energy, and shows that energy justice scholars are ideally placed to take advantage of this, given what the concept brings to energy research through its focus on 'just' decision-making in the energy sector. It highlights the importance of education in ensuring that the energy justice concept is utilised in research and education, and following that a knowledge transfer to policy-makers. The second half of the section highlights a pitfall for energy justice, and that is due to the lessons learned from how the environmental and climate justice concepts developed.

2.2 A Critical Account of the Emergence of the Energy Justice Concept

This exploration of the emergence of the energy justice concept in both the academic arena and in practice is the first in the literature. Exploring when and how it emerged in use is necessary in order to understand: (1) its potential application in practice and policy development; and (2) its potential longevity, value and impact for energy research.

There was not much in the literature at the beginning that detailed the emergence of the concept of energy justice. Even two early monographs which aimed to explore energy justice in detail did not reference its beginnings.[3] Further, in a first review of the concept entitled '*Energy justice: a conceptual review*', the authors do not actually review the origin of the energy justice concept itself, they conduct an academic literature review of its development in academic research and with little mention of its use in practice.[4]

This chapter highlights that there are three specific phases of research that mark the beginning of energy justice research and practice and these are outlined in the following paragraphs. There are three clear distinguishable phases. The first is its use in practice, and in particular, by NGOs. The second is its early use in academia and this is notable in that energy justice as a concept was not advanced or examined by the literature. The final, third phase, is where energy justice is defined as a concept and the research literature builds upon these concepts.

1. *Its use in practice*

Energy justice is a term that has been used in practice (i.e., in non-academic life, such as in the commercial and public sectors) far longer than in research, albeit to a very limited degree. There are two NGOs that have used the term pre-dating academia—one in the US (since 1999)[5] and in the UK[6] (at the very least in 2009 or before). There is another later reference to its use in 2011 by the Chief Executive of National Energy Action (UK) who referred to it in the context of the UK energy sector only and which is a charity whose focus is on ending fuel poverty.[7]

2. *Its early use in academia*

The term energy justice was first used in academic research literature in 2010 in an article entitled '*Energy justice and sustainable development*', however, the article is more on sustainable development than energy justice.[8] Indeed, apart from at the beginning when energy justice is defined essentially as energy poverty there is little further mention of it, and it receives little attention in the conclusion where it is clear sustainable development is the focus of the article. This is similar to an article in 2013 entitled '*Energy justice and ethical consumption: comparison, synthesis and lesson drawing*' which is about ethical consumption in the energy sector and does not address the energy justice concept itself—nor however does the author claim to—and in addition, the author states there is no definition of what it means.[9] Then there is a book entitled '*Energy Justice in a changing climate*' published in late 2013, however, the emphasis was not on exploring the energy justice concept itself but in relating the term to other issues in relation to climate change—which is a rather limited perspective since the concept, or what it means, is never fully debated.[10]

3. *Its use in academia as a defined concept*

In early 2013 the term 'energy justice' began to receive more attention in the literature and become an object of study. This is when scholars started to define it as a concept and develop its frameworks. In an article in early 2013 energy justice was defined as having three central tenets.[11] This was followed by an article exploring specifically, energy justice across the energy life cycle or system in early January 2014.[12] Thereafter the literature on energy justice as a concept has increased and there now is a seminal article in Nature Energy[13] and even a review paper.[14]

In terms of defining the concept there are two main definitions. There is the first from 2013 that defined energy justice as having three central tenets[15] and what was referred to as a *triumvirate of tenets*—distribution, procedural and recognition justice (sometimes as referred to as justice as recognition) which were applied throughout the energy system.[16] Second, a principled approach to energy justice was advanced that is based on eight core principles from 2014 and which has been worked on since[17] and these include: availability, affordability, due process, transparency and accountability, sustainability, intra-generational equity, inter-generational equity, and responsibility. These are the two frameworks for thinking on energy justice and defining it as a concept. There has been one addition which has considered energy justice within an energy system (i.e., the application of energy justice at each activity in the energy life cycle).[18] These defined concepts of energy justice compete with each other and at the same time complement each other.

A major limitation of the approaches outlined above—the triumvirate of tenets, the energy life cycle (systems) approach and the principle-based approach—is that there is little reflection of how these transfer into practice and are 'enforced' in practice, i.e., how energy justice becomes a delivered outcome through policy. Few scholars (as outlined above) have even referred to the use of energy justice in practice, despite it having a longer history of use than in academia.

In exploring how energy justice can become a delivered policy outcome, i.e., making that link between academia and practice, Fig. 2.1 represents the energy justice conceptual framework based on the main literature to date that focuses directly on analysing the concept.

The energy justice scholarship community in this context needs to take note of Popper's (1963)[19] and Kuhn's (1962)[20] arguments in developing a knowledge base—i.e., a research community builds layers of understanding from a common base. For example, the discipline of economics is just one example where thinking and modelling techniques from neoclassical economists have gained prominence while econometrics, and behavioural economics have also risen in importance of late. This was achieved through building on the core models and concepts, and also by collaboration, not by significant lone research and continuous additions to the concept instead of challenging the core assumptions itself—albeit they did not engage in sufficient critical reflection. Similarly this is how other disciplines have developed over time and one can note both Popper's (1963, 2002) and Kuhn's (1962) arguments (despite them having differing views on the process of development) where they discuss the journey of the development of scientific knowledge.

In looking at the energy justice conceptual framework, we begin by looking at the core tenets of energy justice to see if they are present, before then broadening their scope to see where the issue fits within the energy life cycle (or energy system) in the context of having a worldview, i.e., a cosmopolitan perspective. Then we look at how to apply energy justice in practice and to seek how the problems, issues and/or challenge they are researching can be addressed (or not) by the principles.

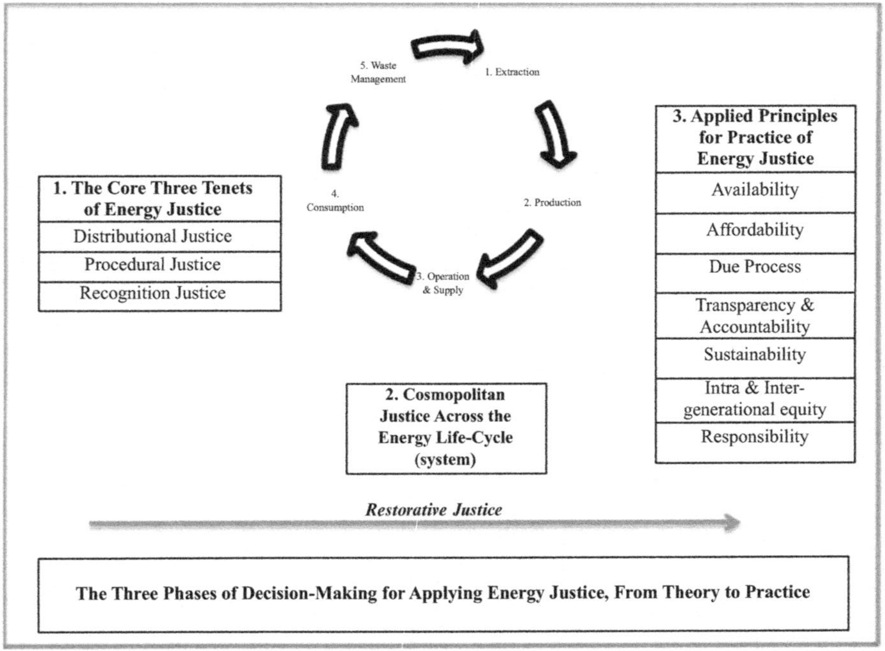

Fig. 2.1 The Energy Justice Conceptual Framework. (*Source*: Created by the author for—Heffron and McCauley 2017)

2.3 Energy Justice: From Theory to Practice and Restorative Justice

Figure 2.1 identifies three clear phases of decision-making for applying energy justice from theory to practice. The application of restorative justice at each phase aims that ensure energy justice is applied in practice. The question arises: how does restorative justice achieve this? Restorative justice is primarily used in and emerged from criminal law and deserves greater attention in future research.

Restorative justice arose from society questioning a range of issues after an injustice had occurred and what was the response to the victim. Restorative justice aims to repair the harm done to people (and/or society/nature), rather than solely focusing on punishing the offender—as societies use the legal system for. Further, restorative justice can assist in pinpointing where prevention needs to occur. While the application of restorative justice is a long-standing debate with the literature in the area dating from the 1990s,[21] recent international events (i.e., such as the global financial crisis of 2007–2009 and the September 11 attacks in the US[22] have prompted society to further explore and apply this type of justice more in decision-making, policy-making and subsequently then into law, resulting in delivered outcomes (should the legal system be robust on enforcement).

Restorative justice makes society deliberate on how to respond to injustices (harms) that have occurred and also in defining what injustices society should give attention to in the first place.[23] While it is has been applied mainly in relation to criminal law, one of the areas it has been applied beyond that is in corporate crime.[24] In the context of the energy sector, this is significant, as one can immediately think of its application post energy-accidents, for example, where it is clear the energy company is responsible for the accident, i.e., the US BP Deepwater Horizon accident.

The application of restorative justice when applying energy justice decision-making forces decision-makers to engage with justice concerns and consider the full range of issues, as any injustice caused by an energy activity would have to be rectified. In some cases, these costs of 'restoration' would be prohibitive and consequently that energy activity would cease or not be proposed. It would ensure that the three energy justice approaches of three tenets, the energy system and/or the eight principles are applied as these identify the areas where restorative action would have to be applied. Then they will all assist in determining a restorative 'cost' of the proposed action which can feed directly into policy decision-making.

Hence, if restorative justice were applied to the energy sector it would ensure that decision-making was made in light of considering the potential harm of that decision and consequently the true cost of that decision. In some cases this is already the case in the energy sector but the terminology of 'restorative justice' is not used. There are examples of this below in practice in three recent phenomena in the energy sector that are having a big impact on the energy sector. It is clear from these examples discussed in brief below that restorative justice provides closure to the energy decision-making process, that it forces the policy-maker to think about what the final outcome will be, and how policy will ensure this. This is evident in relation to practice in three recent phenomena in the energy sector (outlined below): (A) Environmental Impact Assessments and the post-acceptance monitoring phase; (B) a Social-License-to-Operate that will develop cooperation with the local community over the life-span of the energy infrastructure; and (C) the Energy Financial Reserve Obligation where the company needs to demonstrate they have the financial capacity to clean and restore energy infrastructure at the end of its lifespan.

(A) *Environmental Impact Assessments (EIAs)*

The aim of an Environmental Impact Assessment (EIA) is for international, national and local communities to achieve a balance between development and the environment. There are many other methods and strategies for balancing development and the environment but an EIA is a formalised process that has had international and national consensus on its development over time. This article does not aim to go into particular depth on EIAs, but briefly, the EIA process has placed certain limitations on development and ensured that development that does occur is achieved with environmental protection as a core aim from the beginning of the process.[25] Already at the international level the EIA is promoted for use in nearly all projects funded by international development agencies—such as the World Bank, the OECD and the United Nations Environment Programme (UNEP). This area of law is still developing fast and was further reformed in the EU in 2017 with the intention to become more inter-related to climate change. Significantly, while it is not the case at the moment, reform measures include more of a requirement that there will be monitoring of the energy infrastructure project once it has received its EIA approval, to ensure that the project developer has met their environmental obligations once the project is built.

(B) *Social Licence to Operate (SLO)*

The Social-Licence-to-Operate (SLO) is a fast-emerging principle concept in energy policy in general and is, in particular, developed around the mining law and policy community.[26] There are a number of papers which explore the origin of the SLO and its use in the mining sector—with one seminal paper[27]—and it is likely that in the future the vast majority of the energy infrastructure will need an SLO before beginning operation (Prno and Slocombe 2012; Morrison 2014).[28] The SLO in essence builds on an EIA and ensures the energy project operator works with the local community for the lifespan of the project rather than as was previously the case, just satisfying the local community at the outset of the project.

(C) *Energy Financial Reserve Obligation (EFRO)*

Energy Financial Reserve Obligation (EFRO) is a general term for the obligation that companies should have when operating energy infrastructure. In particular, the EFRO applies in terms of companies with waste obligations—or indeed the companies that should have waste obligations. These can also be referred to as clean-up obligations and environmental bonds, and the nuclear energy industry contributes to waste management funds immediately from the point of operation whereas in the coal industry, the operator only has to have the financial reserve capacity to do so.[29] Indeed this has become a major issue and there are a multitude of reports focusing on it in relation to the operation of coal assets in Australia and the US.[30] For example, in the US, under the Federal Surface Mining Control and Reclamation Act (SMCRA) 1997 (and in Australia the Financial Assurance under the Environmental Protection Act 1994),[31] energy companies are required to remediate the lands where mining activity has occurred. However, many companies were allowed to self-bond and therefore when they went bankrupt there was still no finance available for meeting reclamation obligations[32] and the EFRO counters this corporate behaviour.

2.3.1 *Restorative Justice Applied Across the Commercial Energy Project*

From these three examples, it is demonstrated (and see Figure 2.2) how restorative justice applies across an energy project and ensures the local population, society and nature is not subject to harmful actions.

Fig. 2.2 Project Risk across the Project Development in the Energy Sector. (*Source*: Created by author [Heffron 2020]. Key: EIA—Environmental Impact Assessment; SLO—Social Licence to Operate; and EFRO—Energy Finance Reserve Obligation)

2.4 From Energy Education to Energy Policy-Making

One of the main reasons why energy justice has a significant opportunity as a concept to impact upon the energy research and practice is because of the sustained development of energy research at universities. In examining energy research at third-level education, one can highlight the potential longevity, value and impact in energy research that energy justice has the potential to have. In this section the study of energy research is examined and it is demonstrated how 'energy research' has become ingrained at universities and institutes of technology. Consequently, this presents an opportunity for the 'energy justice concept' that crosses the disciplines to make a significant impact at third-level education. In ensuring that future energy decision-makers (and policy-makers) who become stakeholders in the energy sector acquire knowledge on 'energy justice', universities play one of the most important roles in ensuring that this happens. This section examines energy research at universities and also identifies some possible pitfalls that energy justice scholars may face in the future.

The growing community of energy justice scholars need to ensure that the energy justice concept has internal aims within academia (constant normative and evidence-based evolution of the concept) and external aims beyond academia, i.e., where decision-making and policy formulation in the energy sector is made with energy justice 'thinking'. These internal and external aims need to be developed from a solid base of literature which can also be utilised in the practice of teaching on energy justice.

Energy research is growing across universities. It is evident that energy is truly one of the only areas of research that remains today as transcending across all disciplines. This is supported by energy being one of the only areas of research that is supported across and by universities with cross-university energy research centres or initiatives being supported at sixteen of the to twenty universities in the world—if one uses the *Times Higher Education* rankings[33]—see Table 2.1.

In addition, in many universities there is even a further focus on good energy practices through a variety of activities and these come in many forms. For example, the most notable is that there is a Green Metric Ranking of world universities and interestingly nearly all the top twenty universities on this list all produce more than 100 per cent of their own energy needs.[35] This latter development is increasing with universities worldwide seeking to build their own energy generating resources.

Table 2.1 Interdisciplinary Energy Research Centres and/or Initiatives in the Top 20 World Universities[34]

Top 20 World Universities According to the Times Higher Education 2016 Rankings					
No.	*University*	*Energy Centre*	*No.*	*University*	*Energy Centre*
1	University of Oxford	✓	11	University of Chicago	✓
2	California Institute of Technology	X	12	Yale University	✓*[a]X
3	Stanford University	✓	13	University of Pennsylvania	✓
4	University of Cambridge	✓	14	University of California, Los Angeles	X
5	Massachusetts Institute of Technology	✓	15	University College London	✓
6	Harvard University	✓	16	Columbia University	✓
7	Princeton University	✓	17	Johns Hopkins University	X
8	Imperial College London	✓	18	Duke University	✓
9	ETH Zurich—Swiss Federal Institute of Technology Zurich	✓	19	Cornell University	✓
10	University of California, Berkeley	✓	20	Northwestern University	✓

[a]Closed in 2016

Significantly, the role of universities in education on energy issues (though it refers to sustainable development) is highlighted in chapter 36 (promoting Education, Public Awareness and Training) of Agenda 21, the Action Plan of the 1992 United Nations Conference on Environment and Development. In academic literature, it is clear that universities have a role in energy education and the focus is mainly on skills development as well as job potential for those who study in this area.[36] In the context of energy justice, it is notable that some universities have been recruiting specifically for energy justice scholars to academic posts (University of Sussex, UK, and Michigan Technological University, US) while others have courses on energy justice (University of Minnesota).

However, even more education is needed on energy and sustainability issues to reduce the impact of the energy sector on the environment. For too long, this has been avoided. In many ways, and echoing David

Orr's words, it is now time for people with BAs, BSs, LLBs, MBAs and PhDs to correct the wrongs they have inflicted on the planet and to educate us on how to improve our use of energy resources[37]—i.e., it is time people began to transfer their education into policy-making on energy issues. In this context, there is a lack of leadership in the area of energy education[38] and there are calls for energy scholars and educators to extend their roles beyond that of only education, and on to college and university committees.[39] The latter view is particularly interesting in the context of the earlier mentioned example of universities developing their own energy resources. Hence, there is the possibility for energy researchers to apply their research into actual practice, not to mention contributing to policies concerning energy investments in terms of the university endowment.

Energy research has clearly developed within universities, however, there needs to be more interdisciplinary research. There is a need for increased integration of ideas with most research ending up not being interdisciplinary but multi- and trans-disciplinary, and indeed Becker et al. (1997) argue that '*attempts to cope with the complexity of issues raised by sustainability cannot simply aim at adding some new pieces to an already existing knowledge base*' but rather there needs to be a '*paradigm shift towards a new knowledge base*' characterized by '*practices of 'integration'*'.[40] And this is where energy justice as a concept and the energy justice research community have an advantage; they have an interdisciplinary aim and a focus on a theme that encourages, and already has encouraged, practices of integration. Educating the next generation of energy students with a defined interdisciplinary concept of energy justice will ensure to some degree that energy justice scholarship will impact upon policy-making in the future.

2.5 Pitfalls for the Energy Justice Concept

In looking at the current prominence of energy research at universities it is important to consider the previous prominent incumbents. Individually and jointly, environmental and climate change university-wide centres were supported but these seem to have decreased and/or disappeared over the last two decades.[41] For all the positives of environmental and climate change movements—and there are many—its effectiveness for two concepts—climate justice and environmental justice—have to be called into question. That is not to say that both climate justice and environmental justice have not achieved success. They have. But despite their successes, the world is still producing more carbon dioxide emissions than ever before.

According to many reports by leading researchers, academics and international institutions it is not about whether society is staying within a 1.5°C or 2°C rise in temperature, but of 4°C degrees. Indeed, recent reports highlight that seven climate records have been broken this year: the melting of Arctic ice; consecutive hottest months; hottest day in India ever; highest temperature in Alaska; consecutive and biggest annual increase in CO_2; hottest Autumn in Australia ever; and highest-ever amount of destruction in Australia's Great Barrier Reef.[42] What is striking about this list is that the effects of climate change are being experienced across the world. This is not to mention the increase in extreme weather events (a feature of climate change) being experienced across the world also. These latter issues are just a selection of issues that could be listed, but they highlight nevertheless that society's laws (if present in some cases) and therefore the application of justice in environmental and climate change decision-making are not effective.

Hence, in reality, a revision of what has been achieved by climate justice and environmental justice is needed. Questions need to be asked about whether they have: (1) just slowed down or stopped previous excess energy, environment and climate change injustices; or (2) have focused more on mitigation initiatives; or (3) have been putting the building blocks in place for more concerted global efforts on these issues—and from which energy justice can take advantage of.

While it is not the aim of this paper to delve into these questions—though, it must be noted they are worthy of further exploration on their own and they form part of a future research project that develops from this paper—one can consider briefly the aims of environmental and climate justice detailed. Environmental justice really began in the late 1970s and has had three main features: (1) how individual actions can contribute to the environmental movement; (2) ensure environmental risks are distributed equally; and (3) promote alternatives that reduce greenhouse gas emissions and assist communities affected by climate change.[43] Climate justice scholarship began in the 1990s and its theories and concepts primarily has a focus also on assisting those affected by climate change, sharing the burdens and benefits of climate change, mitigation and adaptation and also reducing the main cause of climate change, CO_2 emissions.[44] Considering the sustained increase in carbon emissions, it is clear that environmental and climate change justice have had a limited impact in terms of decreasing emissions of CO_2.

As is evident from the above, the aim of environmental and climate change law also has a focus on more 'preventative action or mitigation'—i.e., note that environmental justice is not about the elimination of environmental risks but distribution of them. Further, the definitions of both environmental justice and climate justice have been diffused over time and their value has not transferred consistently in interpretations across the disciplines. This is in part due to environmental and climate change scholarship decreasing at universities with interdisciplinary centres not establishing themselves across universities. This has contributed to a lack of opportunity and/or motivation to work with others beyond your discipline and to have a concept that crosses all disciplines. It is advanced here that too much lone scholarship and narrative-building exercises on environmental and climate change justice has occurred, where additions were made to concepts before the concepts themselves were assessed for the merit, values and potential for impact.[45] Too many researchers have been happy to fit their research into the label of environmental or climate justice rather than engage directly with the environmental and climate justice scholarship. This is an area where energy justice scholarship can grow in learning and ensure that it crosses over into policy.

In the context of energy justice scholarship developing in a similar way, one can use Ludwig Wiggenstein's concept of 'family resemblances' where some phenomena seem related because they have a range of 'overlapping and crisscrossing' similarities rather than because they have specifically unique characteristics in common.[46] Hence, what is and what is not energy justice scholarship is important to determine, and those engaged in energy justice scholarship need to build outwards from what the concept is and what it means to their research. Energy justice has the opportunity to avoid these latter pitfalls of environmental and climate justice scholarship and to build a more solid and lasting foundation to its core meaning and value, in essence, to transfer the energy justice concept from education and into practice.

2.6 Conclusions and Next Steps

Energy justice scholarship is developing at a fast pace and already has had some notable successes as outlined in Sects. 2.2 and 2.3. There is a great third-level education basis for research and education that can have a direct impact upon the energy sector, and therefore influence the future energy mix used by the human population and contribute to a more sustainable economy, where environment and climate change mitigation are key policies.

This chapter has three specific policy relevant contributions and these are, in particular, within the context of (1) critically exploring the theoretical explorations of energy justice frameworks, and therefore building on this by (2) analysing through education (as applied to third-level education) energy justice's role as a decision-support tool for policy-makers, and (3) considering the ways in which energy justice might be negotiated and implemented in relation to economic policy-making.

(1) Critical Account of the 'Energy Justice Concept'
The critical account of the energy justice concept builds evidence for policy-makers to justify its use. It highlights how energy justice scholars need to improve their message (if they are to be serious about policy engagement) and an interdisciplinary concept will enable this. In order to achieve this, this article provides a diagrammatic structure to the energy justice concept. Further, it explains why the dimension of restorative justice which is common to society in its use in criminal law and could and should have a significant impact in the energy sector.

(2) Energy Justice Education
Policy-makers and educators need to ensure energy justice is part of the energy curricula. Education and research at third-level education needs to improve and needs to be developed in an interdisciplinary way. Already energy research is supported by a sustained platform for energy research scholarship at universities and energy justice scholars should build on that potential. Interdisciplinarity is particularly effective for energy and climate change research and ensuring energy justice is at the core of energy research will result in the next generation of energy professionals having a core grounding in energy justice.

(3) Engaging with Energy Justice with Cost and Economic Policy-making
This view builds on earlier literature[47] in engaging with how energy justice can engage with cost and economic policy-making. It is important given the primacy in society placed on the cost of decision-making and the utilisation of cost–benefit analysis, which will be the focus of the next chapter.

2.6.1 *Final Thoughts*

Energy justice has an emerging inter-, cross-, and trans- disciplinary research area, and has achieved notable successes and there is no reason to suggest this cannot continue. Indeed, more so than with environmental justice and climate justice it has inspired scholars from all disciplines to engage with 'justice' concerns. By engaging in 'justice' concerns researchers have begun to engage in law and policy outcomes and to think about how their research can apply in practice, or what is the value of their research to the real world—and engagement with the law and the regulatory process is noted as a challenge for energy justice in the future. In considering this, there is great motivation, as one need only look at the creation of 'green' investment funds, and the decision of the Norwegian sovereign wealth fund to no longer consider fossil fuel investments, as examples where reasoning is needed to ensure decisions such as these have support in research and that they are not just one-off phenomena. And an increase of interdisciplinary research and education, and the development in energy justice and its concepts, can achieve just that.

Notes

1. This chapter is based on previous work completed for the following article and I thank the publisher and also my co-author Professor McCauley for permission for the adapted re-use of the information: Heffron, R. J. & McCauley, D. 2017. The concept of energy justice across the disciplines. Energy Policy, 105, 658–667.
2. Initiative for Energy Justice. 2019. The Energy Justice Workbook. Available at: https://iejusa.org/wp-content/uploads/2019/12/The-Energy-Justice-Workbook-2019-web.pdf (last accessed 1 May 2021).
3. Guruswamy L. 2016. Global Energy Justice: Law and Policy. West Academic Publishing: Minnesota, US; and Sovacool, BK and MH

Dworkin. 2014. Global Energy Justice: Problems, Principles, and Practices. Cambridge University Press: Cambridge, UK

4. Jenkins, K, McCauley, D, Heffron, R, Stephan, H & Rehner, R. 2016. Energy justice: a conceptual review. Energy Research and Social Science, 11, 174–182.
5. Energy Justice Network (US). 2016. Available at: http://www.energyjustice.net/about (last accessed 20 October 2016). And see more concerning its accomplishments, available at: http://www.energyjustice.net/accomplishments (last accessed 1 May 2021).
6. Centre for Sustainable Energy (UK). 2016. available at: https://www.cse.org.uk/contact (last accessed 1 May 2021).
7. Saunders, J. 2011. Energy justice—the policy challenges. Energy justice in a changing climate: defining an agenda, InCluESEV conference, 10 November 2011, London. In p.423, Hall, S. M. 2013. Energy justice and ethical consumption: comparison, synthesis and lesson drawing, Local Environ. 18 (4) 422–437.
8. Guruswamy, L. 2010. Energy justice and sustainable development, Colo. J. Int. Environ. Law Policy 21, 231.
9. Hall, S. M. 2013. Energy justice and ethical consumption: comparison, synthesis and lesson drawing, Local Environ. 18 (4) (2013) 422–437.
10. Bickerstaff, K., Walker, G. P. and Bulkeley, H. (Eds.). 2013. Energy Justice in a Changing Climate: Social Equity and Low-Carbon Energy. Zed Books, UK.
11. McCauley, D., Heffron, R. J. Stephan, H. and Jenkins, K. 2013. Advancing Energy Justice: The triumvirate of tenets. International Energy Law Review, 32 (3), 107–110.
12. Heffron, R. J. and McCauley, D. 2014. Achieving Sustainable Supply Chains through Energy Justice, Applied Energy, 123, 435–437.
13. Sovacool, B, Heffron, R. J., McCauley, D & Goldthau, A. 2016. Energy decisions reframed as justice and ethical concerns. Nature Energy, 1. https://doi.org/10.1038/nenergy.2016.24.
14. Jenkins, K, McCauley, D, Heffron, R, Stephan, H & Rehner, R. 2016. Energy justice: a conceptual review. Energy Research and Social Science, 11, 174–182.
15. McCauley, D., Heffron, R. J. Stephan, H. and Jenkins, K. 2013. Advancing Energy Justice: The triumvirate of tenets. International Energy Law Review, 32 (3), 107–110.
16. Heffron, R. J. and McCauley, D. 2014. Achieving Sustainable Supply Chains through Energy Justice, Applied Energy, 123, 435–437.
17. Sovacool, B, Heffron, R. J., McCauley, D & Goldthau, A. 2016. Energy decisions reframed as justice and ethical concerns. Nature Energy, 1. https://doi.org/10.1038/nenergy.2016.24.

18. Heffron, R. J. and McCauley, D. 2014. Achieving Sustainable Supply Chains through Energy Justice, Applied Energy, 123, 435–437; and Jenkins K, McCauley DA, Heffron RJ & Stephan H. 2014. Energy Justice, a Whole Systems Approach. Queen's Political Review, II (2), pp. 74–87.
19. Popper, K. 2002. Conjectures and Refutations: The Growth of Scientific Knowledge. Routledge Classics. (First published 1963, Routledge & Kegan Paul).
20. Kuhn, T. 1962. The Structure of Scientific Revolutions. Chicago, IL, US: University of Chicago Press.
21. Galaway, B. and Hudson, J. 1996. Restorative Justice: International Perspectives. Criminal Justice Press/Willow Tree Press: NY, US.
22. Zehr, H. 2014. The Little Book of Restorative Justice. GoodBooks (Skyhorse Publishing): NY, US.
23. Sullivan, D. and Tifft, L. 2006. Handbook of Restorative Justice: A Global Perspective. Routledge: Oxford, UK.
24. Wietekamp, E. G. and Kerner, H. J. 2002; 2011. (eds.). Restorative Justice: Theoretical Foundations. Routledge: Oxford, UK.
25. Tromans, S. 2012. (2nd Ed.). Environmental Impact Assessment. Bloomsbury Professional Ltd: West Sussex, UK.
26. For more see: On Common Ground Consultants Inc. 2014. What is the Social License? Available at: http://socialicense.com/definition.html (last accessed 1 May 2021).
27. Heffron, R. J. et al. 2018. The emergence of the 'social licence to operate' in the extractive industries? *Resources Policy*, Available at: https://doi.org/10.1016/j.resourpol.2018.09.012.
28. Prno, J. and Slocombe, D. S. 2012. Exploring the origins of 'social license to operate' in the mining sector: Perspectives from governance and sustainability theories. Resources Policy, Vol. 37 (3), 346–357; and The Guardian (Morrison, J.). 2014. Business and society: defining the 'social licence'. 29 September 2014. Available at: https://www.theguardian.com/sustainable-business/2014/sep/29/social-licence-operate-shell-bp-business-leaders (last accessed 1 May 2021).
29. Dondo, S. J. 2014. Financial Assurance for Mine Closure: A Regulatory Perspective from the Argentine Context. CSRM Occasional Paper, Centre for Social Responsibility in Mining (CSRM), Sustainable Minerals Institute (SMI), University of Queensland.
30. See the following literature: (1) International Business Times (Gallucci, M.). 2016. When A Coal Company Goes Bankrupt, Who Is Left To Clean Up The Mess? (last accessed 27 January 2017). Available at: http://www.ibtimes.com/when-coal-company-goes-bankrupt-who-left-clean-mess-2264097 (last accessed 1 May 2021); (2) The Guardian (Robertson, J.), 2016. Coal giants abandon unprofitable mines, leaving rehabilitation

under threat. Available at: https://www.theguardian.com/environment/2016/jan/29/coal-giants-abandon-unprofitable-mines-leaving-rehabilitation-under-threat (last accessed 1 May 2021); and (3) Miller, C. G. 2005. Financial Assurance for Mine Closure and Reclamation. (International Council on Mining & Metals). Available at: https://www.icmm.com/document/282 (last accessed 1 May 2021).

31. Federal Surface Mining Control and Reclamation Act (SMCRA) 1977. Available at: http://www.osmre.gov/lrg.shtm (last accessed 1 May 2021); and Financial Assurance under the Environmental Protection Act 1994. Queensland Government Department of Environment and Heritage Protection. Available at: http://www.ehp.qld.gov.au/assets/documents/regulation/era-gl-financial-assurance-ep-act.pdf (last accessed 1 May 2021).
32. Bloomberg (Biesheuval, T., Riseborough, J. and De Sousa, A.), 2015. Why Bankruptcy Might Be the Mining Industry's Last Best Hope (3 December 2015). Available at: http://www.bloomberg.com/news/articles/2015-12-03/why-bankruptcy-might-be-the-mining-industry-s-last-best-hope (last accessed 1 May 2021) and ABC Australia News (Lannin, S.). 2015. China economist warns major miners may collapse in 2016 (18 December 2015). Available at: http://www.abc.net.au/news/2015-12-17/china-economist-warns-that-iron-ore-miners-will-collapse/7037802 (last accessed 1 May 2021).
33. Times Higher Education. 2016. World University Rankings 2017. Available at: https://www.timeshighereducation.com/world-university-rankings/2017/world-ranking (last accessed 1 May 2021).
34. Times Higher Education. 2016. World University Rankings 2017. Available at: https://www.timeshighereducation.com/world-university-rankings/2017/world-ranking last accessed 30 October 2016.
35. UI Green Metric Ranking of World Universities. 2016. Available at: http://greenmetric.ui.ac.id/overall-ranking-2015/ (last accessed 1 May 2021). And additional reports on this are available at: https://www.timeshighereducation.com/news/the-20-greenest-universities-in-the-world/2018495.article (last accessed 1 May 2021).
36. Duke, C., Osbourne, M., and Wilson, B. 2013. A new Imperative: Regions and Higher Education in Difficult Times. Manchester University Press: Manchester, UK. (see in particular, Chapter 7).
37. Orr, D. 1994. Earth in Mind: In Education, Environment, and the Human Prospect, Island Press, Washington DC.
38. Martin, S. and Jucker, R. 2005. Educating earth-literate leaders. Journal of Geography in Higher Education. Vol. 29 (1), 19–29.

39. Martin, J. and Samuels, J. E. (Eds.). 2012. The Sustainable University: Green Goals and New Challenges for Higher Education Leaders. Johns Hopkins University Press: Baltimore, Maryland, US.
40. Becker, E., Jahn, T., Stiess, I. and Wehling, P. 1997 (37). Sustainability, A Cross-Disciplinary Concept for Social Transformations, Management of Social Transformation Policy Papers 6, UNESCO: Paris, France—In Jones, P., Selby, D. and Sterling, S. (Eds.). 2010. Sustainability Education: Perspectives and Practice across Higher Education. Earthscan: London, UK.
41. This is revealed by checking the same universities as those in Sect. 2.4 in Table 2.1 conducted by the authors.
42. The Guardian, 2016. Seven climate records set so far in 2016. (17 June 2016—Adam Vaughan). Available at: https://www.theguardian.com/environment/2016/jun/17/seven-climate-records-set-so-far-in-2016 (last accessed 1 May 2021). This is just a newspaper report connecting to the issue—however, there are many international reports.
43. Mickelson, K. 2007. Critical Approaches. In Bodansky, D., Brunnee, J. and Hey, E. (eds.). 2007. The Oxford Handbook of International Environmental Law. OUP: Oxford, UK.
44. For more on this, see: Lyster, R. 2015. Climate Justice and Disaster Law. Cambridge University Press: Cambridge, UK.
45. Indeed, this is in part what happened to neoclassical economic thinking which rather than challenging and evaluated itself, instead too many economic researchers utilised and added to it, and as a result of an unchecked, or unquestioned or unevaluated 'core' it contributed in time to the financial crisis of 2007–2009.
46. Wittgenstein, L. 1958. Philosophical Investigations—we utilise this excellent example, having read that it is used in a similar way by other academics—from p. 15. Susskind, R. and Susskind, D. 2016. The Future of the Professions. Oxford University Press: Oxford, UK.
47. Heffron RJ, McCauley D and Sovacool BK. 2015. Resolving Society's Energy Trilemma through the Energy Justice Metric. Energy Policy, 87, 168–176.

References

Becker, E., T. Jahn, I. Stiess, and P. Wehling. 1997 (37). Sustainability, A Cross-Disciplinary Concept for Social Transformations, Management of Social Transformation Policy Papers 6, UNESCO: Paris, France—In P. Jones, D. Selby, and S. Sterling (Eds.). 2010. *Sustainability Education: Perspectives and Practice across Higher Education*. London, UK: Earthscan.

Heffron, R.J. 2020. Justice in the Energy Transition. Special Issue 'Decarbonisation Pathways for Oil and Gas'. The Oxford Institute for Energy Studies, March

2020, Issue 121. Accessed 1 May 2021. https://www.oxfordenergy.org/wpcms/wp-content/uploads/2020/03/OEF121.pdf.

Heffron, R.J., and D. McCauley. 2017. The Concept of Energy Justice across the Disciplines. *Energy Policy* 105: 658–667.

Kuhn, T. 1962. *The Structure of Scientific Revolutions.* Chicago, IL: University of Chicago Press.

Morrison, J. 2014. *The Social License: How to Keep Your Organization Legitimate.* UK: Palgrave Macmillan.

Prno, J., and D.S. Slocombe. 2012. Exploring the Origins of 'Social License to Operate' in the Mining Sector: Perspectives from Governance and Sustainability Theories. *Resources Policy*, 37 (3), 346–357.

Times Higher Education. 2016. World University Rankings 2017. Accessed 1 May 2021. https://www.timeshighereducation.com/world-university-rankings/2017/world-ranking.

CHAPTER 3

Economics and Energy Justice

Abstract Economics and energy justice is an underexplored area of research. Too often there is a divergence in what economics wants for society. There has previously been too much focus on economic growth, and it is clear that nowadays this aim results in greater societal inequality. For the energy sector this makes the concept of energy justice very relevant. A key influential factor here was the 2007–2009 economic crisis that caused a recalibration of the discipline that continues until today. Economics plays a vital role in delivering the energy transition and is of high value in ensuring the necessity of ensuring energy justice becomes part of energy economic decision-making processes.

Keywords Energy justice • Energy economics • Societal inequality • Energy infrastructure development • Sustainable world • Energy justice framework

3.1 Introduction

Energy justice has generally lacked engagement with economics. In the literature produced on energy justice there is a very limited amount that engages with the discipline of economics.[1] Currently, economists generally dominate policy formulation in modern society. This is of no surprise as economics provides insights into the trade-offs that societies face, and there is only a limited amount of finance available to governments to

R. J. Heffron, *The Challenge for Energy Justice*,
https://doi.org/10.1007/978-3-030-80097-0_3

distribute to each policy problem. Nevertheless, in terms of policy formulation, society has become too influenced by economists and this applies in particular to the energy sector.

The call for justice in the energy sector has arisen primarily because of the poor management of the sector by policy-makers and economists, including lawyers (who applied the policy through law). The primary focus of economists on economic growth, efficiency, competition and costs has not worked for the energy sector. While in the case of law, it is only in the last few years that the definition of energy law has expanded to include the issue of waste management.[2] Economists have however, led society down many wrong paths in terms of the energy sector, which has suffered many injustices (which will be discussed later).

However, despite this, economists remain the primary influence in energy policy-making. In the UK for example, the Government established a new committee to examine the true cost of energy[3] and notably appointed an energy economist as head of this committee. To gain a perspective on the view of this latter economist, which typifies an economist's perspective on the energy sector, reveals that renewable energy support has only just increased electricity prices and reduced competition.[4]

It is precisely the limited perspective of economists towards justice that this chapter seeks to address. It should be noted that trying to formulate energy policy is complex. The current clear conceptual example of this complexity is via the energy trilemma which contains the competing forces of economics, the environment and politics.[5] There is no perfect solution, but what society can aspire to is achieving a better balance between these three competing aims of energy policy. To date, society has focused more on economics to the particular detriment of the environment.

It is important to remember the injustices the energy sector causes and the major contribution the sector makes to global inequality. The sector is mired by corruption, taxation issues, environmental damage, undocumented GHG emissions, finance issues, market competition distortions, the influence of lobbyists and the powerful influence of multinational companies. With all these problems it is evident as to why the energy sector leads to inequality, and this is further supported by the fact that the energy sector is responsible for the majority of CO_2[6] emissions, and research demonstrates that there is a link between the increase of CO_2 emissions and an increased level of inequality in society.[7]

3.2 Why Is Energy Justice Important, and Not Just Energy Economics?

Society is changing due to the effects of the energy sector and, as it does, there is a need to ensure that justice becomes part of decision-making in the sector. For too long, profit, finance and economics has driven the energy sector, and many of the private companies involved have been referred to as 'robber barons'. The climate records that were broken in 2016 are evidence of the injustices resulting from the energy sector. For example, seven climate records were broken in 2016: the melting of Arctic ice; consecutive hottest months; hottest day in India ever; highest temperature in Alaska; consecutive and biggest annual increase in CO_2; hottest-ever autumn in Australia; and highest-ever amount of destruction in Australia's Great Barrier Reef.[8]

Today, with the aim of reducing CO_2 emissions within society, many countries are going through, or are planning to go through, an energy transition to a low-carbon economy.[9] This transition needs to be a just transition and that is where energy justice has a role. As stated in Sect. 3.1, the energy sector is full of injustices, and as society engages with the energy transition it needs to have 'justice' at the core of it. For too long the energy sector has experienced, and been characterised by, injustices. For example, even now there exists far too much fossil fuel in the global energy system.[10] Clearly, at an international level, it should be acknowledged that the transition needs to happen and needs to happen at an accelerated pace, with recent scholarship noting it is not happening fast enough.[11]

It should be highlighted that transitioning away from fossil fuels in society is proving very difficult and in reality is taking place very slowly. For example, in 2016, of the UK's primary energy needs, fossil fuels provided 81.5 per cent, down only half a per cent from 2015.[12] Consider other examples from the UK in relation to investment in energy infrastructure and also foreign aid: in 2016, £18.6 billion (10.3 per cent of total investment in the UK) was invested of which 34 per cent was in oil and gas extraction, 54 per cent in electricity, 11 per cent in gas, with the remaining in coal extraction and coke and refined petroleum products industries.[13] Now while the amount of that investment in electricity is not calculated in more detail, considering the majority of the electricity sector in the UK is using fossil fuels,[14] one could make the assumption that the majority of this investment is similarly towards fossil fuels; though again further research is needed on this point. Nevertheless the picture is clear, the UK still heavily supports fossil fuel in terms of new investments. This is also aligned with UK foreign investment policy where through development aid, the UK supported fossil fuel projects by a ratio of nearly two to one.[15]

To achieve the energy transition, major investment is needed. To meet a 2°C future limit worldwide temperature rise, an estimated $208 billion in investment in low-carbon energy sources will be needed annually over the next twenty-five years.[16] Only when this investment is made, will energy justice become a consideration in policy-making process. Improved justice during the energy transition can aid in reducing inequalities in modern society. Inequality in society is increasing worldwide, and it represents one of the major research challenges in present day research scholarship (across many disciplines). That inequality is increasing in society is a clear example of policy failure; energy justice scholarship can contribute to finding solutions, and therefore is clearly important as the energy transition builds momentum.

3.3 The Economics of Energy Sector and Energy Justice

3.3.1 Economics Has Led to Injustices

The energy sector is responsible for a litany of injustices around the world, and this is the case whether a country is considered a developed or developing country. Indeed, developed countries have not been very successful in managing their energy sectors successfully when considering they continue to produce CO_2 at record levels. Over several decades neoclassical economics has dominated policy formulation within societies and energy policy has been no exception. Indeed, despite even the pressure caused by the financial crisis of 2007–2009, there has been little change.[17]

A feature of the development of neoclassical economic thinking has been 'secrecy' in its development. It is well documented that Friedrick von Hayek and many other leading economists (many were future Nobel Prize winning economists and von Hayek was also a Nobel Prize winner) used to meet in an invitation-only club called the Mont Perlerin Society.[18] Indeed, Karl Popper, the renowned philosopher, was invited to the society's meetings and had his calls for openness rejected.[19] The energy sector which has adopted neoclassical economics is mired by similar examples of secrecy. Some of this lack of transparency is being reformed through initiatives such as the Extractive Industries Transparency Initiative (EITI) however, that has only limited action overall.

The prevalence of neoclassical economic thinking still reigns in the energy sector. There are two major examples of this which are detailed below, and the first is the issue of energy policy failure and the second the issue of energy subsidies. The focus on these two issues is because they are noted gaps in the literature on energy justice and energy economics, and they reflect the desire for energy justice to be used as a policy tool.[20] The final issue discussed is also underexplored in the energy justice literature, and that is how economics as a discipline is moving towards a key focus on inequality.

3.3.2 Energy Policy Failure

The energy sector is littered with examples of policy failure. What is disappointing perhaps is the lack of belief in the potential of new policy. For example, a high profile energy economist recently stated that success in fracking in the US was not down to policy but to technology.[21] There is the clear alternative argument that success in fracking was down to policy failure. The fracking industry has been subject to light touch regulation and has been allowed to ignore the environmental damage of energy production. An example of this is how the fracking industry in the US did not have to reveal what chemicals they used in the process.[22] This sounds very familiar and is the way coal, oil and gas have dominated the energy sector for years.

There tends to be an overstatement of the influence of technology in the energy sector. Research demonstrates that it takes a long time before energy technology is commercially viable.[23] In addition, it would take longer for some forms of energy to be commercially viable if they were not favoured by a system which advocated economic growth, efficiency, competiveness and cost, i.e., such as neoclassical economics. The question should be asked that why there has been no revision of economic thinking in the energy sector when policy failures have continuously re-occurred. The answer is that neoclassical economics remains of significant influence in all areas of the economy despite its failures elsewhere and the energy sector is no different.[24]

3.3.3 Energy Subsidies

Economists are noted for researching trends and data in different sectors of the economy. It is therefore very confusing as to why some trends and data have been ignored in relation to the energy sector, and in particular around the issue of energy subsidies. In the energy economics community, there remains a fundamental issue as to what is the cost of different energy sources. As mentioned earlier, the fact that the UK Government has conducted several cost reviews into the cost of energy sources is commendable but also revealing in that it has not occurred before; indeed, it has been noted in the literature that there is a significant need for a new research agenda on energy subsidies.[25]

However, it is a worry that the economist in charge of this latter initiative views renewables as only having developed due to subsidies.[26] This is disappointing considering the subsidies to fossil fuels globally accumulated to $5.3 trillion in 2015, equivalent to 6.5 per cent of global GDP.[27] It should be noted that all energy sources receive subsidies, but fossil fuels receive the majority and this is also the case in the UK too (as stated in Sect. 3.2). Further, across Europe there are many legal arbitration cases currently between Governments and investors in terms of the subsidy support they were guaranteed for producing renewable energy. The financial amounts that these cases concern are not as significant as the annual subsidies to fossil fuels in these countries (for example, in Spain and Italy). The question that needs to be asked is: why have economists ignored the data and trends on subsidies over the last forty to fifty years? In this time economists have pushed for policies of privatisation and market liberalisation while ignoring the data from energy subsidies, all of which contributes to a serious market distortion.

3.3.4 The Study of Economics Moves the Focus to Addressing Inequality

The above examples are just two, in a long list of many examples, that could have been stated about what gives rise to inequality in the energy sector. Indeed, there are debates on the rise of inequality in society due to neoclassical economics, issues in international taxation, and the longstanding failure in terms of energy waste management. There are other scholars in the area who note also the destructive influence of neoclassical economics in relation to climate change issues.[28]

The issue in terms of energy justice is that in policy formulation in the energy sector to date, there has been a lack of 'justice' incorporated into policy. Debates such as whether a policy is fair and equitable have been missing, and this mirrors some of the influential economic literature that is moving towards addressing societal inequality through economics.[29] Furthermore, debates on whether a policy had characteristics of distribution, or procedural, or recognition justice have all but been absent. This is what energy justice brings to the policy-making process. It aims to promote the interests of individuals into the energy policy formulation process, and in essence reduce the potential for injustices to occur because of 'policy capture' by certain interest groups.

3.4 The Energy Trilemma: A Critique

The majority of economics-led energy research has led to the retention of the status quo in the energy system. Focusing on low cost and/or efficient outcomes has led to a continued reliance on the use of fossil fuels in the short term and as a result building low-carbon energy infrastructure or developing a low-carbon economy has been a secondary concern for energy policy.

This point can be illustrated by the World Energy Council (WEC) who advanced the notion of the 'energy trilemma' (as mentioned earlier). The challenge of the energy trilemma is to balance three competing aims which are: energy security, environmental sustainability and energy equity (affordability and accessibility).

The WEC is an economics-led institution that has placed 'affordability' as one of the three competing aims of the energy trilemma which results in society aiming to provide low-cost energy. However, a focus on low-cost energy will mean the continued use and development of fossil fuels, and in essence a retention of the status quo of the energy sector. Fossil fuels remain cheap energy sources because they do not pay for externalities such as the long-term storage of their waste product CO_2, the damage already incurred because of CO_2, other wastes such as SO_2, and they also receive some of the highest subsidies globally—far more than low-carbon energy resources.[30]

Hence, an institution such as the WEC should just list the word 'economics' as one of three aims rather than just affordability (and accessibility), as then the aim would be to look at a more broad range of 'economic' issues. A more just and reasonable focus for energy decision-making (i.e., on balancing the energy trilemma) would include other economic concerns such as: energy finance (project finance); energy prices (i.e., oil and gas); electricity prices; insurance costs; subsidy support (in all its forms); tax incentives; and affordability.

To understand with more clarity why the WEC has a narrow view on the economics and the resulting effect, it is necessary to view the origin of the use of the energy trilemma and the WEC. The first time the WEC used the word 'trilemma' was in 2011, and not in 2005 when they produced their first reports. The economics angle of the 'energy trilemma' was discussed as 'social equity' at first, which in 2011 included 'affordability' and 'accessibility'.[31] This then evolved to where it is now described as 'energy equity', and the goal of the energy trilemma index produced is that the 'Energy Trilemma *Index quantifies the* energy trilemma *and comparatively ranks 125 countries in terms of their ability to provide a secure, affordable, and environmentally* sustainable *energy system*'.[32] Again, the use of the word 'affordable' (which is singled out over accessibility) is arguably wrong, and means that their view of 'energy equity' is in reality about affordability. Such a focus on affordability will retain the status quo of the energy sector, and encourage low-cost energy solutions which centre on fossil fuels, which as stated earlier do not pay anything for their long-term waste storage. The WEC should be using other mechanisms to think about the 'economics' of the energy sector as there are far more energy economic concerns than just affordability. The creation and support of short-term policies that are not sustainable and that contribute to energy injustices but deliver better prices, should be sacrificed for medium to longer term sustainable and just energy policies.

In the future, energy decisions and models such as these will need to incorporate justice at their core—a more balanced energy trilemma can be represented as in Fig. 3.1. If understood literally, the WEC is actually stating that we should have a trade-off with 'equity' (which to the WEC means affordability and is their only reference to some form of 'justice' in the energy sector) with energy security and the environment. This thankfully does not represent the view of many researchers who now see 'energy justice' at the core of decision-making in the energy sector. Further and significantly, perhaps the WEC needs to revise its own thinking in light of its recent report stating they are searching for ways to 'balance' the energy trilemma.[33] Is the 'balancing factor' not ensuring justice in energy decision-making, i.e., delivering a *just and equitable* way to manage the competing aims of the energy trilemma? 'Equity' as the WEC defines it (i.e., they define it as affordability) is not 'justice' in the energy sector. The energy sector is more than about energy or electricity prices and consumption by consumers.

3.5 The Right to Choose which Energy Source

In general, the prevailing economic view is that the choice of which energy sources society should use should be based on cost. The UK in particular, highlights how an energy policy is focused on cost. This is in contradiction to its energy policy's main goal of developing a low-carbon economy or

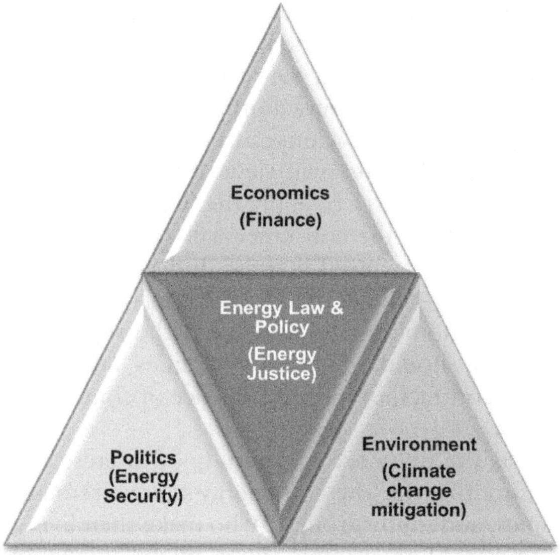

Fig. 3.1 A more just and balanced 'Energy Trilemma'. (*Source*: Adapted by author from Heffron, R.J. 2015. *Energy Law: An Introduction*. Heidelberg, Germany: Springer)

energy transition. A specific example of this issue is through the policy and law for capacity markets in the electricity sector across the EU. In the UK, the capacity market has been described as a 'weak link' in the UK energy transition[34] with the majority of capacity payments going to fossil fuels.

Further, and somewhat contradictory to the UK energy transition policy initiatives, is the recent view that emanated from the House of Lords Select Committee on Economic Affairs that capacity auctions should be technology neutral.[35] This technology neutral stance presents low-cost fossil fuels with a dominant position (which they are in already from the previous capacity auctions) due to their lower costs and does not align with the goal of an energy transition.

Similarly, it is evident how the rhetoric that surrounds the energy trilemma concept has moved to discussing low-cost solutions and energy affordability.[36] All this points towards the continued used of low-cost fossil fuel energy sources.

To supplement this perspective economists have focused on utilising 'willingness to pay' methods for energy analysis, i.e., what are consumers willing to pay for different energy sources. This switches the narrative on to the individual, and does not reveal other issues such as the subsidies to different energy sources and previous costs of policy failures for fossil fuels. Furthermore, it contradicts its own view of ways in which an individual might act, i.e., in self-interest. To apply the 'willingness to pay' method is to expect the answer that the consumer will choose the cheapest energy source, as this is in their own self-interest. Indeed, the prevalence of consumers having an open 'choice' has long been recognised as being too much a focus of economists who advocated the study of the science of choice.[37] The choice should be made by societies, and rather it should be in essence a social contract, or indeed a science of contract (as espoused by Oliver Williamson).[38]

Finally, there is the influence of a variety of interest groups in society that need to ensure that the low-cost energy sources remain. These are the energy companies, and lobby groups[39] who make their living from exploiting energy resources. For example, only ninety companies globally are responsible for circa 66 per cent of the world's CO_2 emissions.[40] It is clear that these companies have a superior power in society given the evidence that air pollution increases mortality, morbidity and shortens life expectancy, particularly in low- and medium-income countries where it is one of the leading causes of these types of damage to health.[41] It is a key interest of these companies to ensure that low-cost energy sources remain in the system.

There is also the well-documented problem of stranded assets.[42] The valuation of these companies is critically dependent upon these reserves. In addition, the scale of overstatement is probably greater than realized as evidenced by the recent issue that was highlighted by the fine received by KPMG in the US. This case involved KPMG being fined $6.2 million due to auditing a company who estimated their oil reserves circa one hundred times their value; the problem was that this company had bought these assets for only $5 million and just two years later estimated them at $480 million.[43]

Achieving energy justice by advancing information that can inform society about which energy source to choose can reduce the current economics-driven view of choosing the low-cost energy solution or the willingness-to-pay method. Energy justice can provide a more robust and broader solution as to why society should choose different energy sources.

3.6 Conclusion and Future Outlook

The energy sector is a key driver of the modern economy. In most reports it accounts for near circa 10 per cent of global GDP and is similar to health expenditure in that context as one of two of the most important sectors to the international economy. It has been and remains a sector of the economy that causes many injustices, and that is why new research and policy tools need to be advanced. The chapter focuses on contributing to the debate in literature on economics and energy justice, and also focuses on addressing societal inequality.

Analytical tools such as energy justice can provide society (including policy-makers, regulators, jurists, and think tanks) with a decision-making tool that provides a more accurate analysis from which to make decisions.[44] It achieves this by capturing issues across the energy life cycle and also having a focus on the redistribution of economic benefits of the sector, i.e., reducing the inequalities in the energy sector.

Notes

1. Heffron, R. J. & McCauley, D. 2017. *The concept of energy justice across the disciplines.* Energy Policy, 105, 658–667.
2. Heffron, R. J. and Talus. K. 2016. *The Evolution of Energy Law and Energy Jurisprudence: Insights for Energy Analysts and Researchers.* Energy Research and Social Science, 19, 1–10.
3. There are multiple reports of this, and for one of these, see: BBC. 2017. *Energy review examining household and environmental costs* (6 August 2017). Available at: http://www.bbc.co.uk/news/uk-40839433 (last accessed 1 May 2021).
4. P. 3. Helm, D. 2017. *Burn Out: The Endgame for Fossil Fuels.* New Haven, US: Yale University Press.
5. Heffron RJ, McCauley D and Sovacool BK. 2015. *Resolving Society's Energy Trilemma through the Energy Justice Metric.* Energy Policy, 87, 168–176.
6. Ekwurzel, B. et al. 2017. *The rise in global atmospheric CO_2, surface temperature, and sea level from emissions traced to major carbon producers.* Climatic Change. 144. 579–590.
7. Chancel, L. and Piketty, T. 2015. *Carbon and inequality: from Kyoto to Paris.* Paris School of Economics (November 2015).
8. The Guardian, 2016. *Seven climate records set so far in 2016.* (17 June 2016—Adam Vaughan). Available at: https://www.theguardian.com/environment/2016/jun/17/seven-climate-records-set-so-far-in-2016

(last accessed 1 May 2021). This is just a newspaper report connecting to the issue—however, there are many international reports.
9. McCauley, D. 2017. *Energy Justice: Re-Balancing the Trilemma of Security, Poverty and Climate Change*. Basingstoke, UK: Palgrave Macmillan.
10. Figueres, C. et al. 2017. *Three Years to Safeguard our Climate*. Nature. 546 (7660) 593–595. (29 June 2017).
11. Ibid., Figueres, C. et al. (2017).
12. Carbon Brief. 2017. *Six charts show UK's progress on low-carbon energy slowing down*. (31 July 2017). Available at: https://www.carbonbrief.org/six-charts-show-uk-progress-on-low-carbon-energy-slowing-down (last accessed 1 May 2021).
13. Department of Business, Energy & Industrial Strategy (BIES)/United Kingdom Statistics Authority (UKSA). 2017. *UK Energy in Brief 2017*. Available at: https://www.gov.uk/government/uploads/system/uploads/attachment_data/file/631146/UK_Energy_in_Brief_2017.pdf (last accessed 1 May 2021).
14. Ibid., BIES/UKSA (2017).
15. CAFOD. 2017. *UK Support for Energy in Developing* Countries. Available at: https://cafod.org.uk/content/download/27353/269740/version/2/file/Policy%20briefing%20UK%20Support%20for%20Energy%20in%20Developing%20Countries%20Oct%202015.pdf (last accessed 1 May 2021).
16. Bloomberg New Energy Finance. 2016. *Mapping the Gap: The Road from Paris (Finance Paths to a Two-Degree Future)*. Available at: http://about.bnef.com/white-papers/mapping-the-gap-the-road-from-paris/ (last accessed 1 May 2021).
17. Davies, H. 2010. *The Financial Crisis: Who is to Blame?* Cambridge, UK: Policy Press.
18. Offer, A. and Soderberg, G. 2016. *The Nobel Factor: The Prize in Economics, Social Democracy, and The Market Turn*. NJ, US, Princeton University Press.
19. Offer, A. and Soderberg, G. 2016. *The Nobel Factor: The Prize in Economics, Social Democracy, and The Market Turn*. NJ, US, Princeton University Press.
20. Sovacool, BK and MH Dworkin. 2015. *Energy justice: Conceptual insights and practical applications*. Applied Energy, 142, 435–444.
21. Helm, D. 2017. *Burn Out: The Endgame for Fossil Fuels*. New Haven, US: Yale University Press.
22. (1) Bamberger, M. and Oswald, R. 2014. *The Real Cost of Fracking*. Boston, US: Beacon Press. And (2) Zuckerman, G. 2013. *The Frackers*. London, UK: Penguin Books.
23. Smil, V. 2017. *Energy and Civilization: A History*. MA, US: MIT.
24. Heffron, R. J. & McCauley, D. 2017. *The concept of energy justice across the disciplines*. Energy Policy, 105, 658–667.

25. Sovacool, BK. 2017. *Reviewing, Reforming, and Rethinking Global Energy Subsidies: Towards a Political Economy Research Agenda.* Ecological Economics 135, 150–163.
26. P. 3. Helm, D. 2017. *Burn Out: The Endgame for Fossil Fuels.* New Haven, US: Yale University Press.
27. Coady, D. et al. 2017. *How Large Are Global Fossil Fuel Subsidies?* World Development. 91, 11–27.
28. Elliot, B. 2014. *Natural Catastrophe Climate Change and Neoliberal Governance.* Edinburgh, UK: Edinburgh University Press.
29. (1) Bookstaber, R. 2017. *The End of Theory. Financial Crises, the Failure of Economics, and the Sweep of Human Interaction.* Princeton University Press: NJ, US; (2) Piketty, T. 2015. *The Economics of Inequality* (translated by Goldhammer, A.). Belknap Press of Harvard University Press: MA, US; (3) Stiglitz, J. E. 2012. *The Price of Inequality.* Penguin Books: London, UK; and (4) Scheidel, W. 2017. *The Great Leveler.* Princeton University Press: NJ, US.
30. IEA, OPEC, OECD, and World Bank Joint Report, 'Analysis of the Scope of Energy Subsidies and Suggestions for the G-20 Initiative' (June 2010) www.iea.org/weo/docs/G20_Subsidy_Joint_Report.pdf (last accessed 1 May 2021); and Global Studies Initiative, 'Untold Billions: Fossil-Fuel Subsidies, Their Impacts and the path to Reform' (2010) p. 33 www.iisd.org/gsi/sites/default/files/transparency_ffs.pdf (last accessed 1 May 2021).
31. This focus on 'affordability' and 'accessibility' is the same economic bias that makes us focus on increasing economic welfare through competition and gains in efficiency which will result in lower prices which can be passed on to consumers—whether this fully works in the energy sector is open to question and generally energy markets need state intervention to ensure fairer, or more just outcomes.
32. World Energy Council, 2016a: 6. The World Energy Trilemma Index—2016—Benchmarking the sustainability of national energy systems. World Energy Council: London, UK. Available at: https://www.worldenergy.org/publications/2016/2016-energy-trilemma-index-benchmarking-the-sustainability-of-national-energy-systems/ (last accessed 1 May 2021).
33. World Energy Council, 2015. Priority actions on climate change and how to balance the trilemma. World Energy Council: London, UK. Available at: https://www.worldenergy.org/publications/2015/world-energy-trilemma-2015-priority-actions-on-climate-change-and-how-to-balance-the-trilemma/ (last accessed 1 May 2021).
34. Energy Live News. 2017. *Capacity Market weak link in UK's energy transition* (13 March 2017). Available at: http://www.energylivenews.

com/2017/03/13/capacity-market-weak-link-in-uks-energy-transition/ (last accessed 1 May 2021).

35. House of Lords. 2017. *The Price of Power: Reforming the Electricity Market.* Available at: https://publications.parliament.uk/pa/ld201617/ldselect/ldeconaf/113/113.pdf. (last accessed 1 May 2021). The government response to this does not provide further clarity, see: BEIS. 2017. *Government Response to the Economic Affairs Committee's Inquiry into the Economics if UK Energy Policy.* Available at: http://www.parliament.uk/documents/lords-committees/economic-affairs/The-Economics-of-UK-Energy-Policy/Government-response-Energy-Market-Report.pdf (last accessed 1 May 2021).
36. Heffron, R. J. & McCauley, D. 2017. *The concept of energy justice across the disciplines.* Energy Policy, 105, 658–667.
37. Buchanan, J. M. 1975. *A Contractarian Paradigm for Applying Economic Theory. American Economic Review.* 65, 225–30: quoted in Williamson, O. E. 2002. *The Theory of the Firm as Governance Structure: From Choice to Contract.* Journal of Economic Perspectives. 16 (3), 171–195.
38. Williamson, O. E. 2002. *The Theory of the Firm as Governance Structure: From Choice to Contract.* Journal of Economic Perspectives. 16 (3), 171–195.
39. Cave, T. and Rowell, A. 2014. *A Quiet Word: Lobbying, Crony Capitalism and Broken Politics in Britain.* London, UK: Vintage Books.
40. Heede, R. 2014. *Tracing anthropogenic carbon dioxide and methane emissions to fossil fuel and cement producers 1854–2010.* Clim. Change 122, 229–241.
41. Cohen, J. A., Brauer, M. et al. 2017. *Estimates and 25-year trends of the global burden of disease attributable to ambient air pollution: an analysis of data from the Global Burden of Diseases Study 2015.* Lancet. 389, 1907–1918.
42. Caldecott, B. et al. (2016). *Stranded Assets and Thermal Coal: An analysis of environment-related risk exposure.* Available at: http://www.smithschool.ox.ac.uk/research-programmes/stranded-assets/satc.pdf (last accessed 1 May 2021).
43. *Financial Times.* 2017. *KPMG slapped with $6.2m fine over oil company audit errors.* (15 August 2017). Available at: https://www.ft.com/content/0f0393de-81d9-11e7-a4ce-15b2513cb3ff (last accessed 1 May 2021).
44. Sovacool, B. K. and Dworkin, M. H. 2014. Global Energy Justice: Problems, Principles, and Practices. Cambridge, UK: Cambridge University Press.

CHAPTER 4

A Case Study on Distributive Justice: Utilising Energy Taxation and Sovereign Wealth Funds

Abstract The energy sector is characterised by inequality. There is limited literature on ensuring that distributive justice is a key policy goal of the influential practitioner area of energy taxation. Too often energy taxation policy is developed in isolation and a more holistic perspective is needed which incorporates the entire tax system and the energy justice perspective. A focus on distributive justice as an over-arching energy taxation policy goal is particularly important, as a retention of the current status quo will continue to see countries lose the majority of the benefits of their own energy resources to foreign markets and consumers. Distributive justice can also ensure increased accountability, transparency and governance in their energy sectors and hence contribute to societal energy and climate goals.

Keywords Energy justice case study • Distributive justice • Energy taxation: Sovereign Wealth Funds • Norway • Democratic Republic of Congo

4.1 Introduction[1]

There have been major changes over the last five years in tax policies worldwide. One of these changes has been the reform of the US tax code led by the previous US President Trump administration and advanced through the House and the Senate via the Republican party. The majority

R. J. Heffron, *The Challenge for Energy Justice*,
https://doi.org/10.1007/978-3-030-80097-0_4

of commentators and also the Democrat party made it clear that these changes would result in an unfair distribution towards the wealthy and corporate elite. That this situation has arisen, and in such an open and transparent way, demonstrates a problem of our times. It is therefore of vital importance that there are public interest groups and/or individuals who bring their voices to policy debates that challenge the policy-makers.

Controversy too surrounds the taxation of multinational companies (MNCs) from all business sectors and this chapter highlights the issue in the context of the energy sector. This is a sector that has long been recognised as one where inequality is rife internally, and that it is responsible for much societal inequality (with a recent Special Outlook within *Nature* on these issues).[2] There has been some limited progress on reforming taxation in the energy sector over the last decade, with the continued success of the Extractive Industries Transparency Initiative[3] that places disclosure obligations on companies and governments. Nevertheless, there remain significant problems, and in particular the issue of inequality because of a lack of tax revenue received and redistributed from the extractive industries by host governments.

This chapter focuses on the issue of taxation and inequality in relation to the management of natural resources. The aim is to provide a case study type analysis of one aspect of energy justice: distributive justice. This can demonstrate that there are many options to focus on for researchers when exploring energy justice.

The central question of this chapter arises from a distributive justice perspective, and this is to determine whether through taxation a fairer distribution of the benefits of a country's natural resources can be achieved. In this context, the aim is to advance the hypotheses that: (1) policy on energy taxation is too often formulated in isolation and not integrated within the overall energy system; and (2) the creation of a Sovereign Wealth Fund is one method of a more integrated tax policy and has the key feature of ensuring distributive justice in the energy sector.

At its core, this is a conceptual analysis that searches specifically for how distributive justice in the area of energy taxation can be increased. The comparative element of the analysis examines the policies of Norway and the Democratic Republic of Congo (DRC). Finally, the chapter contributes to the growing literature in relation to distributive justice in taxation and energy literature, while also advancing the emerging literature on Sovereign Wealth Funds (SWFs); with the latter being identified as one potential solution of how to increase distributive justice in energy taxation policy.

This chapter begins in Sect. 4.2 with a focus on distributive justice and highlights some of the recent literature in economics, energy law and policy, and taxation. Section 4.3 explores how the problems of energy taxation, and how it is a policy area that is formulated in isolation, i.e., there is no holistic and integrated thinking. Section 4.4 then discusses one solution that emphasizes a more holistic approach to energy taxation and this is the establishment of a Sovereign Wealth Fund (SWF). A SWF can ensure that distributive justice is a core goal of energy taxation policy. This section presents a comparison of Norway with a SWF and a country without one, the DRC. Finally, the chapter concludes and highlights how increasing distributive justice through establishing a SWF aligns with energy law principles.

4.2 Distributive Justice as a Policy Goal and in the Literature

4.2.1 Introduction

Distributive justice is fast becoming a popular area of focus in law and public policy literature and also in other disciplines. One can argue it has always been central to the political debate in that it is a foundation of a democracy or more specifically perhaps a 'social democracy'. This chapter does not intend to engage in those debates which are worthy of extended discussions in themselves, rather, the focus here is on why distributive justice remains lacking in the area of taxation and more specifically in relation to energy taxation. This section covers in brief those areas in the literature that research distributive justice such as economics, energy law and policy, and tax law and policy.

4.2.2 Distributive Justice and Economics

Economists for years have been working on the issue of distribution (i.e., in essence they have advocated for distributive justice). Several of these scholars have now received Nobel Prizes for their work in this area and closely related areas, mainly: Angus Deaton, Joseph Stiglitz, Paul Krugman and Amartya Sen. One economist who may join this group in the future is Thomas Piketty[4] whose work on taxation and wealth distribution has received significant attention recently. Unfortunately, as demonstrated by the earlier example of what is happening in the US, the work of these academics has not translated into policy outcomes there, but it still influence policy in other countries.

In assessing the issue of distributive justice in the energy sector there is unfortunately a lack of literature in the area. The majority of energy economists focus on costs of production, and impacts to price, etc., but there is limited literature that has reflected on distributive justice. Further, many energy economists echo the view of one economist who in is his mining economics text stated that the major focus of economics in relation to mining (which includes all the extractives industries) should be profitability.[5] Indeed the same author went even further in his textbook and suggested that a social objective (and even environmental) for a mining company is 'self-deluding'.[6] Hence it can be stated that an issue such as distributive justice is clearly not at the forefront of the private sector actors, for example, in the mining sector.

4.2.3 Distributive Justice and Energy Law and Policy

In energy policy research literature, distributive justice is already a key theme.[7] It has been a focus of researchers increasingly since 2013 and forms part of three central tenets of the 'energy justice' concept, alongside procedural and recognition justice.[8] However, energy researchers have identified distributive justice as the key element as it allows for more engagement with policy-makers.[9] The energy sector like many areas of commerce has faced calls for reform, and a renewed focus on transparency and ethics alongside calls for a fairer and more equitable energy system.[10] Again similar to other sectors, the energy sector is dominated by multinationals and international finance, and the issue of taxation plays a large role in the operations of such firms. In some cases, the issue of taxation is a lead contributor as to the decision of whether to build, buy or sell an energy asset.

More specifically, energy law scholarship to date has hesitated in making judgment in relation to advocating for distributive justice in the energy sector. Energy law scholars have been more interested in the construction of tax regimes rather than thinking of designing these tax regimes with an element of distributive justice. However, more recently since 2015, the issue of distributive justice has increased in the literature in energy law. Scholars have included it as they have developed a guiding set of principles for energy law,[11]an ongoing development of the discipline,[12] and development within its interdisciplinary boundaries.[13] All these factors are leading to distributive justice having a more prominent role in the discipline and therefore impacting more on future public policy outcomes.

4.2.4 *Distributive Justice and Taxation*

These developments in energy economics, law and policy scholarship mirror the growing importance of distributive justice in the tax discipline. For many taxation scholars, distributive justice has always remained a core value of their research (see the work of Reuven Avi-Yonah[14]). Indeed, tax law and policy has certainly become a popular societal issue over the last few years, and it has been described as a noisy subject.[15] And this has translated into legal academia, where last year eleven out of the top twelve most downloaded academics were tax law specialists (on the Social Science Research Network).[16] The first was the aforementioned Reuven Avi-Yonah who has an obvious distributive justice theme running throughout his research, and this demonstrates in part how the issue of distributive justice is rising in prominence.

It should be noted however, that the goal of distribution has long been a tax policy goal but perhaps in many ways has received limited attention until more recently (as stated above).[17] Indeed, recent scholarship has concluded that distributive justice should be recognised as the cornerstone of tax law, i.e., as the 'first or sovereign virtue of a society's tax system'.[18] Unfortunately however, there are many examples of recent literature that do not address or focus on distributive justice despite topics of research that should, for example, such as tax fraud.[19] It nevertheless has been advanced that Adam Smith has argued that distributive justice was a key tax policy goal, but legal certainty was needed in order for distributive justice not to be just an illusory goal, and that this still applies today;[20] and this is certainly an issue for many developing countries when establishing their energy taxation policies.

4.2.5 *Summary*

It should be noted that in thinking about taxation and its overall role in the economy, it is surprising that there is not more of a reflection on distributive justice given its relationship with Smith's four principles of taxation. There is a significant lack of distributive justice already in the majority of countries and this happens particularly in relation to the issue of energy taxation. An increased role for distributive justice can improve policy-making in relation to energy taxation.

Further, it should be stated that it is not that the recent rise of distributive justice was as a result of a policy goal, rather it has resulted from the introduction of law in other areas and also the opposition to the actions and behaviour of multinational companies. In many ways a multitude of different developments have resulted in an increased change and rise to prominence of distributive justice. It is almost as if law and public policy in relation to the promotion of distributive justice have been superseded by an invisible hand that has pushed it to the fore.

This chapter explores what that this 'invisible hand' is, and it concludes after this analysis of literature in this section, that it is the increased understanding of the 'interconnectedness' of different issues in society. In essence, it could be stated that society is becoming more knowledgeable in relation to interdisciplinary issues[21]—and this is why this section has covered distributive justice from an economic, law and policy and taxation perspective. And it should be added that education in taxation is recognising tax as a interdisciplinary discipline; see the recent establishment of the University of Oxford Taxation Masters which is a joint programme between the Faculty of Law and Oxford University Centre for Business Taxation based at Saïd Business School.

Finally, it is clear that distributive justice is of noted concern in relation to taxation in developing countries.[22] This has been recognised in the literature, and perhaps follows the trend of developed countries to use the taxation system to increase distributive justice, making it one of their three main goals of taxation.[23] In exploring energy taxation and distributive justice there is an addition to the literature here. It also highlights how societies, whether considered as developed or developing nations, can benefit from the application of distributive justice in energy taxation policy.

4.3 Energy Taxation Policy in Isolation

4.3.1 Introduction

Energy taxation policy has too often been formulated in isolation. It should be developed in a more holistic way across the energy industry or system. While other areas of commerce have benefited from a near-invisible hand—as mentioned in Sect. 4.2 earlier—that is restoring distributive justice, the energy sector has not. For example, in a recent practitioner and academic text on energy taxation, the issue of distributive justice received limited attention.[24] While the text acknowledges it does not cover all issues, it states that in relation to taxation '*The central task for policymakers is to design fiscal regimes for the extractive industries that raise sufficient* revenue, *provide adequate incentives to invest and are implementable at reasonable cost to both government and taxpayers.*'[25] In essence, the issue of distributive justice has to be inferred from the quote above and that is similar to the majority of energy taxation literature. The use of limited and vague words such as 'sufficient' and 'adequate' already suggests that the balance of power lies with the multinational companies who develop the majority of resources worldwide.

The energy sector is responsible for significant inequality in society (as highlighted earlier in Sect. 4.1) and distributive justice in energy taxation can play a key role in rectifying that. Fiscal regimes for the energy sector need to be developed that cover and fund all energy activities in a nation, and potentially provide finance for other obligations of a state to its taxpayer (i.e., such as health and/or social welfare systems). The benefits should not accrue in an unfair way to multinationals and their home countries. This section demonstrates why energy taxation policy happens in isolation and why distributive justice has not featured prominently to energy taxation policy formulation.

4.3.2 Taxation and the Energy System (the Life Cycle)

Energy taxation policy and why it is formulated in isolation can be best explained using the example of the previously mentioned Energy Life Cycle diagram as shown in Fig. 4.1.

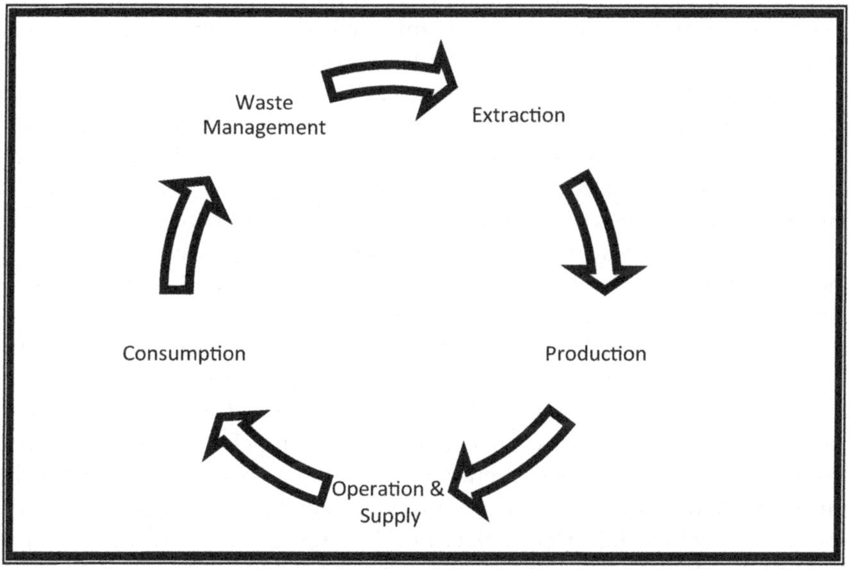

Fig. 4.1 The Energy Life Cycle.[26] (*Source*: Created by the Author)

The energy life cycle diagram shows the five main stages of energy activity in the energy sector or system. This is a well-accepted diagram across all energy disciplines in the energy sector (and is also known as 'cradle-to-grave'). What happens in terms of formulating tax policy in the energy sector is that there is no energy system thinking applied to tax policy. There is a piecemeal approach to taxation, where different energy activities and energy sources are subject to different taxation. This undoubtedly distorts the energy sector. It affects decision-making around the choice of energy sources developed and where the revenues flow from different energy activities.

Too often for resource-rich nations, there is limited redistribution from the wealth created by the natural resources. The taxation issue, for example, is focused entirely on stage one of the energy life cycle above, i.e., extraction. This narrow approach to taxation results in few benefits for developing the rest of the energy sector, and also means that it is the multinational companies engaged in extraction who benefit the most by owning, utilising and selling these resources for energy activities later in the process. Indeed, the importance of effective taxation of multinational companies has been noted in the literature specifically in this context.[27]

4.3.3 *Core Energy Tax Policies*

It is recognised that there are valid reasons for countries to have different taxation regimes, however, at the same time it is evident that there is a clear level of convergence in terms of taxation policies across countries.[28] In a seminal text in the area of energy taxation, the core areas of energy taxation are identified, and these include in summary: environment (i.e., generally carbon, and greenhouse gases) electricity production, extraction, nuclear, hydroelectric, and renewable energy.[29] In assessing what is included, at first one could observe that the wide coverage of areas of different energy sources and activities is a positive. Nevertheless, there is little holistic thinking as to how they relate to each other and how if coordinated they could contribute to better policy outcomes.

The European Union (EU) has however recognised this issue (in 2010) and stated that taxation can play a key role in delivering the energy and climate policies of the EU.[30] This has not translated to action by other countries and nor perhaps has it delivered too much success in Europe; though the majority of EU member states are not resource-rich. Overall, in the aforementioned edited volume on energy taxation, there are multiple authors who acknowledge that a well-designed energy taxation system is fundamental to delivering on all energy and climate policy goals.[31]

The issue of energy taxation is complex. There are competing interests in terms of economic growth and development over, for example, the environment and distributive justice in taxation policy. Many developing countries lack the expertise and the institutional structures to deliver effective energy tax policies that could incorporate distributive justice. However, there are solutions, and indeed a leading economist calls for more action and solutions, and highlights the lead role law can play in this area of taxation and energy, environment and climate issues.[32] In the following section, the development of Sovereign Wealth Funds is analysed as these have a long-term, and distributive strategy for utilising revenue from energy and natural resources.

4.4 Sovereign Wealth Funds, Energy Taxation Policy and Distributive Justice

4.4.1 *Introduction*

An example of a more holistic and integrative approach to energy taxation policy is the creation of a Sovereign Wealth Fund (SWF). This integrative approach results in increased distributive justice as the benefits from a SWF are stated to be fiscal stability and the spreading of the benefits from finite resources over successive generations.[33] Although the use of the terms 'distributive justice' or 'distribution' are not used in the majority of literature on SWFs, it is clear that they are used as a key method of achieving an energy taxation regime that is more 'just' in distribution of the revenue raised from the energy sector than if none exists. Previous literature has focused more broadly on the ability of a SWF to improve governance and institutional quality[34] rather than ensure just outcomes.

This section explores SWFs and presents them as a solution for achieving more distributive justice in energy taxation policy. It first highlights what they are, before exploring a model performing SWF and what may happen if there is no SWF (with Congo given as an example). While literature on SWFs is increasing,[35] it remains limited in amount, and this chapter is a first in exploring distributive justice (and equality) and SWFs.

4.4.2 *What Is a Sovereign Wealth Fund?*

There are many definitions of what a Sovereign Wealth Fund is and these emanate from different international institutions, such as the International Monetary Fund (IMF), etc. However, there is a clearer definition expressed in the recent literature on the subject and this is that SWFs are '... *extra budgetary mechanisms holding a (generally natural resource based) fiscal or foreign exchange reserve surplus*'.[36]

An SWF will use revenue raised via taxes on energy resources in that nation to invest for the long term in investments external to that nation (in some cases the SWF may invest domestically). The aim is always to share the benefits of energy sources and to ensure that future generations benefit too. There is limited information on SWFs and not all of them are very transparent, but the value of SWFs internationally is growing and their creation is too, and even more countries are researching their establishments and/or planning to introduce SWFs. Overall, SWFs are currently valued at US$7.4 trillion (2016) a figure that has remained constant since 2014.[37] There are seventy-nine SWFs listed by the Sovereign Wealth Fund Institute's rankings page with fifty-three of these being natural resource (i.e., including all the extractive industries) funded; it should be noted that some countries have more than SWF, for example there are eight in the US.[38]

4.4.3 A Model Sovereign Wealth Fund in Practice

As stated earlier, there is limited literature on SWFs but it is increasing. From a key article which provides a literature review on SWFs it is held that there are key themes in the literature such as: regulation of SWFs, positives and negatives for firms and target countries; investment strategies; and a new area of shareholder activism.[39] This is interesting in that the literature does not focus on the distributive effect of an SWF, despite this being one of its core purposes as stated in the majority of definitions by researchers and also in relation to information provided by the funds themselves. For example, a review of a selection of SWFs such as the Texas Permanent University Fund (US),[40] The Norwegian Government Pension Fund Global,[41] and the Alberta Heritage Fund (Canada)[42] reveals quite clearly that there is a distributive justice core to their key objectives. Here, it is therefore possible to identify a gap in how SWFs have a distributive justice goal as a result of taxation policy for the energy sector.

A model of the best practice of an SWF in operation is the Norwegian SWF (referred to as the *Government Pension Fund Global*) which is ranked first in the international SWFs rankings.[43] The Norwegian SWF has raised its capital by taxation from its energy resources which are oil and gas. There were three significant legal developments which occurred: the first was in 1963 when Norway introduced a new law whereby the State owned all natural resources found in the Norwegian Continental Shelf (NCS); the second was the creation of a state-owned company, Statoil, which was established via legislation in 1972; and the third was the introduction of the fiscal regime whereby the marginal rate of tax on oil and gas from the NCS was 78 per cent (consisting of ordinary tax at 27 per cent and a special tax rate of 27 per cent).[44] Initially, while Norway did not find any oil and gas, since then there have been many oil and gas discoveries. Norway is now the third largest gas exporter and eighth largest oil exporter in the world.

This is not going to be an extensive review of the operation of the Norwegian SWF, but aims to focus and identify the distributive justice elements of Norway's SWF. The mission statement of the Norwegian SWF highlights its distributive justice core: '*The Government Pension Fund Global is saving for* future generations *in* Norway. *One day the* oil *will run out, but the return on the fund will continue to benefit the Norwegian* population.[45] It highlights the aim to provide intergenerational justice, promote a long-term objective, and also to practise sustainability. There is also intragenerational justice in the form of an annual contribution from the SWF to the Norwegian national budget. This amount is 3 per cent of the value of the fund or in essence is to be the annual return on the fund, and this is used to support a range of public benefits such as social welfare, health and education. In the longer term it will also be used to provide resources for environmental problems resulting from the energy sector such as the decommissioning and waste management issues of the energy sector—though this is subject to more research and approval over the next few years. It should also be noted that the Norwegian SWF highlights its transparency and accountability in its decision-making, and ensures responsibility in its investment practices.[46]

4.4.4 Results if No Sovereign Wealth Fund is Present: The Case of Congo

The ambition of the Norwegian SWF is clear. It is motivated by distributive justice as it ensures all the Norwegian population benefit from its energy resources. Many resource-rich countries, however, do not have such motivations and it is unclear who benefits, but it is certain that no element of distributive justice is incorporated into their energy taxation policy. There are many examples that demonstrate this problem and the country of the Democratic Republic of Congo (the DRC) will be used as an example here. The DRC is a country rich in energy resources and until very recently has not used energy taxation policy for distributive justice purposes. The reason to choose the DRC as an example is that it is Africa's biggest producer of copper and cobalt (used in smartphones and electric cars).

The DRC demonstrates clear problems of not having a SWF and in many ways, it identifies that SWFs provide legitimacy to a national government's aim of ensuring distributive justice is applied to tax revenue from energy and natural resources. The DRC has a national mining company, Gécamines, which oversees its mining sector. It receives and is responsible for creating revenue from the DRCs energy and natural resources. It is clear that over the years, as demand in particular for cobalt has increased, that there has been a realisation that the people of Congo have not benefited as much as the multinational companies. As a result the Chairman of Gécamines stated recently that all contracts with foreign companies in the mining sector will be reviewed within the next year due to the imbalance of these contracts.[47] This is a positive development for the population of the DRC but this decision would have more legitimacy if the DRC had a SWF.

Currently, the latter decision is questioned by multinational companies operating in the DRC as there are reports of unaccounted revenue (up to $750) received by Gécamines.[48] Despite this, it is still acknowledged that MNCs have found ways to reduce their tax liabilities, and it is reported in the Paradise Papers leak in 2017 that Glencore, an international mining company, had received $440 million in discounts in 2008;[49] that Glencore, an Anglo-Swiss company is subject to a criminal complaint in Switzerland due to its operations in the DRC;[50] and that the US announced sanctions against one individual involved in Glencore recently in December 2017.[51] Another major company in operation in the DRC is Ivanhoe, and in light of the contract reviews, its founder, stated that '*"I don't mind paying… as long as that royalty goes to develop, help and empower local people," he told the Investing in African Mining Indaba in Cape Town. "I want the accounting of that money to be transparent and absolutely help people around the mines"*.'[52] It is clear that there are even people from the energy companies who are interested in seeing more distributive justice applied in relation to the energy taxation. As highlighted above, while there may be doubt about what will happen to the energy tax revenue, it is clear that the establishment of a SWF would provide legitimacy, accountability and transparency on how tax revenue is spent; equally the actions of multinationals in reducing their tax liabilities can be limited with improved governance mechanisms that the establishment of an SWF will bring. In this way this research builds on previous research which highlights how resource funds can improve governance and institutional quality.[53]

4.4.5 *Summary*

There are obvious benefits to the DRC in creating a SWF, and the question needs to be asked: why has this not been discussed, or implemented yet, or why has the international community not proposed it?[54] The IMF has advocated SWFs (or resource funds) in the past[55] but it has not been overly active in promoting them (but this is an area for research on its own). However, the reality is perhaps that a SWF would provide too much legitimacy and result in higher tax revenues. Indeed, the German Society for International Cooperation (GIZ), calculated that between 2011 and 2014, tax revenue from the mining sector was equivalent to just 6 percent of GDP[56] and this is far from the 46 per cent recommended by the World Bank.[57]

There may be concern in the DRC that energy tax increases would result in the withdrawal of some MNCs but that should not be a consideration in deciding to establish an SWF. While further research is needed on the impacts of foreign companies due to the creation or ongoing operation of SWFs, it is noticeable that several large MNCs have even reduced or pulled out of their operations in Norway recently, though they have been replaced by other smaller energy companies.[58] There is clearly an abundance of resources and lower operational costs in Congo, and the tax rates are very low (compared with the Norwegian rate earlier in this section) so the business opportunity will remain for MNCs. The energy sector needs reform in the DRC and its population need to benefit, as currently there is little visible benefit, and especially in light of multiple reports that state the mining labour force consists of circa 40,000 children.[59]

There are clearly many issues in the DRC's energy sector but it is interesting to note the conflict that is provided by the following three issues: allegations of corruption by both the MNCs and the DRC government (as highlighted earlier); the noted high returns available for companies by the International Trade Administration (ITA) of the US Department of

Commerce from their mining sector;[60] and all these issues in a country where just 9 per cent of its circa 79 million population have access to electricity.[61] The establishment of a SWF would address some of these concerns and ensure redistribution occurs from the country's wealth in energy and natural resources.

4.5 Conclusions, and Law and Policy Implications

Given the rampant existence of inequality in the world there is a need to ensure fairer and more just outcomes from the policy-making process. This chapter focused on the energy sector and specifically energy taxation policy, and calls for more distributive justice which is a theoretical concept increasing in importance in taxation and energy research literature (via the energy justice concept). One method of achieving distributive justice is for resource-rich nations to develop SWFs to deliver distributive justice in their energy taxation policies. A SWF can result in redistribution of resources across society as well as orienting the economy towards a long-term and sustainable future. This chapter demonstrated the need for resource-rich developing countries in particular, to move away from the short-term benefits that multinational companies encourage when they extract energy resources within their countries.

Distributive justice is emerging as demonstrated in Sect. 4.2 as a key theoretical concept in economic, energy and taxation literature. It is linked to the establishment and operation of SWFs and their potential for reducing inequality in society through its redistributive effect on tax revenue generated from the energy sector. In developing new energy law, specifically energy taxation law, a set of guiding principles has recently been published. Such guiding principles can be a force of change, for example, one can witness worldwide the example of one of the most established environmental law principles, i.e., the 'polluter pays' principle. In this context, these principles of energy law can '*act as a guide to policymakers, academics, lawyers, judges and arbitrators when adjudicating, enforcing, making or formulating documentation, laws, regulations, judgments, etc. on energy law*'.[62] Energy law is stated as having seven guiding principles as given in Table 4.1 and these can assist in guiding the development of an SWF that ensures distributive justice moves from a theoretical concept into practice.

These principles of energy law should act as a guide—and its notable that energy justice is one of the core principles. Energy decision-making

Table 4.1 Principles of Energy Law[63]

1. The Principle of Natural Resource Sovereignty
2. The Principle of Access to Modern Energy Services
3. The Principle of Energy Justice
4. The Principle of Prudent, Rational and Sustainable Use of Natural Resources
5. The Principle of the Protection of the Environment, Human Health and Combating Climate Change
6. Energy Security and Reliability Principle
7. Principle of Resilience

needs to have a *long-term perspective* and should be *integrated*. Energy taxation policy should not be developed in isolation (as demonstrated in Sect. 4.3) and the establishment of SWFs are one solution that can ensure a long-term and integrated energy taxation policy that has distributive justice as one of its key objectives.

Overall, policy-makers will benefit from demonstrating a long-term policy that incorporates a SWF where it would be open and transparent, even despite far higher tax rates. It would ensure that investors see a long-term vision, for example in the DRC (this case study is outlined in detail in Sect. 4.4) that is enabled by supporting legislation to provide legal certainty as to the Government's aims. Achieving this, although there are difficulties involved, has the benefit of providing a platform for securing investor confidence, as investors then can act due to the reduction in risk around new energy infrastructure projects. Indeed, new energy law that is based on the guiding principles above will provide this clarity and certainty for investors and also for the public, two of the key stakeholders in the energy sector in the DRC where the latter are often forgotten.

While exploring in detail these energy law principles and SWFs is for future research it is worth noting that SWFs also have their own set of principles of operation (though they are voluntary)—the Santiago principles[64]—which are also in need of future scholarly research. However, the formulation and application of revised and/or new energy law on energy taxation can result in a positive societal experience and one that has far more benefits and is more distributively '*just*' than any retention of the current status quo.

Finally, the effect of solving this distributive justice issue would have an overall impact on achieving energy justice, and would enable other elements of justice such as the procedural, restorative, cosmopolitan and recognition ones.

Notes

1. This chapter is modelled on previous work completed for the following article and I thank the publisher for permission: Heffron, R. J. 2018. The application of distributive justice to energy taxation utilising sovereign wealth funds. *Energy Policy*, 122, 649–654.
2. Nature, 551, (30 November 2017)—Available at: https://www.nature.com/nature/journal/v551/n7682/index.html#out (last accessed 1 May 2021).
3. Extractive Industries Transparency Initiative. Available at: https://eiti.org/ (last accessed 1 May 2021).
4. Piketty, T. 2014. *Capital in the Twenty-First Century* (translated by Goldhammer, A.). Cambridge, MA: Belknap Press of Harvard University Press.
5. P. 405. Crowson, P. 2008. *Mining Unearthed*. Aspearmont UK: London, UK.
6. P. 405. Crowson (2008).
7. Heffron, R. J. & McCauley, D. 2017. *The concept of energy justice across the disciplines*. Energy Policy, 105, 658–667.
8. McCauley, D., Heffron, R. J. Stephan, H. and Jenkins, K. 2013. *Advancing Energy Justice: The triumvirate of tenets. International Energy Law Review*, 32 (3), 107–110.
9. Sovacool, B, Heffron, R. J., McCauley, D & Goldthau, A. 2016. *Energy decisions reframed as justice and ethical concerns. Nature Energy*, https://doi.org/10.1038/nenergy.2016.24.
10. Heffron and McCauley (2017).
11. Heffron, R. J., Ronne, A., Bradbrook, A., Tomain, J. P. and Talus, K. 2018. *A Treatise for Energy Law*. Journal of World Energy Law & Business, 11 (1), 34–48.
12. Heffron, R. J. and Talus. K. 2016. *The development of energy law in the 21st century: a paradigm shift?* Journal of World Energy Law and Business, 9 (3), 189–202.
13. Heffron, R. J. and Talus. K. 2016. *The Evolution of Energy Law and Energy Jurisprudence: Insights for Energy Analysts and Researchers. Energy Research and Social Science*, 19, 1–10.
14. Reuven Avi-Yonah, 2018. University Webpage Profile: https://www.law.umich.edu/FacultyBio/Pages/FacultyBio.aspx?FacID=aviyonah (last accessed 1 May 2021).
15. Deloitte. 2013. *Responsible Tax: Sustainable tax strategy*. Available at: https://www2.deloitte.com/content/dam/Deloitte/uk/Documents/tax/uk-tax-responsible-tax-v2.pdf (last accessed 1 May 2021).

16. See the data from the following two academic blog posts: Available at: (1) http://taxprof.typepad.com/taxprof_blog/2018/01/ssrn-tax-professor-rankings-1.html and (2) http://taxprof.typepad.com/taxprof_blog/2018/01/11-tax-profs-blow-up-the-ssrn-download-rankings.html (last accessed 1 May 2021).
17. Gribnau, H. and Vording, H. 2017. *The Birth of Tax Law as a Legal Discipline*. Harris, P. and de Cogan, D. (Eds.). 2017. *Studies in the History of Tax Law*, Volume 8. Oxford, UK: Hart Publishing.
18. P. 167. Duff, D. 2017. *Tax Policy and the Virtuous Sovereign: Dworkinian Equality and Redistributive Taxation*, (pp. 167–89). In Bhandari, M. (ed). 2017. *Philosophical Foundations of Tax Law*. Oxford University Press: Oxford, UK.
19. De la Feria, R. 2018. *Tax Fraud and the Rule of Law*. Oxford University Centre for Business Taxation, Working Paper Series 18/02 (January 2018).
20. Gribnau and Vording (2017).
21. Nature, 2015. Special Issue on *Interdisciplinarity*. Available at: http://www.nature.com/news/interdisciplinarity-1.18295 (last accessed 1 May 2021)
22. Bird, R. M. and Zolt, E. M. 2005. *Redistribution Via Taxation: The Limited Role of the Personal Income Tax in Developing Countries*. 52 UCLA L. Rev. 1627.
23. Avi-Yonah, R. S. 2006. *The Three Goals of Taxation*. Tax L. Rev. 60, no. 1, 1–28.
24. Daniel, P., Keen, M., Swistak, A. and Thuronyi, V. (Eds.). 2017. *International Taxation and the Extractive Industries*. Oxford, UK: Routledge.
25. P. 1. Daniel et al. (2017).
26. Heffron and Talus. 2016. *The Evolution of Energy Law and Energy Jurisprudence: Insights for Energy Analysts and Researchers*. Please Note: The diagram was adapted by those authors from the: US EPA, Climate Change and the Life Cycle of Stuff, available at http://epa.gov/climatechange/climate-change-waste/life-cycle-diagram.html (last accessed 1 May 2021).
27. Daniel et al. (2017).
28. Sandford, C. 2000. *Why Tax Systems Differ? A Comparative Study of the Political Economy of Taxation*. Fiscal Publications: Bath, UK.
29. Pistone, P. and Villar Ezcurra, M. (Eds.). 2016. *Energy Taxation, Environmental Protection and State Aids: Tracing the Path from Divergence to Convergence*. Amsterdam, The Netherlands: IBFD.
30. Traversa, E. and Wolff, S. 2016. *Energy Tax Policy in an EU Context: Non-Discrimination, Free Movement and Tax Harmonisation*. In Pistone and Villar Ezcurra, M. (Eds.). 2016.

31. Pitrone, F. 2016. *Design of Energy Taxes in the European Union: Looking for a Higher Level of Environmental Protection.* In Pistone and Villar Ezcurra, M. (Eds.). 2016.
32. Tirole, J. 2017. *Economics for the Common Good.* Princeton, NJ: Princeton University Press.
33. Rietveld, M. and Toledano, P. (Eds.). 2017. *The New Frontiers of Sovereign Investment.* New York: Columbia University Press
34. Tsani, S. 2013. *Natural resources, governance and institutional quality: The role of resource funds. Resources Policy.* Vol. 38 (2) 181–195.
35. Alhashel, B. 2015. *Sovereign Wealth Funds: A Literature Review.* Journal of Business and Economics. Vol. 78, 1–13.
36. P. 5, Rietveld and Toledano (2017).
37. Carpantier, J. F. and Vermeulen, W. N. 2018. *Emergence of Sovereign Wealth Funds. Journal of Commodity Markets* 11 (C), 1–2. https://doi.org/10.1016/j.jcomm.2018.01.002
38. Sovereign Wealth Fund Institute. 2018. Available at: https://www.swfinstitute.org/sovereign-wealth-fund-rankings/ (last accessed 1 May 2021).
39. Alhashel (2015).
40. Texas Permanent University Fund (US). 2018. https://www.utsystem.edu/puf (last accessed 1 May 2021).
41. The Norwegian Government Pension Fund Global. 2018. https://www.nbim.no/en/the-fund/ (last accessed 1 May 2021).
42. Alberta Heritage Fund (Canada). 2018. http://finance.alberta.ca/business/ahstf/index.html (last accessed 1 May 2021).
43. Sovereign Wealth Fund Institute. 2018. Available at: https://www.swfinstitute.org/sovereign-wealth-fund-rankings/ (last accessed 1 May 2021).
44. All the data in this sub-section on *A Model SWF in Practice* is from the website of The Norwegian Government Pension Fund Global. 2018. https://www.nbim.no/en/the-fund/ (last accessed 1 May 2021).
45. The Norwegian Government Pension Fund Global (2018).
46. The Norwegian Government Pension Fund Global (2018).
47. *Financial Times.* 2018. *DRC mining co to renegotiate all contracts within next year* (6 February 2018). Available at: https://www.ft.com/content/d6cb308a-0b4e-11e8-8eb7-42f857ea9f09 (last accessed 1 May 2021).
48. The Carter Center. 2017. *A State Affair: Privatizing Congo's Copper Sector.* (Atlanta, GA, US). Available at: https://www.cartercenter.org/resources/pdfs/news/peace_publications/democracy/congo-report-carter-center-nov-2017.pdf (last accessed 1 May 2021).
49. ICIJ (Fitzgibbon, W.). 2017. *Paradise Papers Research Raises Questions Over Glencore's $440m Congo Discount.* (14 December). Available at: https://www.icij.org/investigations/paradise-papers/paradise-papers-research-raises-questions-glencores-440m-congo-discount/ (last accessed 1 May 2021).

50. The Guardian. 2017. *Paradise Papers prompt criminal complaint against Glencore*. (21 December). Available at: https://www.theguardian.com/business/2017/dec/21/paradise-papers-prompt-criminal-complaint-against-glencore (last accessed 1 May 2021).
51. The Guardian. 2017. *Paradise Papers: US puts sanctions on billionaire over dealings in DRC*. (22 December). Available at: https://www.theguardian.com/news/2017/dec/22/paradise-papers-us-sanctions-billionaire-dealings-drc (last accessed 1 May 2021).
52. *Financial Times*. 2018. *Ivanhoe founder Robert Friedland joins debate over DRC mining code* (7 February). Available at: https://www.ft.com/content/44800d7c-0be4-11e8-839d-41ca06376bf2 (last accessed 1 May 2021).
53. Tsani (2013).
54. US Department of State. 2015. 2015 *Investment Climate Statement—Democratic Republic of the Congo*. Available at: https://www.state.gov/e/eb/rls/othr/ics/2015/241522.htm (last accessed 1 May 2021).
55. Calder, J. 2014. Administering Fiscal Regimes for Extractive Industries: A Handbook. Washington DC, US: IMF.
56. Radley, B. 2016. *The limits of corporate social responsibility and the possibilities for harnessing mining to reinstitute processes of state-led local development in the DRC*. In F Reyntjens, S Vandeginste & M Verpoorten (Eds.), *L'Afrique des Grands Lacs Annuaire*, 2015–2016 (pp. 169–186). Paris: L'Harmattan.
57. World Bank. 2008. *Democratic Republic of Congo Growth with Governance In the Mining Sector*. Available at: http://siteresources.worldbank.org/INTOGMC/Resources/336099-1156955107170/drcgrowthgovernanceenglish.pdf (last accessed 1 May 2021).
58. The Norwegian Government Pension Fund Global (2018).
59. Multiple reports available on this: Amnesty International. 2018. *Is my Smartphone powered by Child Labour?* Available at: https://www.amnesty.org/en/latest/campaigns/2016/06/drc-cobalt-child-labour/ (last accessed 1 May 2021).
60. International Trade Administration (ITA)—U.S. Department of Commerce. 2018. *Congo (DR)—Mining and Minerals*. Available at: https://www.export.gov/article?id=Congo-Democratic-Republic-Mining-and-Minerals (last accessed 1 May 2021).
61. International Trade Administration (ITA)—U.S. Department of Commerce. 2018. *Congo (DR)—Energy*. Available at: https://www.export.gov/article?id=Congo-Democratic-Republic-Energy (last accessed 1 May 2021).

62. P. 48. Heffron, R. J., Ronne, A., Bradbrook, A., Tomain, J. P. and Talus, K. 2018. *A Treatise for Energy Law*. Journal of World Energy Law & Business, 11 (1), 34–48.
63. P. 40. Heffron et al. (2018).
64. International Forum of Sovereign Wealth Funds. 2018. *Santiago Principles*. Available at: http://www.ifswf.org/santiago-principles-landing/santiago-principles (last accessed 1 May 2021).

References

Alhashel, B. 2015. *Sovereign Wealth Funds: A Literature Review. Journal of Business and Economics* 78: 1–13.

Crowson, P. 2008. *Mining Unearthed*. London, UK: Aspearmont UK.

Daniel, P., M. Keen, A. Swistak, and V. Thuronyi, eds. 2017. *International Taxation and the Extractive Industries*. Oxford, UK: Routledge.

Gribnau, H., and H. Vording. 2017. The Birth of Tax Law as a Legal Discipline. In *Studies in the History of Tax Law*, ed. P. Harris and D. de Cogan, vol. 8. Oxford, UK: Hart Publishing.

Heffron, R.J., and D. McCauley. 2017. The Concept of Energy Justice across the Disciplines. *Energy Policy* 105: 658–667.

Rietveld, M., and P. Toledano, eds. 2017. *The New Frontiers of Sovereign Investment*. New York, NY: Columbia University Press.

The Norwegian Government Pension Fund Global. 2018. Accessed 1 May 2021. https://www.nbim.no/en/the-fund/.

Tsani, S. 2013. Natural Resources, Governance and Institutional Quality: The Role of Resource Funds. *Resources Policy* 38 (2): 181–195.

CHAPTER 5

Implementing Energy Justice into the Energy Transition through Human Rights

Abstract Energy justice research has realized that the energy sector was missing an overall *raison d'être*—the permeation of justice throughout the sector. This chapter opens the door to a more practical element that is needed in energy justice research, and focuses on how energy justice can be implemented. National legal courts are the arenas where energy justice can be enforced, and where societies can seek to have justice enforced through protection of a variety of human rights. One hundred legal cases from around the world covering the activities of the energy life cycle are analysed to highlight the key human rights and forms of justice that are being implemented today.

Keywords Energy justice • Energy transition • Energy justice circle • Human rights • Procedural justice

5.1 Introduction

Energy justice has become a leading research topic over the last decade. In essence there has been a realisation that the energy sector was missing an overall *raison d'être*, and that is to have justice permeating throughout the sector. All researchers can connect with this topic, as all decision-making in the energy sector should be delivering just outcomes for society. In a normative way, energy justice presents us with the vision for what the energy

R. J. Heffron, *The Challenge for Energy Justice*,
https://doi.org/10.1007/978-3-030-80097-0_5

sector should be characterised by as it develops over the next decades. It is vital to have energy justice given the environmental impacts of the sector and its contribution of carbon emissions to the climate change problem.

This chapter is the crux, in essence, the heart of this book on energy justice and advances energy justice in a new direction with the focus on human rights and their protection. The book has explored different key angles of energy justice in looking at its interdisciplinary nature, the importance of economics and a further case study on distributive justice. This chapter builds on all that work and provides a direct link for how energy justice can be implemented in practice. And that is where society can seek to have energy justice implemented. There are a number ways this can occur, but the final way and the opportunities of last resort are the national legal courts of countries. This chapter explores this aspect of energy justice and marks a turning point in energy justice research. It marks a first major method of exploring how energy justice can move from theory to practice, and this is the aim of this expert insight.

The momentum for this chapter on implementing energy justice has received impetus from recent developments in the United States. Early in January 2021, the new US President Joe Biden appointed Professor Shalanda Baker as Deputy Director of Energy Justice in the Department of Energy.[1] This new appointment will bring energy justice and its elements to internal US energy policy, but also externally wherever the US is influential across the world (i.e., through USAID programs and international organisations such as the World Bank, IMF, etc.). Following energy justice implementation efforts over the next few years will be exciting, but it also highlights how this is an underexplored area in energy justice and energy scholarship generally.

Crossing into the policy agenda and ensuring energy justice is implemented and practised is vital if society is to meet its impending energy and climate goals of 2030 and beyond. Indeed, significant climate science research demonstrates that action on climate change is moving too slowly.[2] Action is needed and society needs to ensure that more 'just' outcomes result from energy decision-making. These just outcomes are characterised by five forms of justice: distributive, procedural, restorative, recognition and cosmopolitan justice. There are benefits too for energy companies, because if they achieve energy justice they reduce the risk profile of their projects. The application of justice across the project life cycle in planning, construction, operation and decommissioning can result in a continued and successful social licence to operate,[3] and can then therefore contribute in a major way to lowering the risk profile of the project, which in turn lowers the cost of the project.[4]

In thinking of sustainable economic recoveries worldwide, low-carbon energy development can deliver this, but also deliver for governments a more equal, fair and equitable (i.e., just) energy policy that can meet its climate targets. Section 5.2 highlights some of the early literature that discusses energy justice from theory to practice. In Sect. 5.3, one method of how energy justice can be implemented— through the legal system—is examined, and this involves the instances where energy disputes arise across the energy life cycle. Section 5.4 discusses then how in different energy activities across the energy life cycle there are legal cases and the making of decisions that reflect the five forms of justice and human rights. These outcomes should deliver further justice into the future and define new limits and boundaries of the energy sector where rights and justice come to the fore in energy decision-making. In essence national courts are where energy justice can be enforced and are the arenas where societies can seek to have justice enforced through a variety of human rights protections. One hundred legal cases from around the world and covering the activities of the energy life cycle are analysed to highlight the key human rights and forms of justice that are being implemented today.[5]

5.2 Energy Justice from Theory to Practice

When considering energy justice research it is important to realise the growth in scholarship around the area which is significant across all interdisciplinary journals over the last decade. It is incredibly exciting to see and there is widespread adoption across all disciplines of the energy justice concept. Of huge importance is that finally there is a common goal within the energy sector, a realisation that the energy sector has to produce just outcomes. In the past, researchers focused on different issues to try and explore justice without ever thinking about what justice they were looking for. For example, people spent time exploring issues of safety, energy security and delivering affordable energy to the population, and some were also concerned with infrastructure.[6] However, today it is great to see many people have at the backs of their minds the goal of justice as the overarching aim of their research.

Energy justice is a concept that has grown significantly since 2013. In many ways it has emerged owing to the importance and nature of the energy sector. The energy sector is vital to an economy as stable energy supplies ensure economic stability. The nature of the energy sector is one that is centred around risk, and with a poor record of environmental, social and governance issues.[7] Over time society began to address these issues, with practice and research in climate and environmental justice.

Surprisingly however, the root cause of the climate and environmental issues, i.e., the energy sector, remained untreated and underexplored.[8]

Indeed, if energy justice was applied in practice there would be limited need for much action in terms of environmental and climate change issues. Energy justice can prevent the damage that happens to the environment and could lower carbon dioxide emissions. At its simplest, energy justice is about the application of ***human rights*** across the energy life cycle, from extraction to production to operation (and supply) to consumption to waste management (including decommissioning). Energy justice provides a comprehensive framework for action, and centres on the five forms of justice[9] which are worth reviewing again and are given in brief below:

- Distributive justice—this concerns the distribution of benefits from the energy sector and also the negatives, for example, are energy revenues shared sufficiently?
- Procedural justice—the focus here is on legal process and questions will surround whether processes have been followed, if there is access to justice, etc.
- Restorative justice—any injustice caused by the energy sector should be rectified, for example, decommissioning practices would be a classic example.
- Recognition justice—is concerned with the recognition of rights of different groups and in particular local and/or indigenous communities.
- *Cosmopolitanism justice*—in essence this stems from the view that in energy we are all citizens of the same world and therefore the cross-border effects from the energy activities need to be considered.

A key practitioner guide—*The Energy Justice Workbook*[10]—from the aforementioned Professor Baker (now the new US Energy Justice Director) written on energy justice identifies the key framework for applying energy justice from theory to practice (see Fig. 5.1). This is an area for further research exploration and will be elaborated in the rest of this chapter.

5.3 Implementing Energy Justice: How Can Energy Justice Happen in Practice?

In terms of thinking how energy justice can be implemented, there are a number of ways. This expert insight focuses on how this takes place through the legal system. It is advanced here, that in the practice of justice

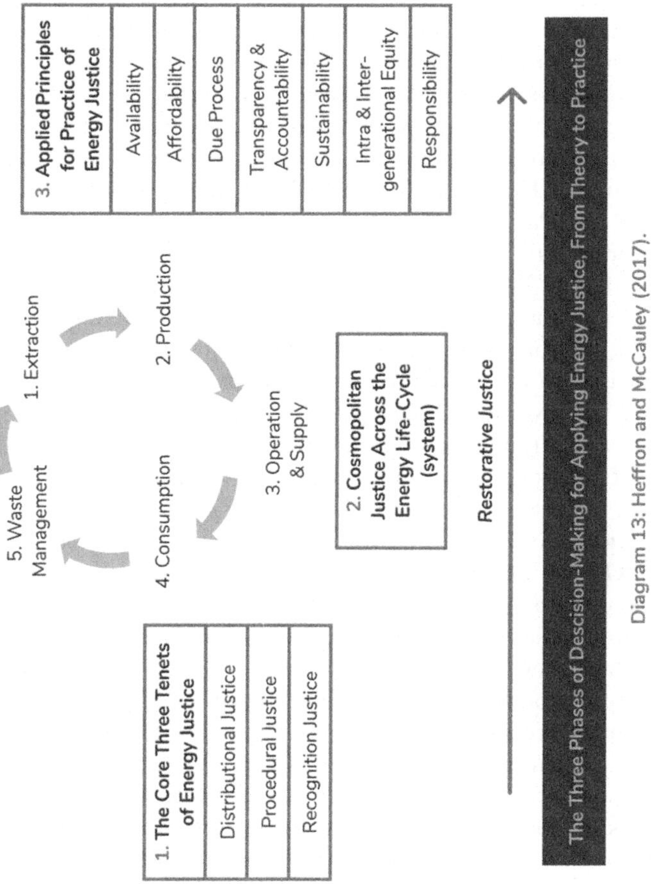

Fig. 5.1 Energy Justice from Theory to Practice. (*Source:* Initiative for Energy Justice [2019])

the opportunity of last resort to ensure justice is implemented is through the legal system. The points within the legal system which are this 'opportunity of last resort for energy justice' will be the national courts within countries, the points at which judges will give their decisions.

At first instance it is necessary to consider that within law and policy there are three interrelated levels where changes can take place: the international, national and local levels.[11] Many people will be already be familiar with change at the international level, and especially today, for example, in terms of renewable energy development and building more sustainable economies. The United Nations (UN) has promoted two initiatives in a major way since 2015: the seventeen UN Sustainable Development Goals (SDGs) and the Paris COP21 Agreement. Both these initiatives have placed a clear plan for the development of sustainable low-carbon economies by 2030. The Paris COP21 Agreement is particularly influential for how countries will achieve their future energy and climate targets; and that is why 2021 will be instrumental for energy justice as new targets are agreed in Glasgow (UK) at the annual UN climate change conference due to take place in November 2021.

There are also a range of other international initiatives that are outside the control of national governments but at the same time are ensuring more energy justice. These international initiatives influence change at both the national and local levels, and these include justice risks such as: the UN SDGs; the 2015 Paris Agreement; climate change action; rise in imagery and data; bankruptcy rules; rules of foreign investment; economics; taxation; disclosure and transparency; project finance; insurance; and environmental impact assessments.[12]

These international initiatives influence what happens at a national level. And in this context, this is where there is a real influence on the behaviour of citizens and corporations as energy justice is secured in two ways: (1) new law is introduced to ensure justice takes place; and (2) a dispute arises over an energy issue and the two parties go to the national legal courts to advance justice on a certain issue. Researchers from all disciplines need to realise what justice they are seeking and how it will result, i.e., which of the two ways mentioned above will be needed—or maybe both? This discussion around how justice is delivered has received little if any attention in the literature to date.

National courts are the places of last resort for justice. This is clearly evident for criminal acts where people become victims and society aim to ensure justice is carried out against those accused of the criminal acts. It is exactly the same for all energy issues; these national courts represent the final place where justice can be sought. If legislation is not in place and/or is not sufficiently detailed, an individual (or company or government) can go to the courts to seek an answer. Here, national courts have a futuristic role; they aim to interpret what justice is according to the law and what it should be according to current society objectives.

In essence, courts are vital to how energy justice will be secured should the necessary law not be introduced. It is well documented that one of the roles of courts is to ensure that the law is kept up-to-date with public policy or with social justice (as it is broadly conceived). Indeed, in a landmark review of the importance of the court system in the 1980s, it was stated that '*Courts are generally looked to in order to satisfy a mounting appetite for social justice on a wide front.*'[13] This remains the case today, and this is why in aiming to secure energy justice's application in society the role of national courts needs to be understood. Within these court systems is where energy justice resides and has the potential to be applied more in practice, and this is the focus of the next section.

This justice can be represented in a protection of what society classifies as human rights. These rights include the right of/for: life, health, minimum subsistence, freedom, human dignity, water, healthy environment, air, culture, property, adequate housing, security and a fair trial. These are the rights that can be protected through the five forms of justice across the energy life cycle activities. This can be expressed diagrammatically in the energy justice circle shown in Fig. 5.2. To develop this and to explore what kind of justice is aimed at, and therefore what types of human rights are protected, one hundred legal cases were examined from around the world across the five stages of the energy life cycle. These are detailed in Appendix 5.1 with twenty cases chosen from around the world on energy activities since 2015 (where possible, and where language translation was allowed or was available).

5.4 Implementing Energy Justice Through National Courts and Protecting Human Rights

5.4.1 Implementing Energy Justice Across Energy Activities

In this section decisions taken at a national level in the court system are examined. National court decisions made by legal judges from different countries around the world were selected that represent cases from the

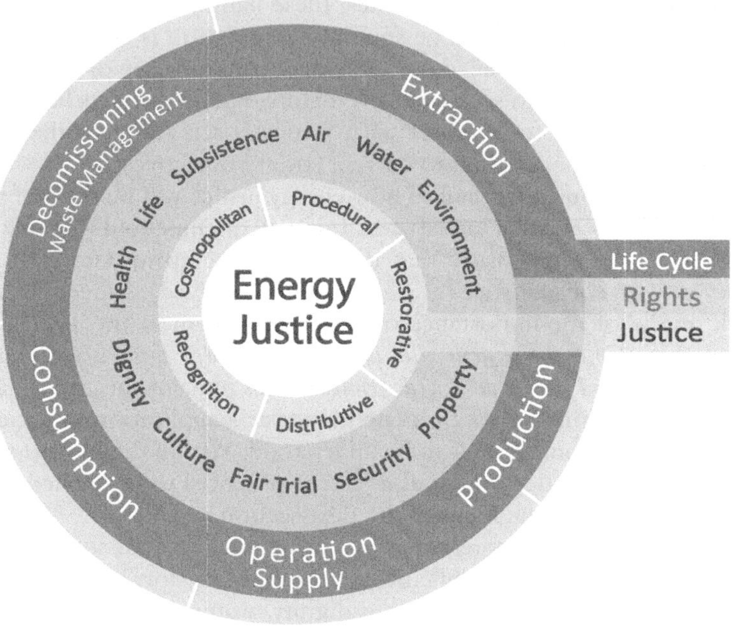

Fig. 5.2 The Energy Justice Circle. (*Source*: Created by Raphael Heffron [2021])

energy life cycle (see Fig. 5.1 earlier), and where it is from extraction—to production—to supply/generation—to consumption—to waste manage ment/decommissioning. What is clear from these decisions (with the case data listed in Appendix 5.1) is that the elements of energy justice are being applied in courts around the world. Unfortunately, however, it demonstrates that energy justice and how it is applied today is based around process rather than being outcome driven.

This latter issue has problems for delivering climate-driven energy goals in that decision-making is delaying the delivery of these just outcomes, and is too often delayed in debates on process. It should be noted that process—i.e., procedural justice—is of value, but what is needed is more combination of achievements. At the same time, it demonstrates that energy justice is being implemented primarily through procedural justice. It demonstrates that it is the 'processes' that exist in society that are and can be targeted to deliver energy justice.

5.4.2 Extraction

In legal cases on extraction, it is clear that all five forms of justice are present, but that predominant among these are procedural and recognition justice. This provides a clear indication that there is a preventative action (procedural justice) where permission has not been granted for projects (generally fossil fuel projects). Further, there are different communities that have not been recognised in the energy extraction process.

Of importance here is that energy justice and its application has been applied in both the developed and developing world. One of the significant cases is from Colombia, where *Demanda Generaciones Futuras v. Minambient* (5 April 2018) (*Future Generations v. Ministry of Environment and Others*). In this case concerning deforestation for extractive activities, there are elements of distributive, recognition, cosmopolitan, and restorative justice. Specifically mentioned within the case are the rights of future generations, and also the Colombian obligation to the rest of the world, where the Amazon (and Colombia's part of the Amazon area) is described as the 'lungs of the world'.

However, in other cases, the courts place limits on behaviour rather than delivering just outcomes. For example, in Guyana, Esso Exploration (a subsidiary of Exxon) had been successful in seeking twenty-three year permits for oil exploration. This would take the company through until 2043 and does not represent responsible business activity. Fortunately, a scientist (Dr Troy Thomas) challenged the permit and had it reduced to five years—*Thomas v. EPA, 7 October 2020 (Guyana)*. This is a point of procedural justice in terms of the permit but there is also an element of cosmopolitan justice whereby Thomas had submitted to the courts that this decision '*exposes Guyana and the rest of the world to serious, if not irreparable, harm and adverse consequences from* climate change *(Thomas v. EPA)*'.

There is a link here in the extraction process in that human rights are increasingly being protected through the court system with the following rights identified, such as: the rights of life, health, minimum subsistence, freedom, human dignity, water, healthy environment, culture, property, adequate housing, security and a fair trial. As was stated earlier, to what level are these rights have been protected in these energy decisions is open to question; there will be differences from country to country. However, it is without doubt that the mention and protection of rights is featuring within these legal cases on extraction.

5.4.3 *Production*

In legal cases on production, again procedural justice is a dominant feature. It can be advanced upon reviewing these cases that there are new challenges to production. The legal court system is recognising the obligations of a country and what it has signed up for in terms of energy and climate targets. In some countries there are clear attempts by energy producers to bypass processes in the system or to try and obfuscate the process and continue ahead with the project. Hence, that is why in the production phase of the project procedural justice features strongly.

Similar to legal cases in the extractive phase, what is noticeable here is that again there is an emerging feature of a link between procedural and cosmopolitan justice. And again, this is evident in both developing and developed countries. In Argentina (*Hahn et al. v. APR Energy S.R.L (II) 2021*) and in Kenya (*Save Lamu et al. v. National Environmental Management Authority and Amu Power Co. Ltd, 26 June 2019, Kenya*) these legal cases highlight the problems of some energy producing infrastructure acquiring an environmental permit properly, and the contribution of this infrastructure to national and international global energy and climate targets. This corresponds to the UK case (*ClientEarth v. Secretary of State for Business, Energy and Industrial Strategy, 21 January 2021*) whereby it was held a gas production plant would violate planning and international commitments of the UK.

It is clear that in this production phase of the energy life cycle that energy producers are finding it difficult to legitimately conform to procedural justice in their actions. As stated earlier, they try to obfuscate the process. This is evident in Japan, for example (*Yokosuka Climate Case, 2021*), whereby a coal producer is alleged (the final decision has still to be determined) to have improperly exploited a streamlined assessment process for replacements or upgrades that the Japanese Government created after the Fukushima Daiichi nuclear accident. This is similar to a case in Argentina (*Carballo et al. v. MSU S.A., UGEN S.A., & General Electric, 2021*) where it is being held that the environmental impact assessment process was flawed to enable the development of the production facility.

Human rights have been identified in case law in terms of production, and they include the majority of rights to the environment, health, cultural, social and property issues, access to justice, life and water. An interesting feature of legal cases here in the production phase, and in terms of human rights, centres on the rise of restorative justice. Cases from Poland,

Brazil and Peru all highlight the need for restorative behaviour where the rights to environment, health and water have to be rectified by these energy companies.

5.4.4 Operation and Supply

There is a switch of emphasis in legal cases on operation and supply with these cases focusing primarily on distributive justice. That should be expected, given the nature of operation and supply, but nevertheless it highlights that there does exist support for fairer distribution of energy and its benefits across society. There are also cases that concern procedural and recognition justice.

The legal cases here reflect how costs are distributed across the energy sector and whether it is fair. The questions relate to whether particular stakeholders such as consumers and energy companies are receiving fair treatment in terms of energy prices. For example, in *Case GRDF SA v. Eni Gas & Power France SA C-236/18 2019*, it was highlighted that a key function of energy markets is to ensure consumer benefits. In Australia there was again distributive justice, but also an element of recognition justice, where vulnerable customers were not accounted for, and policies that should have been accountable for these customers were not applied (*AER v. EnergyAustralia Pty Ltd [2020] FCA 1647*). And in the UK, the imposition of a price cap on an energy company was challenged, but at the same time the courts decided not to quash it, due in part to its value to energy consumers (*R (British Gas Trading Limited) v. Gas and Electricity Markets Authority [2019] EWHC 3048 (Admin)*).

In this phase of operation and supply, the link to human rights is less obvious. There are human rights issues of property, culture, water and health but these are less obvious in this phase of what is the more technical stage of the energy life cycle. However, issues do arise over pipelines, and this has been an issue in relation to an oil pipeline in the case *Center for Food and Adequate Living Rights et al. v. Tanzania and Uganda 2020.* This case is an example of where a lack of procedural justice is evident, again with no evidence of sufficient impact assessment work completed by the project developers or requested by the relevant authorities. Rights to property were also behind the case of a Peruvian farmer who took action against a German energy company over damages to his farm—*Lliuya v. RWE AG 2015.* This type of case will no doubt increase as it gets easier to prove damage as a result of polluting activity, and there is major research underway on this kind of science, called 'attribution science'.[14]

5.4.5 *Consumption*

Consumption is a very interesting stage of the energy life cycle because it is where many of us—citizens—actually engage fully in the energy sector. Generally, we all utilise energy in our daily activities whether it be via electricity or some type of fuel for transport or even cooking. The predominant forms of justice that feature here are as expected, distributive and procedural, however, there are interesting legal cases involving the other forms of justice which demonstrate a rise in the important of energy justice. Many of the main cases involve issues where the customers in essence have been taken advantage of in terms of the contracts they have signed, their ability to switch provider and also some element of customer discrimination (and here there is a cross-over to recognition justice). These types of cases will continue, and these types of justice are central to ensuring justice is implemented at this consumption phase.

In the US, there is an interesting case involving a mix of distributive and restorative justice, where the City of Baltimore (*Mayor & City Council of Baltimore v. BP p.l.c., 6 March 2020 (US)*) has taken legal action against energy companies. The reason is that the city of Baltimore expects that energy companies need to pay their 'fair share' of costs, which are expected to be circa $123.9 million to pay for seawalls needed to protect infrastructure, property and lives from climate-driven sea-level rise. The energy companies were sued '*for their contribution to* climate change *by producing, promoting, selling, and concealing the dangers of* fossil fuel *products*'. This type of case is likely to increase, as the risk associated with climate change rises in cost and insurance becomes more and more difficult to obtain.

The surprising issue here is that there are no specific mentions of human rights in these cases on consumption. It is possible to allude to the protection of certain rights such as environment, subsistence or even property; however, the actual decisions do not refer to them. This demonstrates a lack of engagement by consumers or a lack of resources to take action around consumption issues. Or indeed, in many cases, energy companies will be responding to their customer preferences, and in such cases there is misinformation etc. this concerns economic rights of a consumer which does not cross into the area of human rights in today's understanding.

5.4.6 *Decommissioning and Waste Management*

This final stage of the energy life cycle has become more active over recent years. Restorative justice, as should be expected, is the dominant form of justice in this activity, and there are multiple human rights issues here that the legal courts are willing to protect. It seems certain that accountability for actions on decommissioning and waste management is happening across the world, and that a key issue is that this accountability comes with a cost, i.e., if companies are held accountable there will be an obligation to pay for the clean-up of the energy activity.

One of the particularly interesting cases comes from India where there is a realisation that no longer can policy on decommissioning and waste management take place after the fact, i.e., it needs to be considered from the outset of a project. In this case—*Sukhdev Vihar Residents Welfare Association & Ors. v. Respondent: The State of NCT of Delhi & Ors. (2017)*—the court held that it could not '...allow the public at large to suffer the consequences of the indiscriminate dumping ...' and that policy and legislative action needs to happen '... right at the initial stage rather than provide for remedies post environmental damage'. Indeed, a significant blight of the energy sector has always been the lack of action around this energy activity of decommissioning and waste management. If there is no action, it acts as a hidden subsidy to energy companies and also dangerously sends a message to the public that various energy activities are cheap, when the reality is that they as the taxpayer will end up paying for the clean-up as well as suffering the effects of environmental pollution.

The link with human rights is clear in these cases, as there are clear links with rights for the environment, health, property, water and air. It is here that there is also the consideration of rights for future generations of peoples, as the judge in the highest court in the Philippines stated that if there was no action it ' ... would also affect the rights of the generations yet unborn to live in a balanced and "healthful ecology," guaranteed under Section 16, Article II of the 1987 Constitution'—*West Tower Condominium Corp v. First Philippine Industrial Corporation et al., 16 June 2015 (Philippines)*. The right to a healthy environment is a feature of many cases, and addresses the high, continuous and cumulative impact of the lack of decommissioning and waste management in countries around the world. Cases in this section are mixed, representing both the global north and south.

5.5 Conclusion: Next Steps to Achieving Energy Justice through Human Rights

As stated earlier, the energy sector in essence stood in need of a *raison d'être*, and energy justice has achieved that aim. Research in the area has exploded over the last decade. In part due to this, US President Joe Biden and his team have had the vision of appointing an academic to the administration specifically for energy justice. This is a testament to the strength of the energy justice concept itself. It also highlights the opportunity and the need for more research in the area of energy justice and its implementation into practice. It is an under-researched issue and a research area that could empower policy-makers in the future to make more informed energy decisions that deliver just outcomes for society.

This chapter aims to provide a platform for future researchers and explores this implementation of energy justice issues. It takes a legal approach by looking at what is happening today in national courts around the world. The premise here, is that it has become visible as to which types of injustices are occurring, and how national courts aim to rectify these injustices by making decisions that protect human rights. This is represented by the energy justice circle in Fig. 5.2 which aims to highlight how energy activities of the energy life cycle are intertwined with the forms of justice and also human rights. The human rights we see protected in these legal decisions are the rights to life, health, minimum subsistence, freedom, human dignity, water, healthy environment, air, culture, property, adequate housing, security and a fair trial.

This insight aims to set off a new wave of energy justice research that explores how energy justice will be implemented into the energy transition through national courts that will protect the human rights of its citizens. National courts offer the final opportunity to hold a government or energy company accountable for its actions and to ensure that the energy sector is characterised by justice. It is clear that in looking across the energy life cycle and the five key stages of activity, that there are governments and energy companies being held accountable across the world. In particular, it is clear that energy justice is being implemented in both the global north and south.

Appendix 5.1: Legal Cases Analysed

Data availability: the data below and the judgments (and case summaries) for the one hundred cases are available via standard legal databases on case law and/or the national court system of those countries, and the decisions can be searched for using the references below.

100 Legal Cases Analysed

Extraction (20 legal cases)

1. *Demanda Generaciones Futuras v. Minambient*, **5 April 2018** (Colombia)
2. *Greenpeace Nordic Ass'n and Nature and Youth v. Ministry of Petroleum and Energy*, **4 January 2018** (Norway)
3. *Sentencia C-035/16*, **8 February 2016** (Colombia)
4. *KEPCO Bylong Australia Pty Ltd v Independent Planning Commission*, **18 December 2020** (Australia)
5. *Thomas v. EPA*, 7 **October 2020** (Guyana)
6. *Australian Conservation Foundation Inc. v. Minister for the Environment*, **29 August 2016** (Australia)
7. *Claire Stephenson v. Secretary of State for Housing and Communities and Local Government*, 6 March 2019 (UK)
8. *H.J. Banks & Co. v. Secretary of State for Housing, Communities, and Local Government*, **23 November 2018** (UK)
9. *Gloucester Resources Limited v. Minister for Planning*, **8 February 2019** (Australia)
10. *Clyde River (Hamlet) v. Petroleum Geo-Services Inc*, **26 July 2017** (Canada)
11. *Lho'imggin et al. v. Her Majesty the Queen*, **16 November 2020** (Canada)
12. *Gabriela Simonetti Grez y otros con Servicio de Evaluación Ambiental*, **20 August 2018** (Chile)
13. *Sentencia 4360-2018 de la Corte Suprema de Justicia, Sala de Casacion Civil, M.P. Luis Armando Tolosa Villabona)*, **5 April 2018** (Colombia)
14. *350 Montana v. Bernhardt*, **9 March 2020** (US)
15. *Sierra Club Canada Foundation v. Canada (Environment and Climate Change)*, **pending** (Canada)
16. *Friends of the Earth v. UK Export Finance*, **pending** (UK)
17. *Anjali Sharma and others v. Minister for The Environment (Commonwealth)*, **pending** (Australia)
18. *Waratah Coal Pty Ltd v. Youth Verdict Ltd and others*, **pending** (Australia)
19. *Marktgemeinde Straßwalchen and Others v. Bundesminister für Wirtschaft, Familie und Jugend*, **9 September 2015** (EU)
20. *Dimitar Yordanov v. Bulgaria*, **6 September 2018** (ECHR)

(*continued*)

(continued)

Production (20 legal cases)

1. *Earthlife Africa Johannesburg v. Minister of Environmental Affairs and others*, **8 March 2017** (South Africa)
2. *Smith v. Fonterra Co-Operative Group Limited* [2020] NZHC 419, **6 March 2020** (New Zealand)
3. *McLennan, R (on the application of) v Medway Council & Anor*, **10 July 2019** (UK)
4. *ClientEarth v. Secretary of State*, **21 January 2021** (UK)
5. CAA de NANTES, 5ème chambre, 05/03/2019, 17NT02791-17NT02794, Inédit au recueil Lebon (France)
6. *Save Lamu et al. v. National Environmental Management Authority and Amu Power Co. Ltd*, **26 June 2019** (Kenya)
7. *Wildland Ltd. and the Welbeck Estates v. Scottish Ministers*, **30 August 2017** (UK)
8. *Corporación Privada para el Desarrollo de Aysén y otros con Servicio de Evaluación Ambiental*, **4 January 2018** (Chile)
9. *Milieudefensie and others v. Shell*, **pending** (Netherlands)
10. *Sabo and Others v. Parliament and Council*, **14 January 2021** (EU)
11. *Carballo et al. v. MSU S.A., UGEN S.A., & General Electric*, **pending** (Argentina)
12. *Hahn et al. v. APR Energy S.R.L (II)*, **pending** (Argentina)
13. *OAAA v. Araucaria Energy SA.*, **pending** (Argentina)
14. *Citizens' Committee on the Kobe Coal-Fired Power Plant v. Kobe Steel Ltd., et al.*, **pending** (Japan)
15. *Yokosuka Climate Case*, **pending** (Japan)
16. *Instituto brasileiro do meio ambiente e dos recursos naturais renovaveis v. Siderurgica sao luiz ltda, geraldo magela martins*, **pending** (Brazil)
17. *ClientEarth v. Polska Grupa Energetyczna*, **22 September 2020** (Poland)
18. *Fridays for Future Estonia v. Eesti Energia*, **pending** (Estonia)
19. *Álvarez y otros contra Perúi*, **pending** (Peru)
20. *An Taisce v. An Bord Pleanála*, **9 September 2015** (Ireland)

(continued)

(continued)

Operation and Supply (20 legal cases)

1. *Nabha Power Limited v. Punjab State Power Corporation Limited*, **5 October 2017** (India)
2. *Tempus Energy and Tempus Energy Technology v. Commission*, **15 November 2018** (UK)
3. *Germany v Commission*, **10 May 2016** (EU)
4. *Sierra Club v. United States Department of Energy*, **15 August 2017** (US)
5. *Atchafalaya Basinkeeper v. U.S. Army Corps of Engineers*, **6 July 2018** (US)
6. *Appalachian Voices v. Federal Energy Regulatory Commission*, **19 Feb 2019** (US)
7. *Lliuya v. RWE AG*, **pending** (Germany)
8. *In re Trunkline Gas Co.*, **request for rehearing to FERC** (US)
9. *Deutsche Umwelthilfe v. Stralsund Mining Authority*, **pending** (Germany)
10. *Conservation Council of Western Australia v. Hatton and Woodside*, **pending** (Australia)
11. *Center for Food and Adequate Living Rights et al. v. Tanzania and Uganda*, **pending** (East African Court of Justice)
12. *ExxonMobil Production Deutschland GmbH v. Bundesrepublik Deutschland*, **20 June 2019** (EU)
13. *Interocean Oil Development Company and Interocean Oil Exploration Company v. Federal Republic of Nigeria*, **6 October 2020**
14. *Transglobal Green Energy, LLC and Transglobal Green Panama, S.A. v. Republic of Panama*, **2 June 2016**
15. *Lotus Holding Anonim Şirketi v. Turkmenistan*, **6 April 2020**
16. *UAB E energija (Lithuania) v. Republic of Latvia*, **22 December 2017**
17. *Repsol Butano SA and DISA Gas SAU v. Administración del Estado*, **11 April 2019** (EU)
18. *Balgarska energiyna borsa AD (BEB) v. Komisia za energiyno i vodno regulirane (KEVR)*, **26 October 2017**(EU)
19. *Petroceltic Holdings Limited and Petroceltic Resources Limited v. Arab Republic of Egypt*, **15 September 2020**
20. *Essent Belgium NV v. Vlaams Gewest and Others*, 29 **September 2016** (EU)

(continued)

(continued)

Consumption (20 legal cases)

1. *Ruling on Modification to Ethanol Fuel Rule*, **22 January 2020** (Mexico)
2. *District of Columbia v. Exxon Mobil Corp.*, **pending** (US)
3. *Beyond Pesticides v. Exxon Mobil Corp.*, **pending** (US)
4. *Association nationale des opérateurs détaillants en énergie (ANODE) v. Premier ministre and Others*, **7 September 2016** (EU)
5. *'Overgas Mrezhi' AD and 'Balgarska gazova asotsiatsia' v. Komisia za energiyno i vodno regulirane (KEVR)*, **30 April 2020** (EU)
6. *Stadtwerke Neuwied GmbH v. RI*, **2 April 2020** (EU)
7. *Oulun Sähkönmyynti Oy*, **2 May 2019** (EU)
8. *EVN Bulgaria Toplofikatsia" EAD v. Nikolina Stefanova Dimitrova and 'Toplofikatsia Sofia' EAD v. Mitko Simeonov Dimitrov*, **5 December 2019** (EU)
9. *Engie Cartagena S.L. v. Ministerio para la Transición Ecológica*, **19 December 2019** (EU)
10. *Promociones Oliva Park SL v. Tribunal Económico Administrativo Regional (TEAR) de la Comunidad Valenciana*, **3 March 2021** (EU)
11. *Acea Energia SpA and Others v. Autorità Garante della Concorrenza e del Mercato and Others*, **14 May 2019** (EU)
12. *Eni SpA and Others v. Premier ministre and Ministre de l'Environnement, de l'Énergie et de la Mer*, **20 December 2017** (EU)
13. *FVE Holýšov I s. r. o. and Others v. European Commission*, **20 September 2019** (EU)
14. *Achema AB and Others v. Valstybinė kainų ir energetikos kontrolės komisija (VKEKK)*, **15 May 2019** (EU)
15. *Elecdey Carcelen SA and Others v. Comunidad Autónoma de Castilla-La Mancha*, **20 September 2017** (EU)
16. *Federal Energy Regulatory Commission v. Electric Power Supply Association and EnerNOC, Inc. v. Electric Power Supply Association*, **25 January 2016** (US)
17. *City of Arcata v. Pacific Gas & Electric Co.*, **pending** (US)
18. *Bihar State Electricity Board etc. v. M/S Iceberg Industries Ltd. and others*, **27 April 2020** (India)
19. *Board of County Commissioners of Boulder County v. Suncor Energy (U.S.A.), Inc.*, **pending** (US)
20. *Mayor & City Council of Baltimore v. BP p.l.c.*, **6 March 2020** (US)

(*continued*)

(continued)

Decommissioning and Waste Management (20 legal cases)

1. *Board of County Commissioners of Boulder County v. Suncor Energy (U.S.A.), Inc.*, **7 July 2020** (US)
2. *Rospriropnadzor v. NTEK*, **5 February 2021** (Russia)
3. *Ali v. Federation of Pakistan*, **pending** (Pakistan)
4. *La Confederación Mapuche de Neuquén contra YPF y otros*, **pending** (Argentina)
5. *Okpabi and others v. Royal Dutch Shell Plc and another*, **pending** (UK)
6. *Milieudefensie et al. v. Royal Dutch Shell plc*, **21 January 2021** (Netherlands)
7. *Hope for Humanity Africa (H4HA) v. South Sudan's Minister for Justice, the Greater Pioneer Operating Company (GPOC) and Dar Petroleum Operating Company Ltd*, **pending** (East African Court)
8. *Nuclear Decommissioning Authority v. EnergySolutions EU Ltd (now called ATK Energy EU Ltd)*, **11 April 2017** (UK)
9. 'Permits under the Environmental Code for facilities in a coherent system for final disposal of spent nuclear fuel and nuclear waste; now question of opinion to the government', **23 January 2018** (Sweden)
10. *Duke Energy Progress, Inc. and * Duke Energy Florida, Inc., * v. the US*, **17 November 2017** (US)
11. *Court On Its Own Motion v. Union of India and Ors*, **16 December 2015** (India)
12. *Naveen Chandra Pant and Another Petitioners v. State Of Uttarakhand and Others S*, **28 March 2017** (India)
13. *West Tower Condominium Corp v. First Philippine Industrial Corporation et al.*, **16 June 2015** (Philippines)
14. *Sukhdev Vihar Residents Welfare Association & Ors. v. Respondent: The State of NCT of Delhi & Ors.*, **2 February 2017** (India)
15. *Inter-Environnement Wallonie ASBL and Bond Beter Leefmilieu Vlaanderen ASBL v Conseil des ministres*, **29 July 2019** (EU)
16. *Sanda v. PTTEP Australasia (Ashmore Cartier) Pty Ltd*, **19 March 2021** (Australia)
17. *Nextera Energy, Inc. v. United States*, **28 June 2018** (US)
18. *Plaintiffs v. Eni*, **10 March 2021** (Italy)
19. *Wyoming v. United States Department of Interior*, **8 October 2020** (US)
20. *Chevron Corporation and 2. Texaco Petroleum Company v. The Republic of Ecuador*, **30 August 2018** (The Hague)

Notes

1. Chabot, H. 2021. She's Bringing her Energy Justice Mission to the Biden Administration. Available at: https://news.northeastern.edu/2021/01/23/shalanda-baker-is-bringing-her-energy-justice-mission-to-the-biden-administration/ (last accessed 1 May 2021); and US Department of Energy. 2021. Shalanda Baker—Available at: https://www.energy.gov/index.php/diversity/person/shalanda-h-baker (last accessed 1 May 2021).

2. Figueres, C., et al., 2017. Three Years to Safeguard our Climate. Nature 546 (7660), 593–595 (29 June 2017).
3. Heffron, R. J. et al. 2018. The emergence of the 'social licence to operate' in the extractive industries? Resources Policy, 101172.
4. R. Heffron, R Connor, P Crossley, V López-Ibor Mayor, K Talus & J Tomain. 2021. The identification and impact of justice risks to commercial risks in the energy sector: post COVID-19 and for the energy transition. Journal of Energy & Natural Resources Law, https://doi.org/10.1080/02646811.2021.1874148 (advance access).
5. I express my thanks to my two research assistants who collected and helped build a short data file on these cases; many thanks indeed to Marie Tritz and John O'Boyle—both Masters students at the University of Dundee at the time.
6. Heffron, R. J. and Talus. K. 2016. The Evolution of Energy Law and Energy Jurisprudence: Insights for Energy Analysts and Researchers. Energy Research and Social Science, 19, 1–10.
7. Sovacool, BK and MH Dworkin. 2014. Global Energy Justice: Problems, Principles, and Practices. Cambridge: Cambridge University Press.
8. Heffron, R. J. & McCauley, D. 2017. The concept of energy justice across the disciplines. Energy Policy, 105, 658–667.
9. Heffron, R. J. & McCauley, D. 2017. The concept of energy justice across the disciplines. Energy Policy, 105, 658–667.
10. Initiative for Energy Justice. 2019. The Energy Justice Workbook. Available at: https://iejusa.org/wp-content/uploads/2019/12/The-Energy-Justice-Workbook-2019-web.pdf (last accessed 1 May 2021).
11. Heffron, R. J. and Talus. K. 2016. The development of energy law in the 21st century: a paradigm shift? Journal of World Energy Law and Business, 9 (3), 189–202.
12. R. Heffron, R Connor, P Crossley, V López-Ibor Mayor, K Talus & J Tomain. 2021. The identification and impact of justice risks to commercial risks in the energy sector: post COVID-19 and for the energy transition. Journal of Energy & Natural Resources Law, https://doi.org/10.1080/02646811.2021.1874148 (advance access).
13. Hopkins, J. D. 1985. The Role of the Courts in American Society: The Final Report of the Council on the Role of the Courts, 6 Pace Law Review, 6 (4), 127–132.

14. Otto, F. et al. United Nations. The science of attributing extreme weather events and its potential contribution to assessing loss and damage associated with climate change impacts. Available at: https://unfccc.int/files/adaptation/workstreams/loss_and_damage/application/pdf/attributingextremeevents.pdf (last accessed 1 May 2021).

Reference

Initiative for Energy Justice. 2019. The Energy Justice Workbook. Accessed 1 May 2021.https://iejusa.org/wp-content/uploads/2019/12/The-Energy-Justice-Workbook-2019-web.pdf.

CHAPTER 6

Conclusion: Ensuring Justice in Energy Infrastructure Development

Abstract This chapter highlights the importance of resolving human rights abuses. In order to ensure no delays to a project it is necessary for the project developer to resolve these current and potential risks concerning human rights. These risks need to be addressed so that the energy infrastructure project is less risky and therefore the costs of borrowing will be reduced. These new energy justice risks have all emerged in essence since the 2007–2009 financial crisis. Managing these risks will resolve the potential for human rights abuses. The chapter then discusses energy justice research and highlights some lessons for young researchers in the future.

Keywords Energy justice • Energy justice risks • Project finance • Lessons for the next generation • Implementing energy justice

6.1 What Will Happen by Resolving Human Rights?

6.1.1 Human Rights and Risk in the Energy Sector

The importance of energy justice lies in ensuring that justice gets permeated throughout the energy sector. Decision-making needs to become dominated by issues of justice, i.e., distributive, procedural, restorative, recognition and cosmopolitan justice. In this way the energy sector can

R. J. Heffron, *The Challenge for Energy Justice*,
https://doi.org/10.1007/978-3-030-80097-0_6

reduce its majority contribution to greenhouse gases and its environmental impact within countries and globally across the world. To ensure that this happens, what is needed is an energy infrastructure that is developed under such decision-making processes where energy justice is evident. No longer should energy infrastructure be built where carbon dioxide emissions and/or environmental impacts remain unaccounted for and mitigation plans are absent or not acted upon. If countries around the world are to meet their energy and climate goals under the Paris Agreement, all new energy infrastructure needs to align with these goals and deliver us our low-carbon and clean economies.

The world is in continual need of new energy infrastructure for multiple reasons: to further economic growth, to increase energy access, to reduce energy poverty, to replace aged infrastructure and to meet carbon dioxide reduction policies. An addition to all these reasons is the present COVID-19 pandemic and the resulting financial crisis. New energy investment will be seen as the catalyst to restart many economies across the world. The figure advanced by Bloomberg (2019) on new energy generation investment by 2050 is $13.3 trillion and it is likely that the world will accelerate towards that figure much faster than planned due to the need to emerge from this current crisis; and with a further $11.4 trillion in distribution and transmission[1] there are a range of reports which state circa $40–50 trillion will be invested in the energy sector more broadly, which includes expenditure in the extractives, in waste management and for upgrading existing infrastructure.

Within this context lies the reason why energy justice is so important. All this investment into the energy sector globally has to occur in a just way if the energy sector is to make its contribution to the Paris Agreement and for addressing societal inequality more broadly. However, even for the commercial world energy justice is of vital importance. And the link here is directly with human rights. If there are situations where court cases are going to be advanced, then all these will affect a project as it goes through its life cycle—from the planning to construction to operation and to the decommissioning phase; this can be expressed as in Fig. 2.2 earlier in Chap. 2.

Hence, from the commercial perspective, ensuring that there are no human rights abuses from the past, or current, and even into the future, in a new energy project will be vital. This is the case because managing human rights is necessary to reduce the risk of the overall project. And for the commercial sector, the less risky a project is the lower the costs of borrowing on finance for that project. So there is now a real incentive to manage these risks and to ensure that energy justice gets applied, and that no projects become subject to an action in court over human rights abuse.

With energy projects, the investor community already considers general commercial risks and political risk, however, neither of these account for the risks that come from the challenges of the energy transition (the switch from fossil fuels to low-carbon energy source) and the global initiative around the Paris Agreement 2015 on climate change, or the UN Sustainable Development Goals (which for the energy sector calls for a massive reduction on the environmental impacts of their projects). Therefore, there is a new set of risks that can be referred to as 'justice' risks. These new justice risks are emerging from society itself and the planned push for a more inclusive society and these 'justice' risks will increase in the future. Indeed, these justice risks have already been on the rise since the financial crisis of 2007–2009, and as a result of COVID-19 they will accelerate even further in their influence, and will have to be fully incorporated into research and practice around energy project developments.

The importance of the role of law in ensuring that justice takes place in project development is of vital importance. The practitioner legal professions will have to identify these justice risks for their clients, so as to avoid the cost of court action where human rights will be protected. Significant scholarship has been completed in the area recently in 2020 by practitioners and academics on energy law and justice from the *International Bar Association*.[2]

The viability of energy projects and the legal processes that need to be followed and addressed are vital in terms of whether a project is rolled out or not. A project can fail for many reasons, and indeed in project management research literature, it is identified that 'law' is a key reason why some projects fail.[3] In addition, there have been cases where projects have only been partly built, or else completed but never turned on, due to unresolved legal issues.

6.1.2 Understanding Risk

To understand commercial risk at its simplest is necessary at the outset. There are many definitions of commercial risk and these may vary according to the company's business sector. However, a broad and clear definition is one that states commercial risk covers all risk except political risk (OECD 2020), with political risk being commonly understood as expropriation, adverse government action (including change in law or tax regimes), and political or civil disturbance.[4] In terms of finance, many definitions state that commercial risk concerns repayment of finance, but again a broader understanding of this can be that commercial risk questions the viability of a project or activity. The different risks generally occur across four stages of a project and its associated activities from planning to development to operational to the decommissioning stage. However, in the past it has been clear that the decommissioning phase has not always been considered,[5] even though this phase is a feature of justice risks.

In the context of the energy sector and this chapter, commercial risk refers to energy projects at whatever stage they have reached, but there is a specific focus in thinking of planned new energy infrastructure projects, i.e., those that governments have outlined in their energy policy objectives; again in contrast, justice risks issues are considered throughout the project so as to include operation and decommissioning phases.

In terms of general commercial risks, all of these will typically be addressed as the subject matter of private-law contracts, and the essence of good risk management is to ensure the risk is contracted for, i.e., the risk is allocated between relevant stakeholders to the project. Exactly which persons or organisations are the stakeholders, is increasingly a very broad question that needs addressing, but in brief it includes public actors and all types of private actors that may be part of or affected by the project. An example of justice risk (i.e., via cosmopolitan justice) is a recent Australian case—*Gloucester Resources Limited v. Minister for Planning [2019] NSWLEC 7*—in which Judge Brian Preston considered stakeholders beyond the Australian border when deciding to not grant permission for a coal mine, i.e., people overseas would be affected by carbon dioxide emissions from coal.

For the interdisciplinary energy scholar, it is important to consider that there are so many issues that can arise that increase the risk to a project (whether it is being planned, constructed, in operation or decommissioned).

6.1.3 Human Rights as the Foundation of Energy 'Justice Risks'

As legal theory suggests in the evolution of energy law, the issue of 'justice' has become an emerging key driver of energy law formulation.[6] Hence, no longer can the energy community ignore these risks as law and policy is changing already to account for these risks. The issue of justice and the risks it brings to energy activities and project development has however been underexplored and also underappreciated in terms of commercial progress by the interdisciplinary energy community.

Irrespective of the COVID-19 pandemic and the new 2020 financial crisis, the energy transition has been underway and that is clear both from energy research and practice literature. What has been evolving is the role for justice in that transition and how it will be achieved. With greater justice, there will be a reduction in commercial risk. Generally, the search for justice is driven by a need to rebalance a relationship that has become unbalanced. That is why governments, companies and individuals enter into contracts. It is also why one goes to court, to ensure compensation or behavioural change as a result of an imbalanced relationship. In this context, what is in essence at stake is that an individual's or group's rights are being infringed. If you can prove that, you can achieve change. Hence, as made clear in Chap. 5, there are many legal cases from around the world, either resolved or in progress, which shows that human rights abuses are being challenged more regularly.

At its simplest, justice in the energy sector means the application of human rights across the energy life cycle (i.e., from extraction to production, operation, supply, consumption and waste management).[7] When these rights are infringed, there is a call for justice. Such a right may already be enshrined in legislation, or society may take the view that it should be and that public policy needs to change (and following that, new legislation will reinforce that policy). An individual or group may then test whether the change has occurred, or is likely to be implemented in the courts, as in the energy and climate change cases discussed in Chap. 5 (and see Appendix 5.1).

Justice risks are the risks that result from society seeking more fairness, equitable solutions, and resolving inequality in a variety of ways. In essence, they aim to address a normative situation, the way society wants the world to be, and they provide a future pathway for societal development, i.e., with energy justice contributing to this in the energy sector. Not all the justice risks are solved in new law and policy initiatives but together they demonstrate that they are clearly having key influences on the way business is developing.

Conditions in society have been changing for a multitude of reasons, but the increase in data, the rise in the availability of technology, the financial crisis of 2007–2009, the COVID-19 pandemic and now the 2020 financial crisis have created what can be referred to as a 'perfect storm of energy justice'[8] whereby the opportunity for justice to permeate the energy sector has arisen. As Plato stated, 'Accidents and calamities ... are the universal legislators of the world.'[9] In this context it is advanced that there is a new classification of risks for energy activities and project development, and these are energy justice risks; see Fig. 6.1. There are twelve identified

Fig. 6.1 Justice Risks in Project Development (Planning, Construction, Operation and Decommissioning). *Source*: Created by Heffron (2020)

risks and these have their roots in the five forms of justice as mentioned earlier, but have been created by advances in societal conditions over the last circa two decades; with the financial crisis of 2007–2009 being the catalyst in many ways.

6.2 The Key Contribution of This Book for Energy Justice Scholarship

Here I want to give my perspective on 'where next' for the concept of energy justice. In this book the key contribution centres around the challenge of energy justice, and that is to correct human rights abuses in the energy sector. To me, this is a key area for future research in that it is about the implementation of energy justice into practice, and also connects with the individual in that it is about protecting human rights. Every day in different places around the world our human rights are being infringed, as energy projects contribute in some form to impacting on our human rights to life, health, minimum subsistence, freedom, human dignity, water, healthy environment, air, culture, property, adequate housing, security and a fair trial.

A focus on ensuring that energy justice is implemented into practice is a key motivation for writing this book, and also the main contribution of this research. I hope, that as a collective set of chapters, it will inspire other people both in research and practice to work on issues around the implementation of energy justice into practice. My work in this text aims to highlight how interdisciplinarity (Chap. 2) and connecting to economics (Chap. 3) are vital in aiming to implement energy justice into practice. Then a case study on distributive justice (Chap. 4) is presented with a direct examination into the practice of energy taxation and its distributive justice aim, highlight how implementing energy justice into practice could work.

The heart of this text is explored in Chap. 5 where there is the specific examination of case law from around the world and how people (and in some cases organisations) are seeking energy justice. They utilise the national legal courts in a country because justice is not achievable without utilising this process. This is the option of last resort in the majority of countries, where the system has failed and the final option is to seek justice in the legal courts. As the case law demonstrates in Chap. 5, more and more cases are being brought to the courts, and this is positive news in that our energy sectors are becoming more fair, equitable and inclusive.

However, for the future perhaps we need this change to happen faster. It is proposed here in the Conclusion that this may already be happening in the context of energy justice risks that feed into the costs of energy infrastructure, i.e., that better management of these risks and their potential human right violations will reduce the cost of borrowing finance for the project. The acceleration of action is still necessary and hopefully both more and varied triggers will emerge so it can be achieved. In this context I presented the picture of the 'perfect storm' of events arising to create this new set of justice risks.

One of the recent triggers is US President Joe Biden appointing an academic specifically on energy justice to his administration. Within the first twenty-four hours of his presidency, he appointed Professor Shalanda Baker as a Deputy Director of Energy Justice into his new administration team and to the Department of Energy. This for me could be a trigger to further increasing the implementation of energy justice into practice. And as noted earlier in this book, Professor Baker had already (through her co-authored *Energy Justice Workbook*) been considering this issue for more than several years, as within that report it directly addresses the issue of how energy justice can transfer from theory into practice.

6.3 Where Next for Energy Justice, and Lessons for the Next Generation of Energy Justice Scholars

Energy justice is now well established and as stated in Chap. 2 there are researchers working across the disciplines on this topic. These are significant positives to take forward and build upon. It is important now to take the next step forward and achieve practical relevance. More research is necessary on how to utilise the concept of energy justice in practice. To achieve this, research projects need to involve other stakeholders in some capacity within the project. This has two aims: it can enrich the project itself and its results, and secondly it can introduce and diffuse the concept more into practice. It can enable researchers to achieve greater impact from their project.

For me, too many researchers are going back to thinking about the concept of energy justice. This is generally fine, but there needs to be a justifiable reason for it. In essence, the researcher needs to explain the weaknesses of energy justice, and how does their improvement to the concept fix the weakness. For example, for myself I have identified the implementation of energy justice into practice as a weakness, and through my consideration of the protection of human rights in national courts I have aimed at achieving energy justice in practice.

Unfortunately, I find that some of the research work taking place is misdirected. Some additions to the framework are presented that are rarely justified, and generally are not justified for a practical relevance. Many of these kinds of articles fail to realise that their 'addition' to the concept is already covered within the energy justice concept. It needs to be remembered that while the energy justice concept is a recent phenomenon, the forms of justice it is based on (distributive, procedural, restorative, recognition and cosmopolitan justice) are hundreds and thousands of years old. The success of energy justice scholars has been to identify the most influential forms of justice that can achieve change in the energy sector. The second success of these scholars has been how they tackled the issue and made it relevant and understandable to the entire research community. Hence, there are many reasons why before sitting down to write some addition to the theory there has to be demonstrable evidence of why such a change is needed.

Such evidence can usually be gathered by (a) considering the practical relevance of your addition and (b) utilising the energy justice framework(s) to explore the issue. Research needs to become more replicatable particularly if we are to convince all stakeholders of its importance. And hence utilising the energy justice frameworks can enable us to resolve that problem. In exploring your research and/or practitioner problem using the energy justice framework your work will be united by that core normative *raison d'être* of aiming for an energy sector as being characterised by energy justice, and thus contributing to a fairer and more sustainable world. This will enable the broader energy community to engage with your work, will ensure it is more highly valued and even potentially more impactful.

For all of us working in this area, we have an obligation to push forward the concept and see if our work can really be translated into practice. I believe we need more comparative work to make this happen and more engagement with stakeholders (as stated earlier). Energy justice should also if applied as a framework offer those in the energy sector a new way to look at energy issues that they are faced with. It should inspire more accountability in the energy sector. More research is needed in this space and particularly on whether fossil fuel projects meet our modern standards of justice and how such projects can be classified as 'just'. Further, is it morally ethical to support such projects given that from a cosmopolitan perspective we all have signed up to the Paris Agreement and its international commitments (for example, through the nationally determined contributions)? Are there not alternative energy infrastructure projects that can we build that are more energy just? Who will be held accountable if we continue to build fossil fuel projects if they are classified as unjust energy projects?

These are exciting questions for us to consider, and I have high hopes for future energy scholarship. For too long, justice has not been at the core of the energy sector, but now it appears that progress has been made. Hence I will finish this text with the words of the Noble Prize winning Irish poet Seamus Heaney,[10] where he states:

> *History says Don't hope on this side of the grave. But then, once in a lifetime the longed-for tidal wave of justice can rise up, and hope and history rhyme.*

Notes

1. Bloomberg, 2019. New Energy Outlook Annual Report Executive Summary 2019. Available at: https://bnef.turtl.co/story/neo2019/page/2/2?teaser=true (last accessed 1 May 2021).
2. Del Guayo, I., Godden, L., Zillman, D.D. Montoya, M.F. and Gonzalez, J. J. 2020. (Editors). *Energy Justice and Law*. Oxford, UK: Oxford University Press.
3. Flyvbjerg, B. 2011. Managing major projects. In: P.W.G. Morris, J.K. Pinto, J. Soderlund (Eds.), The Oxford Handbook of Project Management, Oxford University Press, Oxford, UK (2011).
4. OECD, 2020. Available at: https://rmid-oecd.asean.org/project-risks-mitigation/project-risks/commercial-risks/commercial-risks-over-the-project-life-cycle/ (last accessed 1 May 2021).
5. Heffron, R. J. 2018. Energy law for decommissioning in the energy sector in the 21st century. *Journal of World Energy Law & Business*, 11 (3), 189–195.
6. Heffron, R. J. and Talus. K. 2016. The Evolution of Energy Law and Energy Jurisprudence: Insights for Energy Analysts and Researchers. *Energy Research and Social Science*, 19, 1–10.
7. R.J. Heffron and D. McCauley, 'The concept of energy justice across the disciplines', *Energy Policy*, 105 (2017), 658–67.
8. Heffron, R. J. 2020. Justice in the Energy Transition. Special Issue 'Decarbonisation Pathways for Oil and Gas'. The Oxford Institute for Energy Studies, March 2020, Issue 121. Available at: https://www.oxfordenergy.org/wpcms/wp-content/uploads/2020/03/OEF121.pdf (last accessed 1 May 2021).
9. Plato, *The Laws*, tr. Trevor J. Saunders (Penguin, 1970), 164.
10. Heaney, S. 2018 (Original 1990). The Cure at Troy: Sophocles' Philoctetes. Faber & Faber: London, UK.

References

Bloomberg. 2019. New Energy Outlook Annual Report Executive Summary 2019. Accessed 1 May 2021. https://bnef.turtl.co/story/neo2019/page/2/2?teaser=true.

Heffron, R.J. 2020. Justice in the Energy Transition. Special Issue 'Decarbonisation Pathways for Oil and Gas'. The Oxford Institute for Energy Studies, March 2020, Issue 121. Accessed 1 May 2021. https://www.oxfordenergy.org/wpcms/wp-content/uploads/2020/03/OEF121.pdf.

OECD. 2020. Accessed 1 May 2021. https://rmid-oecd.asean.org/project-risks-mitigation/project-risks/commercial-risks/commercial-risks-over-the-project-life-cycle/.

References

ABC Australia News (Lannin, S.). 2015. China Economist Warns Major Miners May Collapse in 2016 (18 December 2015). Accessed 1 May 2021. http://www.abc.net.au/news/2015-12-17/china-economist-warns-that-iron-ore-miners-will-collapse/7037802.

Alberta Heritage Fund (Canada). 2018. Accessed 1 May 2021. http://finance.alberta.ca/business/ahstf/index.html.

Alhashel, B. 2015. *Sovereign Wealth Funds: A Literature Review. Journal of Business and Economics* 78: 1–13.

Amnesty International. 2018. *Is My Smartphone Powered by Child Labour?* Accessed 1 May 2021. https://www.amnesty.org/en/latest/campaigns/2016/06/drc-cobalt-child-labour/.

Avi-Yonah, R.S. 2006. The Three Goals of Taxation. *Tax Law Review* 60 (1): 1–28.

Bamberger, M., and R. Oswald. 2014. *The Real Cost of Fracking*. Boston, MA: Beacon Press.

BBC. 2017. *Energy Review Examining Household and Environmental Costs* (6 August 2017). Accessed 1 May 2021. http://www.bbc.co.uk/news/uk-40839433.

Becker, E., T. Jahn, I. Stiess, and P. Wehling. 1997 (37). Sustainability, A Cross-Disciplinary Concept for Social Transformations, Management of Social Transformation Policy Papers 6, UNESCO: Paris, France—In P. Jones, D. Selby, and S. Sterling (Eds.). 2010. *Sustainability Education: Perspectives and Practice across Higher Education*. London, UK: Earthscan.

Bickerstaff, K., G.P. Walker, and H. Bulkeley, eds. 2013. *Energy Justice in a Changing Climate: Social Equity and Low-Carbon Energy*. London: Zed Books.

R. J. Heffron, *The Challenge for Energy Justice*,
https://doi.org/10.1007/978-3-030-80097-0

Bird, R.M., and E.M. Zolt. 2005. *Redistribution Via Taxation: The Limited Role of the Personal Income Tax in Developing Countries.* 52 UCLA L. Rev. 1627

Bloomberg. 2019. New Energy Outlook Annual Report Executive Summary 2019. Accessed 1 May 2021. https://bnef.turtl.co/story/neo2019/page/2/2?teaser=true.

Bloomberg (Biesheuval, T., Riseborough, J., and De Sousa, A.). 2015. Why Bankruptcy Might Be the Mining Industry's Last Best Hope (3 December 2015). Accessed 1 May 2021. http://www.bloomberg.com/news/articles/2015-12-03/why-bankruptcy-might-be-the-mining-industry-s-last-best-hope.

Bloomberg New Energy Finance. 2016. *Mapping the Gap: The Road from Paris (Finance Paths to a Two-Degree Future).* Accessed 1 May 2021. http://about.bnef.com/white-papers/mapping-the-gap-the-road-from-paris/.

Bookstaber, R. 2017. *The End of Theory. Financial Crises, the Failure of Economics, and the Sweep of Human Interaction.* Princeton, NJ: Princeton University Press.

Buchanan, J.M. 1975. A Contractarian Paradigm for Applying Economic Theory. *American Economic Review* 65: 225–230: quoted in Williamson, O.E. 2002. The Theory of the Firm as Governance Structure: From Choice to Contract. *Journal of Economic Perspectives* 16 (3): 171–195.

CAFOD. 2017. *UK Support for Energy in Developing* Countries. Accessed 1 May 2021. https://cafod.org.uk/content/download/27353/269740/version/2/file/Policy%20briefing%20UK%20Support%20for%20Energy%20in%20Developing%20Countries%20Oct%202015.pdf.

Caldecott, B. et al. 2016. *Stranded Assets and Thermal Coal: An Analysis of Environment-Related Risk Exposure.* Accessed 1 May 2021. http://www.smithschool.ox.ac.uk/research-programmes/stranded-assets/satc.pdf.

Calder, J. 2014. *Administering Fiscal Regimes for Extractive Industries: A Handbook.* Washington, DC: IMF.

Carbon Brief. 2017. *Six Charts Show UK's Progress on Low-Carbon Energy Slowing Down.* (31 July 2017). Accessed 1 May 2021. https://www.carbonbrief.org/six-charts-show-uk-progress-on-low-carbon-energy-slowing-down.

Carpantier, J.F., and W.N. Vermeulen. 2018. Emergence of Sovereign Wealth Funds. *Journal of Commodity Markets* 11 (C): 1–2. https://doi.org/10.1016/j.jcomm.2018.01.002.

Cave, T., and A. Rowell. 2014. *A Quiet Word: Lobbying, Crony Capitalism and Broken Politics in Britain.* London, UK: Vintage Books.

Centre for Sustainable Energy (UK). 2016. Accessed 1 May 2021. https://www.cse.org.uk/contact.

Chabot. H. 2021. She's Bringing Her Energy Justice Mission to the Biden Administration. Accessed 1 May 2021. https://news.northeastern.edu/2021/01/23/shalanda-baker-is-bringing-her-energy-justice-mission-to-the-biden-administration/.

Chancel, L., and T. Piketty. 2015. *Carbon and Inequality: From Kyoto to Paris.* Paris School of Economics (November 2015).

Coady, D., et al. 2017. How Large Are Global Fossil Fuel Subsidies? *World Development* 91: 11–27.

Cohen, J.A., M. Brauer, et al. 2017. Estimates and 25-year Trends of the Global Burden of Disease Attributable to Ambient Air Pollution: An Analysis of Data from the Global Burden of Diseases Study 2015. *Lancet* 389: 1907–1918.

Crowson, P. 2008. *Mining Unearthed.* London, UK: Aspearmont UK.

Daniel, P., M. Keen, A. Swistak, and V. Thuronyi, eds. 2017. *International Taxation and the Extractive Industries.* Oxford, UK: Routledge.

Davies, H. 2010. *The Financial Crisis: Who Is to Blame?* Cambridge, UK: Policy Press.

De la Feria, R. 2018. *Tax Fraud and the Rule of Law.* Oxford University Centre for Business Taxation, Working Paper Series 18/02 (January 2018).

Del Guayo, I., L. Godden, D.D. Zillman, M.F. Montoya, and J.J. Gonzalez, eds. 2020. *Energy Justice and Law.* Oxford, UK: Oxford University Press.

Deloitte. 2013. *Responsible Tax: Sustainable Tax Strategy.* Accessed 1 May 2021. https://www2.deloitte.com/content/dam/Deloitte/uk/Documents/tax/uk-tax-responsible-tax-v2.pdf.

Department of Business, Energy & Industrial Strategy (BIES)/United Kingdom Statistics Authority (UKSA). 2017. *UK Energy in Brief 2017.* Accessed 1 May 2021. https://www.gov.uk/government/uploads/system/uploads/attachment_data/file/631146/UK_Energy_in_Brief_2017.pdf.

Dondo, S.J. 2014. Financial Assurance for Mine Closure: A Regulatory Perspective from the Argentine Context. CSRM Occasional Paper, Centre for Social Responsibility in Mining (CSRM), Sustainable Minerals Institute (SMI), University of Queensland.

Duff, D. 2017. Tax Policy and the Virtuous Sovereign: Dworkinian Equality and Redistributive Taxation. In *Philosophical Foundations of Tax Law*, ed. M. Bhandari, 167–189. Oxford, UK: Oxford University Press.

Duke, C., M. Osbourne, and B. Wilson. 2013. *A New Imperative: Regions and Higher Education in Difficult Times.* Manchester, UK: Manchester University Press (see in particular, Chapter 7).

Ekwurzel, B., et al. 2017. The Rise in Global Atmospheric CO_2, Surface Temperature, and Sea Level from Emissions Traced to Major Carbon Producers. *Climatic Change* 144: 579–590.

Elliot, B. 2014. *Natural Catastrophe Climate Change and Neoliberal Governance.* Edinburgh, UK: Edinburgh University Press.

Energy Justice Network (US). 2016. Accessed 20 October 2016. http://www.energyjustice.net/about. And See More Concerning Its Accomplishments. Accessed 1 May 2021. http://www.energyjustice.net/accomplishments.

Energy Live News. 2017. *Capacity Market Weak Link in UK's Energy Transition* (13 March 2017). Accessed 1 May 2021. http://www.energylivenews.com/2017/03/13/capacity-market-weak-link-in-uks-energy-transition/.

Extractive Industries Transparency Initiative. n.d. Accessed 1 May 2021. https://eiti.org/.

Federal Surface Mining Control and Reclamation Act (SMCRA). 1977. Accessed 1 May 2021. http://www.osmre.gov/lrg.shtm; and Financial Assurance under the Environmental Protection Act 1994. Queensland Government Department of Environment and Heritage Protection. Accessed 1 May 2021. http://www.ehp.qld.gov.au/assets/documents/regulation/era-gl-financial-assurance-ep-act.pdf.

Figueres, C. et al. 2017. Three Years to Safeguard our Climate. *Nature* 546 (7660): 593–595. (29 June 2017).

Financial Times. 2017. KPMG Slapped with $6.2m Fine over Oil Company Audit Errors (15 August 2017). Accessed 1 May 2021. https://www.ft.com/content/0f0393de-81d9-11e7-a4ce-15b2513cb3ff.

———. 2018a. DRC Mining Co to Renegotiate All Contracts Within Next Year (6 February 2018). Accessed 1 May 2021. https://www.ft.com/content/d6cb308a-0b4e-11e8-8eb7-42f857ea9f09.

———. 2018b. Ivanhoe Founder Robert Friedland Joins Debate Over DRC Mining Code (7 February). Accessed 1 May 2021. https://www.ft.com/content/44800d7c-0be4-11e8-839d-41ca06376bf2.

Flyvbjerg, B. 2011. Managing Major Projects. In *The Oxford Handbook of Project Management*, ed. P.W.G. Morris, J.K. Pinto, and J. Soderlund. Oxford, UK: Oxford University Press.

For More See: On Common Ground Consultants Inc. 2014. What Is the Social License? Accessed 1 May 2021. http://socialicense.com/definition.html.

Galaway, B., and J. Hudson. 1996. *Restorative Justice: International Perspectives.* Monsey, NY: Criminal Justice Press/Willow Tree Press.

Global Studies Initiative. 2010. Untold Billions: Fossil-Fuel Subsidies, Their Impacts and the Path to Reform, p. 33. Accessed 1 May 2021. www.iisd.org/gsi/sites/default/files/transparency_ffs.pdf.

Gribnau, H., and H. Vording. 2017. The Birth of Tax Law as a Legal Discipline. In *Studies in the History of Tax Law*, ed. P. Harris and D. de Cogan, vol. 8. Oxford, UK: Hart Publishing.

Guruswamy, L. 2010. Energy Justice and Sustainable Development. *Colorado Journal of International Environmental Law and Policy* 21: 231.

———. 2016. *Global Energy Justice: Law and Policy.* St Paul, MN: West Academic Publishing.

Hall, S.M. 2013. Energy Justice and Ethical Consumption: Comparison, Synthesis and Lesson Drawing. *Local Environment* 18 (4): 422–437.

Heaney, S. 2018 (Original 1990). *The Cure at Troy: Sophocles' Philoctetes*. London, UK: Faber & Faber.

Heede, R. 2014. Tracing Anthropogenic Carbon Dioxide and Methane Emissions to Fossil Fuel and Cement Producers 1854–2010. *Climate Change* 122: 229–241.

Heffron, R.J. 2018a. Energy Law for Decommissioning in the Energy Sector in the 21st Century. *Journal of World Energy Law & Business* 11 (3): 189–195.

———. 2018b. The Application of Distributive Justice to Energy Taxation Utilising Sovereign Wealth Funds. *Energy Policy* 122: 649–654.

———. 2020. Justice in the Energy Transition. Special Issue 'Decarbonisation Pathways for Oil and Gas'. The Oxford Institute for Energy Studies, March 2020, Issue 121. Accessed 1 May 2021. https://www.oxfordenergy.org/wpcms/wp-content/uploads/2020/03/OEF121.pdf.

Heffron, R.J., and D. McCauley. 2014. Achieving Sustainable Supply Chains through Energy Justice. *Applied Energy* 123: 435–437.

———. 2017. The Concept of Energy Justice across the Disciplines. *Energy Policy* 105: 658–667.

Heffron, R.J., and K. Talus. 2016a. The Development of Energy Law in the 21st Century: A Paradigm Shift? *Journal of World Energy Law and Business* 9 (3): 189–202.

———. 2016b. The Evolution of Energy Law and Energy Jurisprudence: Insights for Energy Analysts and Researchers. *Energy Research and Social Science* 19: 1–10.

Heffron, R.J., D. McCauley, and B.K. Sovacool. 2015. Resolving Society's Energy Trilemma through the Energy Justice Metric. *Energy Policy* 87: 168–176.

Heffron, R.J., et al. 2018a. The Emergence of the 'Social Licence to Operate' in the Extractive Industries? *Resources Policy*. https://doi.org/10.1016/j.resourpol.2018.09.012.

Heffron, R.J., A. Ronne, A. Bradbrook, J.P. Tomain, and K. Talus. 2018b. A Treatise for Energy Law. *Journal of World Energy Law & Business* 11 (1): 34–48.

Heffron, R., Connor, R., Crossley, P., López-Ibor Mayor, V., Talus, K., & Tomain, J. 2021. The Identification and Impact of Justice Risks to Commercial Risks in the Energy Sector: Post COVID-19 and for the Energy Transition. *Journal of Energy & Natural Resources Law*, https://doi.org/10.1080/02646811.2021.1874148 (advance access).

Helm, D. 2017. *Burn Out: The Endgame for Fossil Fuels*. New Haven, CT: Yale University Press.

Hopkins, J.D. 1985. The Role of the Courts in American Society: The Final Report of the Council on the Role of the Courts. *6. Pace Law Review* 6 (4): 127–132.

House of Lords. 2017. *The Price of Power: Reforming the Electricity Market*. Accessed 1 May 2021. https://publications.parliament.uk/pa/ld201617/ldselect/ldeconaf/113/113.pdf. The Government Response to This Does Not

Provide Further Clarity, see: BEIS. 2017. *Government Response to the Economic Affairs Committee's Inquiry into the Economics If UK Energy Policy*. Accessed 1 May 2021. http://www.parliament.uk/documents/lords-committees/economic-affairs/The-Economics-of-UK-Energy-Policy/Government-response-Energy-Market-Report.pdf.

ICIJ (Fitzgibbon, W.). 2017. *Paradise Papers Research Raises Questions Over Glencore's $440m Congo Discount* (14 December). Accessed 1 May 2021. https://www.icij.org/investigations/paradise-papers/paradise-papers-research-raises-questions-glencores-440m-congo-discount/.

IEA, OPEC, OECD, and World Bank Joint Report. 2020. Analysis of the Scope of Energy Subsidies and Suggestions for the G-20 Initiative (June 2010). Accessed 1 May 2021. www.iea.org/weo/docs/G20_Subsidy_Joint_Report.pdf.

Initiative for Energy Justice. 2019. The Energy Justice Workbook. Accessed 1 May 2021. https://iejusa.org/wp-content/uploads/2019/12/The-Energy-Justice-Workbook-2019-web.pdf.

International Business Times (Gallucci, M.). 2016. When A Coal Company Goes Bankrupt, Who Is Left To Clean Up The Mess? (last accessed 27 January 2017). Accessed 1 May 2021. http://www.ibtimes.com/when-coal-company-goes-bankrupt-who-left-clean-mess-2264097.

International Forum of Sovereign Wealth Funds. 2018. *Santiago Principles*. Accessed 1 May 2021. http://www.ifswf.org/santiago-principles-landing/santiago-principles.

International Trade Administration (ITA)—U.S. Department of Commerce. 2018a. *Congo (DR)—Mining and Minerals*. Accessed 1 May 2021. https://www.export.gov/article?id=Congo-Democratic-Republic-Mining-and-Minerals.

———. 2018b. *Congo (DR)—Energy*. Accessed 1 May 2021. https://www.export.gov/article?id=Congo-Democratic-Republic-Energy.

Jenkins, K., D.A. McCauley, R.J. Heffron, and H. Stephan. 2014. Energy Justice, A Whole Systems Approach. *Queen's Political Review* II (2): 74–87.

Jenkins, K., D. McCauley, R. Heffron, H. Stephan, and R. Rehner. 2016. Energy Justice: A Conceptual Review. *Energy Research and Social Science* 11: 174–182.

Kenya—Cortec Mining Kenya Limited. 2019. Cortec (Pty) Limited and Stirling Capital Limited v. Republic of Kenya, ICSID Case No. ARB/15/29.

Kuhn, T. 1962. *The Structure of Scientific Revolutions*. Chicago, IL: University of Chicago Press.

Lyster, R. 2015. *Climate Justice and Disaster Law*. Cambridge: Cambridge University Press.

Martin, S., and R. Jucker. 2005. Educating Earth-Literate Leaders. *Journal of Geography in Higher Education* 29 (1): 19–29.

Martin, J., and J.E. Samuels, eds. 2012. *The Sustainable University: Green Goals and New Challenges for Higher Education Leaders*. Baltimore, MD: John Hopkins University Press.

McCauley, D. 2017. *Energy Justice: Re-Balancing the Trilemma of Security, Poverty and Climate Change*. Basingstoke, UK: Palgrave Macmillan.

McCauley, D., R.J. Heffron, H. Stephan, and K. Jenkins. 2013. Advancing Energy Justice: The Triumvirate of Tenets. *International Energy Law Review* 32 (3): 107–110.

Mickelson, K. 2007. Critical Approaches. In *The Oxford Handbook of International Environmental Law*, ed. D. Bodansky, J. Brunnee, and E. Hey. Oxford, UK: OUP.

Miller, C.G. 2005. Financial Assurance for Mine Closure and Reclamation. (International Council on Mining & Metals). Accessed 1 May 2021. https://www.icmm.com/document/282.

Morrison, J. 2014. *The Social License: How to Keep Your Organization Legitimate*. UK: Palgrave Macmillan.

Nature. 2015. Special Issue on *Interdisciplinarity*. Accessed 1 May 2021. http://www.nature.com/news/interdisciplinarity-1.18295.

Nature, 551. 2017. (30 November 2017). Accessed 1 May 2021. https://www.nature.com/nature/journal/v551/n7682/index.html#out.

OECD. 2020. Accessed 1 May 2021. https://rmid-oecd.asean.org/project-risks-mitigation/project-risks/commercial-risks/commercial-risks-over-the-project-life-cycle/.

Offer, A., and G. Soderberg. 2016. *The Nobel Factor: The Prize in Economics, Social Democracy, and The Market Turn*. Princeton, NJ: Princeton University Press.

Orr, D. 1994. *Earth in Mind: In Education, Environment, and the Human Prospect*. Washington, DC: Island Press.

Otto, F. et al. 2015. United Nations. The Science of Attributing Extreme Weather Events and Its Potential Contribution to Assessing Loss and Damage Associated with Climate Change Impacts. Accessed 1 May 2021. https://unfccc.int/files/adaptation/workstreams/loss_and_damage/application/pdf/attributingextremeevents.pdf.

Peru–Bear Creek v. Peru Bear Creek Mining Corporation v. Republic of Peru. 2021. ICSID Case No. ARB/14/2.

Piketty, T. 2014. *Capital in the Twenty-First Century*. Translated by A. Goldhammer. Cambridge, MA: Belknap Press of Harvard University Press.

———. 2015. *The Economics of Inequality*. Translated by A. Goldhammer. Cambridge, MA: Belknap Press of Harvard University Press.

Pistone, P., and M. Villar Ezcurra, eds. 2016. *Energy Taxation, Environmental Protection and State Aids*. The Netherlands: IBFD.

Pitrone, F. 2016. Design of Energy Taxes in the European Union: Looking for a Higher Level of Environmental Protection. In P. Pistone and M. Villar Ezcurra (Eds.).

Plato. 1970. *The Laws*, tr. Trevor J. Saunders (Penguin, 1970), 164.

Popper, K. 2002. Conjectures and Refutations: The Growth of Scientific Knowledge. Routledge Classics. (First published 1963, Routledge & Kegan Paul).

Prno, J., and D.S. Slocombe. 2012. Exploring the Origins of 'Social License to Operate' in the Mining Sector: Perspectives from Governance and Sustainability Theories. *Resources Policy*, 37 (3), 346–357.

Radley, B. 2016. The Limits of Corporate Social Responsibility and the Possibilities for Harnessing Mining to Reinstitute Processes of State-Led Local Development in the DRC. In *L'Afrique des Grands Lacs Annuaire, 2015–2016*, ed. F. Reyntjens, S. Vandeginste, and M. Verpoorten, 169–186. Paris: L'Harmattan.

Reuven, Avi-Yonah. 2018. University Webpage Profile. Accessed 1 May 2021. https://www.law.umich.edu/FacultyBio/Pages/FacultyBio.aspx?FacID=aviyonah.

Rietveld, M., and P. Toledano, eds. 2017. *The New Frontiers of Sovereign Investment*. New York, NY: Columbia University Press.

Sandford, C. 2000. *Why Tax Systems Differ? A Comparative Study of the Political Economy of Taxation*. Bath, UK: Fiscal Publications.

Saunders, J. 2011. Energy Justice—The Policy Challenges. Energy Justice in a Changing Climate: Defining an Agenda, InCluESEV Conference, 10 November 2011, London. In p. 423, Hall, S.M. 2013. Energy Justice and Ethical Consumption: Comparison, Synthesis and Lesson Drawing. *Local Environment* 18 (4) 422–437.

Scheidel, W. 2017. *The Great Leveler*. Princeton, NJ: Princeton University Press.

Smil, V. 2017. *Energy and Civilization: A History*. Cambridge, MA: MIT.

South American Silver Limited (Bermuda) v. the Plurinational State of Bolivia. 2013. PCA Case No. 2013-15.

Sovacool, B.K. 2017. Reviewing, Reforming, and Rethinking Global Energy Subsidies: Towards a Political Economy Research Agenda. *Ecological Economics* 135: 150–163.

Sovacool, B.K., and M.H. Dworkin. 2014. *Global Energy Justice: Problems, Principles, and Practices*. Cambridge, UK: Cambridge University Press.

———. 2015. Energy Justice: Conceptual Insights and Practical Applications. *Applied Energy* 142: 435–444.

Sovacool, B., R.J. Heffron, D. McCauley, and A. Goldthau. 2016. Energy Decisions Reframed as Justice and Ethical Concerns. *Nature Energy*. https://doi.org/10.1038/nenergy.2016.24.

Sovereign Wealth Fund Institute. 2018. Accessed 1 May 2021. https://www.swfinstitute.org/sovereign-wealth-fund-rankings/.

Stiglitz, J.E. 2012. *The Price of Inequality*. London, UK: Penguin Books.

Sullivan, D., and L. Tifft. 2006. *Handbook of Restorative Justice: A Global Perspective*. Oxford, UK: Routledge.

Texas Permanent University Fund (US). 2018. Accessed 1 May 2021. https://www.utsystem.edu/puf.

The Carter Center. 2017. *A State Affair: Privatizing Congo's Copper Sector*. GA, US: Atlanta. Accessed 1 May 2021. https://www.cartercenter.org/resources/pdfs/news/peace_publications/democracy/congo-report-carter-center-nov-2017.pdf.

———. 2016. Seven Climate Records Set So Far in 2016. (17 June 2016—Adam Vaughan). Accessed 1 May 2021. https://www.theguardian.com/environment/2016/jun/17/seven-climate-records-set-so-far-in-2016. This Is Just a Newspaper Report Connecting to the Issue—However, There Are Many International Reports.

The Guardian. 2017a. *Paradise Papers Prompt Criminal Complaint against Glencore*. (21 December). Accessed 1 May 2021. https://www.theguardian.com/business/2017/dec/21/paradise-papers-prompt-criminal-complaint-against-glencore.

———. 2017b. *Paradise Papers: US Puts Sanctions on Billionaire over Dealings in DRC*. (22 December). Accessed 1 May 2021. https://www.theguardian.com/news/2017/dec/22/paradise-papers-us-sanctions-billionaire-dealings-drc.

The Guardian (Robertson, J.). 2016. Coal Giants Abandon Unprofitable Mines, Leaving Rehabilitation under Threat. Accessed 1 May 2021. https://www.theguardian.com/environment/2016/jan/29/coal-giants-abandon-unprofitable-mines-leaving-rehabilitation-under-threat.

The Norwegian Government Pension Fund Global. 2018. Accessed 1 May 2021. https://www.nbim.no/en/the-fund/.

Times Higher Education. 2016. World University Rankings 2017. Accessed 1 May 2021. https://www.timeshighereducation.com/world-university-rankings/2017/world-ranking.

Tirole, J. 2017. *Economics for the Common Good*. Princeton, NJ: Princeton University Press.

Traversa, E., and S. Wolff. 2016. *Energy Tax Policy in an EU Context: Non-Discrimination, Free Movement and Tax Harmonisation*. In P. Pistone and M. Villar Ezcurra (Eds.).

Tromans, S. 2012. *Environmental Impact Assessment*. 2nd ed. West Sussex, UK: Bloomsbury Professional Ltd.

Tsani, S. 2013. Natural Resources, Governance and Institutional Quality: The Role of Resource Funds. *Resources Policy* 38 (2): 181–195.

UI Green Metric Ranking of World Universities. 2016. Accessed 1 May 2021. http://greenmetric.ui.ac.id/overall-ranking-2015/. And Additional Reports on this Are Accessed 1 May 2021. https://www.timeshighereducation.com/news/the-20-greenest-universities-in-the-world/2018495.article.

US Department of Energy. 2021. Shalanda Baker. Accessed 1 May 2021. https://www.energy.gov/index.php/diversity/person/shalanda-h-baker.

US Department of State. 2015. 2015 *Investment Climate Statement—Democratic Republic of the Congo*. Accessed 1 May 2021. https://www.state.gov/e/eb/rls/othr/ics/2015/241522.htm.

US EPA. n.d. Climate Change and the Life Cycle of Stuff. Accessed 1 May 2021. http://epa.gov/climatechange/climate-change-waste/life-cycle-diagram.html.

Wietekamp, E.G. and H. J. Kerner. eds. 2002; 2011. *Restorative Justice: Theoretical Foundations*. Oxford, UK: Routledge.

Williamson, O.E. 2002. The Theory of the Firm as Governance Structure: From Choice to Contract. *Journal of Economic Perspectives* 16 (3): 171–195.

Wittgenstein, L. 1958. Philosophical Investigations—We Utilize This Excellent Example, Having Read Is Used to a Similar Way by Other Academics—From, p. 15.

World Bank. 2008. *Democratic Republic of Congo Growth with Governance In the Mining Sector*. Accessed 1 May 2021. http://siteresources.worldbank.org/INTOGMC/Resources/336099-1156955107170/drcgrowthgovernanceenglish.pdf.

World Energy Council. 2015. *Priority Actions on Climate Change and How to Balance the Trilemma*. London, UK: World Energy Council. Accessed 1 May 2021. https://www.worldenergy.org/publications/2015/world-energy-trilemma-2015-priority-actions-on-climate-change-and-how-to-balance-the-trilemma/.

———. 2016. 6. *The World Energy Trilemma Index—2016—Benchmarking the Sustainability of National Energy Systems*. London, UK: World Energy Council. Accessed 1 May 2021. https://www.worldenergy.org/publications/2016/2016-energy-trilemma-index-benchmarking-the-sustainability-of-national-energy-systems/.

Zehr, H. 2014. *The Little Book of Restorative Justice. GoodBooks*. NY, US: Skyhorse Publishing.

Zuckerman, G. 2013. *The Frackers*. London, UK: Penguin Books.

Index[1]

[1] Note: Page numbers followed by 'n' refer to notes.

R. J. Heffron, *The Challenge for Energy Justice*,
https://doi.org/10.1007/978-3-030-80097-0

The manufacturer's authorised representative in the EU is Springer Nature Customer Service Centre GmbH, Europaplatz 3, 69115 Heidelberg, Germany. If you have any concerns regarding our products, please contact ProductSafety@springernature.com

Printed and bound by CPI Group (UK) Ltd, Croydon, CR0 4YY

30/09/2026

02225666-0006